Storytimes
for Everyone!

Storytimes for Everyone!

Developing Young Children's Language and Literacy

SAROJ NADKARNI GHOTING
and PAMELA MARTIN-DÍAZ

An imprint of the American Library Association
Chicago | 2013

A children's librarian for more than thirty-five years, **Saroj Nadkarni Ghoting** is now an early childhood literacy consultant. She is the coauthor of the best-selling *Early Literacy Storytimes @ your library* (2005) and *The Early Literacy Kit: A Manual and Tip Cards* (2009). She also conducts face-to-face and online trainings on early literacy, including Every Child Ready to Read @ your library, an early literacy initiative cosponsored by the Public Library Association and the Association for Library Service to Children. She received her BA from Oberlin College in Ohio and her MLS from Catholic University of American in Washington, DC. Visit her website, www.earlylit.net, for more information.

Pamela Martin-Díaz, coauthor of *Early Literacy Storytimes @ your library*, is a branch manager and early literacy coordinator at the Allen County Public Library in Fort Wayne, Indiana. She conducts storytimes in child-care centers and works with community groups to help get the word out about the importance of having all of our children enter school ready to learn. As a trustee of the Fort Wayne Community Schools Board from 2006 to 2010, she became keenly aware of the key role that early literacy plays in positive outcomes for children. Pamela received her BA from Kenyon College in Ohio and her MA in library science from the University of Chicago.

Printed in the United States of America
17 16 15 14 13   5 4 3 2 1

Extensive effort has gone into ensuring the reliability of the information in this book; however, the publisher makes no warranty, express or implied, with respect to the material contained herein.

ISBNs: 978-0-8389-1169-3 (paper); 978-0-8389-9501-3 (PDF). For more information on digital formats, visit the ALA Store at alastore.ala.org and select eEditions.

Library of Congress Cataloging-in-Publication Data

Ghoting, Saroj Nadkarni.
    Storytimes for everyone! : developing young children's language and literacy /
  Saroj Nadkarni Ghoting and Pamela Martin-Díaz.
        pages   cm
    Includes bibliographical references and index.
    ISBN 978-0-8389-1169-3
      1. Children's libraries—Activity programs—United States. 2. Storytelling—United States.
  3. Language arts (Early childhood)—Activity programs. 4. Preschool children—Books and
  reading—United States. 5. Reading—Parent participation—United States. I. Martin-Díaz,
  Pamela. II. Title.
Z718.3.G565 2013
027.62'51—dc23   2013011549

Cover images © Shutterstock, Inc. Text design by Kimberly Thornton in Melior and Din.

⊗ This paper meets the requirements of ANSI/NISO Z39.48-1992 (Permanence of Paper).

Contents

Acknowledgments

WE ACKNOWLEDGE THE MANY PEOPLE WHOSE STORYTIME IDEAS WE HAVE BUILT ON, particularly Virginia Krute of Montgomery County (MD) Public Libraries and Cindy Christin of Bozeman (MT) Public Library. We especially recognize Amy Alapati, also of Montgomery County Public Libraries, for her sustained energy and enthusiasm—she has championed our youngest patrons with programs for them and their parents and caregivers, and early on she integrated American Sign Language into these programs. In addition, the sign-language communication and ASL expertise of Susan Cohen, of the Montgomery County Public Libraries, was invaluable. Heather Grady and Nancy Magi, of the Allen County (IN) Public Library, proved, as always, a source of support and inspiration.

Thanks also to the library staff who gave us ideas in workshops, in e-mails, in person, and through Public Librarians Serving Young Adults and Children (PUB-YAC) and Association for Library Service to Children electronic discussion lists. The ideas and energy that have been shared with us are inspiring.

We thank our readers, who took time from busy schedules to offer insights to make the book more comprehensible, comprehensive, and useful: Katie Ross, youth services librarian, Westerville (OH) Public Library; Terrie Weckerle, project manager, Ready to Read Resource Center, Anchorage (AK) Public Library; Marie Raymond, early literacy coordinator, Scottsdale (AZ) Public Library; and Nancy Wood, early childhood and outreach librarian, Beaumont (CA) Library District.

In addition, Bonnie Banks of Amos Memorial Public Library (Sidney, OH); Renee Edwards of Fairfax (VA) Public Library; Renea Arnold of Multnomah County (OR) Libraries; Susan Bard, Every Child Ready to Read @ your library trainer; Janet Ingraham Dwyer, library consultant, State Library of Ohio; Dorothy Stoltz, Carroll County (MD) Public Library; Jennifer Timmerman, Boone County (KY) Public Library; and Enid Costley, Library of Virginia, offered helpful, insightful comments.

We thank the following individuals for their work and contributions on assessing and evaluating early literacy enhanced storytimes: Stephanie Bailey-White, projects coordinator, Idaho Commission for Libraries; Roger Stewart, professor, Boise State University; Rachel Payne, coordinator of early childhood services, Brooklyn (NY) Public Library; Priscilla Queen, Literacy Department, Douglas County (CO) Libraries; and Lori Romero and Melissa Depper, Child and Family Library Services Department, Arapahoe Library District (Arapahoe County, CO).

Thank you to the staff at ALA Editions, including Jill Davis, Jenni Fry, Christine Schwab, and Katherine Faydash, and especially to Stephanie Zvirin, acquisitions editor, for making this publication come to fruition.

We coauthors are grateful to have had the chance to collaborate once again.

Introduction

STORYTIMES ARE FOR EVERYONE—BABIES, TODDLERS, AND PRESCHOOLERS AND THEIR parents and care providers. Sharing language through books, songs, fingerplays, flannelboards, puppets, and other materials, combined with research-backed tidbits of information adults can use to help children develop a strong foundation for later reading success, is the focus of this book. Caring adults, children with their eyes and minds wide open, and you, the storytime presenter, bring all the elements together to create a storytime that is informative and, most of all, fun. Although much has changed since the publication of our first book, *Early Literacy Storytimes @ your library: Partnering with Caregivers for Success*, storytime still remains one of public libraries' core services. Many parents are reintroduced to the library through their children's huge appetite for books and the opportunity that storytimes provide to support book sharing and reading, as well as social time for both children and adults. More and more libraries are creating interactive early learning environments to encourage adults to talk, read, sing, write, and play with their children in the library. The idea of the library as being that "third place"—neither home nor work—where people feel comfortable socializing, and perhaps learning together, is one that many libraries are embracing.

For a lot of us, storytimes have changed as we have embraced research and become intentional about incorporating parent education as a value-added aspect of our storytimes. In this way, storytimes help parents understand the connection between our joyful activities around books and language and later reading. Through storytimes we can introduce adults and children to the basics of scientific thinking. Vocabularies grow as we purposefully introduce children to new words. When we model behaviors that encourage early literacy development in children and explain to the adults who accompany children why we are doing what we're doing, we add value to a program that is already loved and esteemed. By doing this, we send a powerful message. We understand that many children are not prepared to learn when they go to school, and we acknowledge that we have a professional commitment to do what we can to help change childhood outcomes.

In this book we reintroduce the early literacy enhanced storytime: a traditional storytime with the addition of three early literacy tips or asides directed to the adults, all highlighting one of the early literacy components or skills. Adults learn how storytime activities and activities they can do at home after storytime support young children's literacy development.

Why Should I Do Early Literacy Enhanced Storytimes?

About one-third of children enter school without the requisite skills needed to learn to read. Children who start out behind often do not catch up. There is a 90 percent probability that a child will still be a poor reader at the end of fourth grade if that child is a poor reader at the end of first grade.[1] A solid foundation in early literacy before kindergarten plays a critical role in ensuring that a child has a strong start in formal schooling, regardless of socioeconomic status, home language, or ethnicity.

Through storytime programs offered in the library, child-care centers, and other places in the community, library staff have the opportunity to reach children and adults of all socioeconomic backgrounds. Library staff can model behaviors that promote the development of early literacy skills, and they can discuss how specific storytime activities develop these skills. Our goal is to introduce adults to these early literacy skills and to encourage them to continue practicing these skills at home with their children. By providing them with the research-based skills to help their children develop a solid early literacy foundation, we are helping them create readers who later become lifelong learners.

Evaluations of early literacy enhanced storytimes have shown that there are two factors that motivate parents to do activities that support early literacy with their children: understanding the connection between activities and later reading, and seeing a storytime presenter model these activities in enjoyable ways, which makes the activities look like something parents can do at home, too.

So, to recapitulate, why we should do early literacy enhanced storytimes?

- We want to be part of the solution to help children be successful readers!
- We have access to young children and to their parents and caregivers. We interact with them already.
- We have information about early literacy that can help parents and caregivers prepare their children for learning.
- We do not see young children on a daily basis to help support their early literacy development. However, by sharing early literacy information with adults, we have an opportunity to make a difference in children's early literacy development.
- We have a professional obligation to share this information in a way that is meaningful and appropriate for young children.

Every Child Ready to Read: Changes in Approach

New research has reaffirmed the importance of early literacy skills as an integral part of a child's ability to learn to read. To reflect the shifts that have occurred as a result of research in the field of early childhood education, we have adopted a more comprehensive definition of early literacy from Jaclyn Kupcha-Szrom: "what children know about communication, language (verbal and nonverbal), reading, and writing before they can actually read and write. Early literacy encompasses all of a child's experiences with conversation, stories (oral and written), books, and print."[2]

The second edition of Every Child Ready to Read (ECRR2), a joint effort of the Public Library Association (PLA) and the Association for Library Service to Children (ALSC), builds on the six skills and research from the first edition while explaining and giving supporting evidence for new research. Here we explore two of the major differences between the two editions of Every Child Ready to Read, and we review the research that spurred the creation of the new edition (for a history of the project, see www.everychildreadytoread.org).

The first difference is the focus on five practices (singing, talking, reading, writing, and playing) rather than on the six early literacy skills. The shift occurred because the authors of ECRR2 believe that encouraging these practices without focusing on the skills is a more effective way to help adults get their children ready to read. The practices are less intimidating than the skills. It is still important, however, to show the connection between the practices and how they support early literacy and later reading. The second difference is a reconfiguration and expansion of language development, from oral language to early literacy to literacy. This change is a reflection of the centrality of language experiences to a child's acquisition of early literacy skills and comprehension. The focus on language development includes an emphasis on using informational books to help young children develop their vocabularies and background knowledge. ECRR2 more directly shows the continuum of the practices, early literacy, and the process of reading.

Five Components of Early Literacy

To better align with the new research and ECRR2, in this book we have changed the language we use to articulate what the research indicates. Rather than talking about six skills, we describe five components of early literacy. The term *components* is more inclusive, reflecting, for example, the fact that background knowledge is not a skill but the result of several skills (the *ECRR2 Manual* refers to a similar configuration as "critical dimensions of language and literacy"). Here are the five components:

1. **Phonological awareness:** the ability to hear and play with the smaller sounds in words, beginning with recognizing environmental sounds (e.g., doorbell, animals) and progressing to hearing syllables, rhyme, and sounds at the beginning of words (e.g., /d/ at the beginning of *dog*)
2. **Print conventions and awareness:** knowing that print has meaning, and knowing how to handle a book, follow text on a page, and recognize environmental print
3. **Letter knowledge:** knowing that the same letter can look different and that letters have names and represent sounds
4. **Vocabulary:** knowing the meanings of words, including words for things, concepts, feelings, and ideas
5. **Background knowledge:** prior knowledge, or what a child knows before entering kindergarten from his or her experiences with living and language. Background knowledge is the result of several skills. Narrative skills and print motivation (from the first edition of ECRR) are included in this broader category, which includes experiences with stories and books.

We contend that any of the five practices is a natural and supportive way to enter into conversations with adults about early literacy. It may also make library staff more comfortable talking about early literacy and be less intimidating for parents and caregivers. It is critical, however, to incorporate explicit information on early literacy and later reading so that caregivers realize that how both librarians and parents perform these practices with children makes a difference in their early literacy development.

Organization of This Book

We have divided this book into three parts. The first part, "Learning It," looks at research and information on early literacy and storytime practices. We cover material not explored in our first book and its relationship to the five practices presented in ECRR2, with special emphasis on writing, talking, and playing, and how these foster reading. In addition, we go into detail on two topics that might be new to many library staff: oral language and background knowledge. We also look at the impact of research on storytime practices. Moreover, we zero in on informational books, focusing on mathematics and science, and we present research and ideas on math and science activities to use during or after storytime. Other chapters in this part bring together updated research on English-language learners and discuss how we can best serve them in our storytimes, and look at issues with the use of television and DVDs in storytimes.

The second part, "Doing It," discusses how to prepare an early literacy enhanced program and offers sample storytimes for infants and toddlers, two- and three-year-olds, and preschoolers. Each storytime is complete, including information that librarians can present directly to parents and additional activities that include math and science experiences for older preschoolers.

The third part, "Making It Your Own," helps you build your own early literacy enhanced storytime. It includes a selection of storytime extras (nursery rhymes, song and movement activities, and craft activities) that you can adapt to fit your own situation, early literacy asides for parents, and guidance to help you evaluate your program.

We hope that you will find this book to be a useful tool in incorporating early literacy information and activities into your storytimes. It is not intended to limit what you do but rather to help you expand your repertoire and your understanding of why your work with children and adults is so critical.

NOTES

1. American Federation of Teachers, "Waiting Rarely Works: Late Bloomers Usually Just Wilt," *Reading Rockets*, www.readingrockets.org/article/11360/.

2. Jaclyn Kupcha-Szrom, "A Window to the World: Early Language and Literacy Development," *Zero to Three*, February 2011, 1.

Part I

Learning It

chapter 1

Early Literacy Research

Critical Dimensions of Language and Early Literacy

THIS CHAPTER SUMMARIZES AND EXPANDS ON THE RESEARCH ON EACH OF THE CRITI-cal dimensions of language and early literacy as set forth in the second edition of Every Child Ready to Read (ECRR2). These topics include the following:

Oral language: listening, speaking, and communication skills

Phonological awareness: the ability to hear and play with the smaller sounds in words, beginning with recognizing environmental sounds (e.g., doorbell, animals) and progressing to hearing syllables, rhyme, and sounds at the beginning of words

Print conventions and awareness: knowing that print has meaning, and knowing how to handle a book, follow text on a page, and recognize environmental print

Letter knowledge: knowing that the same letter can look different and that letters have names and represent sounds

Vocabulary: knowing the meanings of words, including words for things, concepts, feelings, and ideas

Background knowledge: prior knowledge, or what a child knows before entering kindergarten from his or her experiences with living and language. Background knowledge is the result of several skills.

Narrative skills and print motivation (from the first edition of ECRR) are included in this broader category, which includes experiences with stories and books.

CONSTRAINED AND UNCONSTRAINED EARLY LITERACY COMPONENTS

The early literacy components can be loosely arranged into two groups—constrained and unconstrained skills. According to Dr. Scott Paris, constrained skills are those that are finite.[1] Constrained skills help a child to read—or to decode, recognize, or sound out words. The skills that are most closely related to decoding are phonological awareness, print conventions and awareness, and letter knowledge—all of which are finite skills:

Phonological awareness: There are about 44 phonemes (individual sounds) in the English language. Although each language has its own unique set of phonemes, only about 150 phonemes constitute all the world's languages.[2]

Print conventions and awareness: Understanding how to handle a book—starting at the front cover, holding it right-side up, turning pages from right to left in English, and knowing the direction of print (from left to right and top to bottom in English) are all aspects of print awareness.

Letter knowledge: There are twenty-six letters in the English alphabet. Each letter has an upper- and lowercase form. There are myriad fonts, but always twenty-six letters.

Unconstrained skills are those that do not have an end—we continue to acquire new vocabulary and background knowledge throughout our lives. Unconstrained skills help children understand what they read. They are a strong predictor of reading success from the fourth grade on, when children read to learn. The following are unconstrained skills:

Vocabulary: Knowing the meanings of words, including the names of things, concepts, feelings, and ideas. There is a finite number of words in the dictionary, but the likelihood of our learning the meanings of all those words in our lifetime is slim. In addition, new words are always being added to language.

Background knowledge: What children have learned before entering kindergarten, including general knowledge about how their world works, knowledge about the structure of story and books, content knowledge, and conceptual thought.

Both constrained and unconstrained skills are critical to a child's later reading. Both sets of skills start to develop from birth, and children progress in these skills according to their age and developmental stage.

The process of reading is divided into two key areas: decoding and comprehension. *Decoding* refers to converting the printed word into spoken language. Some words are recognized by sight. Others require the application of knowledge of letter-sound relationships and patterns, that is, the matching of a letter or combination of letters to their sound, in order to decipher words. *Comprehension* refers to understanding what is being read.[3] Decoding is most directly supported by constrained skills, whereas comprehension is most directly supported by unconstrained skills. It is important to note that vocabulary spans both areas; in addition to having better comprehension, children with larger vocabularies can more easily sound out words with which they are familiar.[4]

Through second grade young children are "learning to read," which is most directly supported by constrained skills. Beginning in the third grade, they "read to learn," which is most directly supported by unconstrained skills. To become readers, children need both constrained and unconstrained skills, as well as early literacy skills, to support the decoding and comprehension areas of reading. These skills start developing at birth, which means that from day one, children's experiences with language and literacy shape their future ability to read.

CHANGES IN ECRR2: FIVE PRACTICES

A major difference between the two editions of ECRR is the shift from the six skills to five practices, or activities. In the first edition, the approach was to start with the skills and then look for activities that supported those skills. For example, phonological awareness—hearing and playing with the smaller sounds in words—can be supported by several activities, including singing songs, having children repeat animal sounds, clapping out syllables, and talking about rhyming words. In ECRR2, adults are encouraged to use five activities to help their children get ready to read: talking, singing, reading, writing, and playing.

However, simply doing these five practices is not enough. It is critical to help adults understand that *how* they do these activities affects their children's early literacy development. We can help adults make connections to their children's later reading by explaining both the hows and the whys of the practices. A public opinion survey conducted by Calgary Public Library as part of a public relations campaign found that parents knew that reading with their children would support later reading. However, they did not connect other activities (talking, singing, writing, and playing) with learning how to read.

OTHER CHANGES IN ECRR2

In ECRR2 the book picture walk has replaced the dialogic reading activity. Although there are some similarities in the techniques of these activities, their goals are different. *Dialogic reading* refers to the interaction between the adult and the child in reading, with the goal of developing the child's vocabulary and narrative skills to increase comprehension. In contrast, the goals of the book picture walk are to help the adult understand what the child knows, using the pictures in the book as a guide, and to help the child predict what will happen in a story.

Dialogic reading can start with younger children who have at least fifty words of expressive vocabulary (in other words, those who can respond with a word or phrase), and the emphasis is on the conversation itself, following the child's lead and using a picture in a book as a conversation starter. For younger children we start by asking what an item in the picture is, labeling it, and having the child repeat the word, and then we add a bit more description. For children with more language, more open-ended questions can be asked, such as what is happening, how the situation got that way, what the character is feeling, when the child has felt that way, and so on. The child's sense of the story as a whole can be developed, but it is not required; each picture can be discussed individually. The goal is to follow the child's language in order to encourage more language. For more information on dialogic reading, see *Early Literacy Storytimes @ your library*. For a bookmark summarizing dialogic reading steps, see www.earlylit.net/workshopmats/ecrrstorytime/handdialbkmk1.pdf.

In ECRR2 the book picture walk takes readers on a "walk" through a book, looking at and talking about the pictures before reading it. Readers use some of the same techniques as in dialogic reading, such as using the pictures in books as the basis of conversation, asking open-ended questions, and relating the pictures to the child's experiences. The goals of the book picture walk are to preview the book to learn what the child already knows and to help the child predict what might happen in the story; later those predictions are verified to see whether they were correct. The book picture walk is geared toward preschool-age children and those in the primary grades. Children must be old enough to have a sense of story and a sense of sequencing.

In ECRR2 another way of sharing books together is called shared book reading, in which adults read the text aloud, conveying the rhythm, the lilt of the author's language, and the words that the author has chosen to tell the story. With shared book reading, which emphasizes verbal interactions between adults and children, adults build on words used in the text and point out conventions of print. A bookmark summarizing the steps of a book picture walk and shared book reading can be found at www.earlylit.net/workshopmats/elest2/6parentpicwalk2.pdf. All of these ways of sharing books—dialogic reading, book picture walks, and shared book reading—are valuable.

Another change in ECRR2 is an emphasis on sharing factual books and information with young children, in order to support a broader vocabulary and increased background knowledge (we address this in more depth in chapter 5).

NATIONAL EARLY LITERACY PANEL RESEARCH

In 2008 the National Early Literacy Panel published a comprehensive study with the goal of identifying early literacy interventions and programs that have the most positive impact on children's ability to learn to read, write, and spell.[5] The study identified alphabet knowledge, phonological awareness, and oral language as essential elements of early literacy instruction. It also found that the rapid naming of letters and digits, as well as objects and colors, is a strong or moderate predictor of later literacy achievement. This does not necessarily mean that parents should drill children in rapidly naming a series of letters. Rather, children's rapid naming ability is the result of their having learned the letters, numbers, colors, and objects.[6] In response to the panel's report, several early literacy experts have also noted the importance of vocabulary and background knowledge to the reading process, in addition to the ability to decode.[7]

In the following sections, we summarize some of the research on oral language and on each of the early literacy components.

Oral Language

Oral language, which encompasses listening, speaking, and verbal communication, is the foundation for both early literacy and later literacy. It is not considered a component because, quite simply, it suffuses all the early literacy components. Children with strong oral language skills find it easier to learn to read than children with less developed oral language skills. The National Institute for Literacy describes the three fundamental skills of oral language as follows:[8]

Listening Skills
- understanding what other people are saying when they speak
- hearing the smaller sounds of spoken language (phonology)
- enjoying listening to stories
- following oral instructions

Speaking Skills
- producing the sounds of language
- understanding what words mean and the connections among words (semantics)
- putting words in the right order (e.g., adjective before noun)
- using conventional forms of words, such as plurals and verb tenses (syntax)
- using language for different purposes, such as to express ideas and feelings, to obtain or give information, and to negotiate disagreements

Communication Skills
- understanding the social rules of conversation, such as taking turns, listening when someone else is talking, and saying hello and good-bye and please and thank you (pragmatics)
- understanding and using the rules of grammar (syntax)
- asking questions to obtain information
- engaging peers and adults by using language

Language acquisition begins at birth; the brain is primed for learning language in the early years. Even before babies can speak words, they use nonverbal language, such as facial expressions, gestures, and body language, to communicate. In order to progress from nonverbal to verbal language, children need to be spoken to directly and to be responded to when they make sounds, and they need nonverbal cues to help them make sense of what they hear. Some families even use sign language with their children before they are able to express themselves verbally. This helps children make themselves understood. However, to promote language learning, it is important for adults to verbalize the word for the sign as they make it, and to encourage children to use their voices along with their signs even if their words are not understandable.

Oral language develops progressively. Infants listen to and become aware of sounds and words. They learn the meanings of words through actions and facial expressions. They learn to communicate their needs by cooing, babbling, crying, and using gestures. Infants recognize their names at about four months of age. Researchers have found that one way babies learn to identify words in a word stream is that they notice the word that directly follows their name.[9] Babies also learn to make sense of language from adults' reactions to their babbling. For example, when a baby says, "Da-da-da-da," parents' animated reaction to what sounds like *dada* or *daddy* helps the baby understand that those sounds are important. Where sound meets meaning, we have language. Infants are also very aware of the rhythm of language. In learning to distinguish words from strings of syllables, they note which syllables are stressed. For example, in English, two-syllable words are usually stressed on the first syllable. The lilt of the language that children hear helps them to make sense of language.

Toddlers often repeat what is said to them. They use language to express their feelings and to learn about what is happening in their world. They begin not only to repeat what is said but also to respond to it. They start to talk in simple sentences, to make their needs and opinions known, and to ask for information.

Preschoolers build larger vocabularies from the language of people around them and from ideas they learn about in books, and their sentences become longer and more complex. They like to share their knowledge on all types of topics. They respond to open-ended how and why questions. They can tell long, involved stories and can recount events in sequence. They talk about past and future events.

Children can only learn language in a social context—from speaking and being spoken to. Researchers Todd Risley and Betty Hart found that the amount of language a child possesses at age nine depends largely on the amount and kind of language that the child heard from his or her family between birth and age three. And the amount of language a child possesses at age nine indicates the child's lifelong literacy prospects.[10] (For more details on this study and its implications, see the section "The Five Practices—Talking" in this chapter.)

Now let's look at each of the early literacy components that arises from oral language: phonological awareness, print conventions and awareness, letter knowledge, vocabulary, and background knowledge. We only touch on the first four components, as our first book addressed them in some detail, but we go into more depth on background knowledge.

Phonological Awareness

Phonological awareness is the ability to hear and play with the smaller sounds in words; it includes recognizing environmental sounds, being able to hear syllables (including breaking words apart and blending them together), rhyming, and identifying sounds at the beginning of words. This early literacy component is critical to a child's ability to sound out words when reading. If children cannot hear the smaller sounds in words, they cannot sound out words by relating letters to sounds.

Phonological awareness begins as infants notice the sounds they hear in their environment; for example, they may turn their heads at the sound of a doorbell ringing or a dog barking. At four months old, an infant's brain distinguishes between language fragments and other nonlanguage sounds, such as a phone ringing or a car honking. These two types of sound are processed in different parts of the brain.[11] Later, with encouragement from adults, children try to reproduce the sounds they hear. If an adult asks, "What sound does a cat make?" a child might respond, "Meow! Meow!" Or an adult might ask a child to say a word (such as *mama*), and the child will try to do so.

Similarly, in all aspects of phonological awareness, development progresses from hearing to recognizing to producing. For example, children first hear rhyme (as adults say nursery rhymes or read books with rhyme), then recognize words that rhyme (e.g., an adult can offer two words and asks whether they rhyme, or offer two words that rhyme and one that does not and ask which two words rhyme), and then are able to make a rhyme (e.g., an adult can say a word and ask the child to say a word that rhymes with it).

The various aspects of phonological awareness develop in complex and interrelated ways. For example, in rhyming a one-syllable word (e.g., *cat*), children are able to isolate the beginning sound, or onset—/k/—but they hear the ending sounds, or rime—/a/ and /t/—as one sound, /at/. Beth Phillips, Jeanine Clancy-Menchetti, and Christopher Lonigan looked at some of the factors that can make phonological awareness difficult to teach.[12] In general, they conclude that the progression starts with larger elements and moves to smaller ones, so it begins with word awareness and moves to awareness of compound words, then syllables, followed by onset and rime (including rhyming), and finally phonemic awareness. But children do not finish developing all of one aspect before moving on to another; there is much overlap.

The final aspect of phonological awareness to develop, phonemic awareness, is the ability to hear and play with the smallest sounds that make up words. (A phoneme is the smallest sound in a word that makes a difference in the word.) In the progression of phonemic awareness, children will hear individual sounds most easily at the beginning of the word, then at the end, then in the middle. For example, they will hear the /b/ in *boy* before the /b/ in *tub*, and they will hear the /b/ in *tub* before the /b/ in *rabbit*. To help children with this skill, adults can read tongue twisters or books with alliteration and ask the child to point out when two words start with the same sound, or ask the child to think of a word that starts with the same sound as a given word.

Print Conventions and Awareness

The concept underlying print awareness is that print has meaning. Print is all around us—in books, magazines, and newspapers, of course, but also on mail, signs, posters, labels, warning stickers, and so on. One aspect of print awareness is recognizing print wherever you see it. Understanding how to handle a book is a combination of several other aspects—starting at the front cover, holding it right-side up, turning pages from right to left in English, and knowing that the direction of print is from left to right and top to bottom in English. When children feel comfortable handling a book, they can pay more attention to the process of learning to read once they start school.

Research has shown that when preschool children share books with adults, they direct about 95 percent of their visual attention to the illustrations, and 95 percent of their talk focuses on illustrations or concepts expressed in the book. With help from adults, children can be guided to explore the print. *Print referencing* is the term for talking about print, nonverbally tracking print, and otherwise using verbal and nonverbal cues to encourage children's attention to and interactions with print.[13] Some examples of print referencing are when an adult runs a finger under words as he or she says them out loud or points out how fonts can reflect the meaning of a word or the way we say words. A recent study looked at longitudinal results from the Sit Talk and Read program, a thirty-week program during which preschool teachers systematically referenced print during shared reading. Print referencing activities included pointing out the words for what was being said aloud (e.g., "Here are the words for *thank you*"), pointing out the author's name and saying what the author does, pointing out the title, showing the direction of print by following the text with a finger, pointing out some characteristics of letters, and picking out letters from a child's name. This technique of adding print referencing to shared book reading resulted in increases in scores for reading, spelling, and comprehension two years later. Furthermore, it was found not to detract from other aspects of early literacy support, such as vocabulary development and language growth.[14] In addition, the technique required only subtle shifts in teacher behaviors, which made it easy to implement. The results of this study are the first to suggest causal links between print referencing and later literacy achievement.

Letter Knowledge

Letter knowledge refers to knowing that the same letter can look different and that letters have names and represent sounds. Especially in English, where one letter can represent multiple sounds, it is a small but important distinction for children to know that letters represent sounds but do not "make" them. English has what is known as deep orthography: there are 44 phonemes, or individual sounds, in English, but 1,100 ways to spell those sounds. In contrast, in Spanish there are about 35 phonemes and 38 ways to spell those sounds.[15] It appears that knowledge of letter names precedes and facilitates knowledge of letter sounds;[16] in turn, knowledge of letter sounds directly promotes awareness of phonemes, decoding, and word recognition.

The precursors to letter knowledge for young children are the abilities to recognize shapes and to understand similarities and differences. Children recognize letters by their shapes: an uppercase *A* has a triangle in it, and a *p* is a circle with a line on the side. Many letters look similar: the only difference between a lowercase *n* and a lowercase *h* is the height of the line. When young children play with a ball, blocks, or puzzles, and adults point out shapes, this supports the development of letter knowledge. Adults support the skills children need for letter knowledge when they describe objects; point out differences in texture, color, and shape; and play matching games.

Vocabulary

Vocabulary is knowing the meanings of words, including words for things, feelings, concepts, and ideas. The more words children know, the easier it is for them to learn to read. Children enter school knowing anywhere from five thousand to twenty thousand words; the actual number depends on how much they have been spoken and read to.[17] Having a large vocabulary helps children with reading in two ways. First, when children are learning to read, they sound out words. It is easier for them to recognize a word they are sounding out if they have heard the word before. Second, if there are too many words in a text that a child does not know, it will be difficult for him or her to understand the whole paragraph or story.

Babies learn words when we speak to them. They try to figure out where one word ends and another begins, and they do this largely on the basis of emphasis on syllables. They also use hints from our gestures (e.g., pointing to objects), facial expressions (e.g., feeling words and associations), and reactions to their babble (e.g., "Oh, he said, 'Dada'!") to understand the meaning of what we say. The more often babies hear a word, the more likely they are to recognize it as a word and learn its meaning. Children learn the meanings of words for things they encounter in their environment first—such as *milk*, *juice*, and *blanket*—and progress to learning more abstract words—such as *share*, *happy*, and *yellow*. Even as their vocabulary grows, they continue to learn words best when they hear them spoken in context, that is, as part of what they are experiencing.

Children learn words through fast mapping.[18] Fast mapping is the connection made between a new word and its underlying concept after only a brief encounter with the word. Fast mapping gives children a general idea of what a word means but not the specifics. So, if a child has seen a dog and knows what it is, when the child sees a cow, he or she "defines" a cow (unknown) in reference to a dog (known). With increased exposure to things and the words for them, children will learn similarities and differences among them and make finer and finer distinctions to arrive at a better understanding of the words that correspond to the things.

Another way that researchers have found that children learn words is through repetition; they learn the words that they hear most often and the words for things that interest them. One way to build on a child's interest while expanding his or her vocabulary is by reading informational books. Again, children learn words best in a meaningful context, rather than through rote memorization, which is why a book about science that has compelling photographs with captions is a better vocabulary-teaching tool than flashcards. Children also need clear information about words. To help preschoolers build vocabulary, it is important for adults to express the meaning of a word on the child's level; for instance, by relating it to something the child already knows.

Adults should use all kinds of words when talking to children—exposure to a wide variety of words is a first step toward later comprehension. Adults tend to use nouns more than other parts of speech when talking to young children. However, for children to build vocabulary, they must also be exposed to verbs, adverbs, adjectives, and prepositions. So, when a child asks, "What's that?" an adult could respond, "It's a microwave oven, a machine that cooks and warms up our food." Children need to hear words for feelings and ideas, words for talking about things that happened in the past or that will happen, and words for talking about things we know. Even with babies, adults should use all sorts of words. Even though they won't understand all of them, their brains are using all those different sounds to lay the groundwork for learning language.

The techniques for sharing books mentioned previously in this chapter—dialogic reading, the book picture walk, and shared book reading—all encourage children's vocabulary development and narrative skills. The question-and-answer format of dialogic reading also stimulates conversation and allows opportunities for adults to expand children's vocabulary through conversation. Overall, the more vocabulary words children know, the more vocabulary they will gain. Learning a word generally leads to learning other words, and so knowledge of words grows vocabulary.

Background Knowledge

Background knowledge, in the context of early literacy, refers to prior knowledge, or what children know before entering kindergarten. Researchers have noted that one of the best predictors of student learning is what children already know before they begin to study new material. Also, the more children know, the easier it is for them to learn even more things. This is because children learn best when they can add new information to what is already familiar to them.[19] Together with vocabulary, background knowledge is a key component of comprehension, or understanding what is being read. To understand what they are reading, children use their own growing knowledge of language and the world, as well as their understanding of print.

The best way to build children's background knowledge is to talk with them about what they are seeing or doing. For example, in the checkout aisle of the grocery store, parents can talk with children about what is happening around them. In an interview we conducted, one parent noted that her daughter thought that the checkout cashiers were all rich—she believed that they kept all the money people gave to them. This story illustrates why it is not enough for adults to expose their children to new experiences; they also need to talk with them before, during, and after the experience, to help them understand it.

Children also need to be able to understand and talk about things that they have not immediately experienced. In a longitudinal study of children participating in Head Start, Catherine Snow, David Dickinson, and Patton Tabors found that exposure to "decontextualized language"—or language that goes beyond the here and now—was the most important factor in children's success with language and literacy.[20] A study by Hart and Risley also showed the significance of going beyond the here and now: children who developed larger vocabularies had parents who used more past-tense verbs in conversations with them during their first three years.[21]

Background knowledge is divided into four areas: general knowledge, story and book knowledge, content knowledge, and conceptual thinking. General knowledge refers to knowledge of things. The more general knowledge children have, the easier it is for them to understand their world. General knowledge includes things such as knowing that the light goes on when you flip the switch, knowing that you need a raincoat when it is raining, and knowing that something is happening outside when the dog barks.

Story and book knowledge refers to understanding the structure of story (beginning, middle, and end; problem resolution). Children become familiar with story motifs, such as things happening in sets of three (e.g., three billy goats, three bears) or "once upon a time." They also learn the language of story, that is, written language, which is different from conversational language.

Content knowledge refers to knowledge of topical facts or information. Young children are naturally curious, and sharing factual information with them about topics of interest to them is one way to help them learn facts and ideas and to make sense of the world.

Conceptual thinking includes knowing concepts such as shapes, colors, and size, as well as the ability to think abstractly about things that are not immediately in front of you. Conceptual thinking is the result of thought processes like remembering, problem solving, and decision making. It involves not only the development of understanding of a specific concept, such as seasons or opposites, but also the use of strategies to encourage understanding and thinking skills. During the first three years of life, children master these thinking and understanding skills: that objects are alike and different, that objects and people exist even if they cannot be seen (object permanence), cause and effect, how to use tools, how to think symbolically (i.e., that one thing can represent another), and how to imitate.[22] Additional aspects of conceptual thinking include sequencing, describing characteristics of objects, sorting and matching, having a sense of time, talking about abstract ideas (e.g., truth, loyalty), talking about the past and future, pretending and imagining, solving problems, and making predictions. Each of these aspects develops in progression, from the more concrete to the more abstract. For example, with sequencing, toddlers understand that their socks go on before their shoes, whereas older children have a sense of the sequence of events over the course of a day or over the course of a story.

Additional information on content and processes related to background knowledge can be found in chapter 5. A chart summarizing the early literacy components can be found at the website www.earlylit.net/workshopmats/elest2/7el compsummary.pdf.

Adults consciously and subconsciously help children gain a foundation in early literacy as they interact with young children. ECRR2 offers adults five practices that provide opportunities to support young children's language and early literacy development in enjoyable ways.

The Five Practices

Children can acquire a strong foundation in early literacy with the help of involved adults who talk, sing, read, write, and play with them. Each of these practices can be varied to develop and nurture early literacy skills. The practices are part of storytimes as well. Library staff can model the behaviors that foster children's early literacy development and articulate to adults the connection that these activities have to children's later reading success. In the following sections, we look at the five practices from ECRR2 as they relate to the components of early literacy. In the next chapter we look at how information on the practices can inform what library staff do in storytime.

TALKING

Talking with children is key to developing their oral language and to cultivating their facility in each of the early literacy components. Adults can be most effective when talking with children when they incorporate gestures, talk a lot, and use a wide variety of words.

For babies and toddlers, language *is* literacy. Parents who use a lot of gestures in communicating with their children will see their babies' language increase at a more rapid rate than those who don't. When parents point things out, babies and toddlers learn to make more gestures, and the number of gestures a child can make predicts his or her vocabulary size at age four and a half. When parents "translate" their child's gestures into words, those words become part of the child's spoken vocabulary within a few months. Gesture can also play a direct role in word learning by giving children an opportunity to practice generating particular meanings with their hands at a time when those meanings are difficult to produce by talking.[23]

A study by Hart and Risley documented the correlation between the number of words that a child hears and the development of his or her vocabulary. The authors followed the language interactions between adults and their children in forty-two families, which were categorized as "professional," "working," or "welfare," and found that children from more talkative families had higher vocabularies regardless of category.[24] Whether adults talked with their children a lot or a little, there was the same amount of talk around the business of everyday life, or "business talk." *Business talk* refers to talking about what needs to get done (e.g., "It's time to go," "Wash your hands," "Don't touch that!"). When parents need children to pay attention, they give them explicit directions, without the distraction of extra language. In taciturn families, business talk tends to make up the majority of language that children hear, whereas in talkative families, there is a lot of extra talk, or "play talk"—chitchat, commentary, expressions of affection, wordplay, open-ended questions, and storytelling.

Risley explained that it is this extra talk that gives children in talkative families an advantage.[25] The reason for this, Hart and Risley found, is that in addition to increasing the sheer number of words a child hears, play talk is richer talk (that is, it contains a wider variety of words), and it is also more responsive and encouraging. There's more information; more back-and-forth; more interesting and unusual words; and a lot more encouragement for questioning, exploring, putting ideas into words, and figuring things out.

When parents talk more with their children, this extra talk automatically becomes that richer, extra language.[26] To encourage parents to talk more with their children, librarians can suggest that they try adding two enriching or positive sentences to what they are saying. For example, a parent might say, "Put your shoes on. We're going grocery shopping." To add two positive sentences, the parent might then say, "It will be a quick trip, but our friends are coming over tomorrow, and I need some ingredients for the dinner I'll be cooking. I was thinking of making lasagna. You like that, too!"

The ways we talk with children also affect the amount and kind of oral language children have. For example, children about nine months old and younger will listen to adults longer if they speak in "parentese," that higher-pitched, slower-paced talk with elongated vowels and clear speech. In addition, according to Hart and Risley, talking with children using more encouragements or positive assurances leads them to learn more language than when talk uses more prohibitions. The more positive the affect during interactions, the more motivated the child is to explore new topics, to try out tentative relationships, to listen and practice, to add words to those he or she has already accumulated, and to notice facts and relationships.[27] So, when we encourage parents and caregivers to speak more with their children, we should also encourage them to make those interactions supportive and respectful, and to elicit children's responses.

It is critical to articulate to parents and caregivers that talking is important, and not just talking to their children, but encouraging their children to talk in turn. Library staff need to share that there are various strategies for encouraging children to talk, including the following:

- verbalizing the child's gestures
- imitating the child's sounds and actions
- repeating what the child says
- using compelling themes
- asking open-ended questions
- "striving for five" interactions (encouraging multiple turns between the adult and the child)
- thinking aloud

The following scenarios expand on the strategies listed above:

A young child may make a gesture or point to something. The adult can put words to what the child wants to communicate. After waiting a few seconds, the adult should ask the child to say the words back to him or her, even if he or she know the words will sound like babble.

When the child is familiar with a particular routine, the adult should stop and wait for the child to say what to do next.

If a child cannot answer a question, the adult can describe what is happening, or, when reading, the adult can describe the pictures in a book. Both of these types of description provide the child with language that he or she will use later.

When a child mispronounces a word or uses incorrect grammar, the adult should simply repeat the word or sentence properly without forcing a correction. For example, if the child says, "We goed to the park yesterday," the adult can respond, "Yes, we went to the park yesterday."

Adults can talk with children about the reasons for anything and everything around them, such as why there are traffic lights or why police cars have sirens.

Adults can encourage children to tell stories and talk about things that have happened and can encourage pretend play or acting out situations or stories. To help develop children's vocabulary, adults can suggest descriptive words, use synonyms of words children are saying, or add a bit of explanation or information that children may not already know.

The adult can repeat what the child says and then wait for the child to speak again. Sometimes this approach encourages the child to

> say more than if the adult asked a direct question. Adults should wait at least five seconds for a child to respond.
>
> Adults can use compelling themes (i.e., themes with rich content and through which children will gain knowledge about their world) to engage children. Themes that are interesting to children help them remember ideas and facts and encourage them to ask questions and think critically.[28]
>
> Dr. David Dickinson, professor at Vanderbilt University's Department of Teaching and Learning, suggests that adults should "strive for five," that is, keep an interaction going through five exchanges (e.g., adult-child-adult-child-adult).[29] The adult can ask questions, but need not; the adult's response can be an answer to a question the child has asked or "Tell me more" or "That's interesting" or "I remember when . . ."
>
> Adults can think aloud—musing openly about what they are doing, while exhibiting curiosity and abstract uses of language—and allow time for children to jump in. (It is also helpful for children to see adults learning new things.)[30]

The quantity of words that children hear certainly matters, but so does content, especially as children get older. Adults should engage children in substantive conversation on a variety of topics. All people, regardless of age, need to explain, to tell, to talk about experiences and the world around them. One way to encourage this kind of interaction with children is to fill conversations with ideas, facts, connections, observations, and feelings that are related to what is happening around them. This kind of talk is most likely to take place when children are participating in familiar activities or routines and during dramatic play.

The relationship between the adult and the child affects how well talking can increase language learning. The Classroom Assessment Scoring System (CLASS) was developed as an observational tool that focuses on the effectiveness of interactions among teachers and children, to encourage creative, nurturing environments and engaging opportunities to learn. It was found that positive relationships between the teacher and children were a major factor in the development of children's language. This tool has some implications for librarians to consider.

In 2013 the CLASS observation tool, designed for preschool through third-grade classrooms, is to be implemented in Head Start programs. A version of the tool is also being developed for those who care for infants and toddlers. The CLASS tool measures the effectiveness of teacher-child interactions in three domains: emotional support, instructional support, and organizational support. The most consistent and robust domain for predicting growth over time is instructional support, in which teachers promote higher-order thinking and creativity and give verbal feedback relevant to performance, which increases children's receptive and expressive language, understanding of prereading concepts, and applied mathematical skills. The emotional support domain is associated with growth in children's expressive (words they express through speaking) and receptive (words they understand when heard) language scores.[31]

The elements that are integral to CLASS are the same ones that we advocate for adults, both parents and caregivers—creating a friendly and warm environment, asking open-ended questions, starting where the child is, following the child's lead, narrating what you are doing and what the child is doing, using unfamiliar words, and relating those to what is familiar to the child.

SINGING

Adults can help children develop their vocabularies by singing songs. Many songs have new words, and adults can take time to explain some of them. Adults can also play with the words in a song to tell a story. However, with singing, the most direct link to early literacy components is to phonological awareness, or the ability to hear and play with the smaller sounds in words. Singing helps children develop phonological awareness because words are separated into syllables in music, often with a different note for each syllable. Singing also slows down the pronunciation of words, which makes each part of a word easier for children to hear. Please note that, although singing supports phonological awareness, it is not sufficient in and of itself to develop phonological awareness. Phonological awareness is integral to the ability to learn how to read, so it needs to be intentionally taught, through talking and playing with initial sounds and rhymes, as children get older.

READING

Pediatricians, teachers, and librarians all give parents the same message—read aloud to your child. Reading to children has been hailed as "the single most important activity for building the knowledge required for eventual success in reading."[32] Research has shown positive correlations between how often parents read to their children and three key early literacy measures—alphabetic knowledge (knowing the letter names and their sounds), early reading (children are helped to sound out and blend letters of familiar words), and invented spelling (children are asked to spell words to the best of their ability). These three skills can reliably predict a child's success in reading in grade school.[33] Children who are read to also develop background knowledge about a range of topics and build a large vocabulary, which assists in later reading comprehension and the development of reading strategies.

Repeated readings of books have been shown to be helpful to preschoolers in increasing vocabulary and comprehension. Studies have shown that young children comprehended and spoke more new words after listening to three repeated readings of picture books than after just one or two exposures to a book; in fact, children did not learn to say any new words after listening to a book just once or twice. Instead, young children comprehended and spoke more new words when they were actively involved during the repeated book readings, such as by answering requests to label new words.[34]

Because books contain many words that do not occur in ordinary conversation, they offer opportunities for children to expand their vocabulary. Sometimes children understand an unfamiliar word from the context of the story or the other information in the book. They also pick up clues from the pictures. This leaves them with a general idea of what the word means. By the time children are pre-school age, it is important for them to have more than this general knowledge of the meanings of words. To that end, it is helpful for adults to give a more specific meaning or to add information to better define a word or to distinguish it from a word with a similar meaning. Strategies to help expand a child's vocabulary using books can be as simple as using synonyms as you read the book, discussing a certain word before starting the book, or asking questions to see what children think about the meaning of a word.[35] Some books have many unfamiliar words, but it is not necessary to do this with each word.

Children who are read to often or who regularly see adults reading and writing for personal tasks and pleasure will come to expect that reading and writing play useful roles in life and are valued activities. Children with limited exposure to reading and writing will have different expectations and understanding.[36] Multiple studies have indicated that a child's interest in and enjoyment of reading have an impact on literacy achievement. For example, "child interest predicted alphabetic knowledge even after [controlling] for the frequency of parent teaching," and "child interest in learning about letters and reading [is] a unique predictor of early literacy skills."[37] Because more than half of children find learning to read difficult, a child's interest in and enjoyment of books and reading (also known as print motivation) is a strong factor in learning to read. Research has shown that children who have positive experiences related to books and reading are more likely to stick with learning to read longer when they get to school.

Reading to children, though, is only a first step in promoting reading development. Numerous studies have shown that it is not only the quantity of reading experiences that is important to children's ability to acquire the requisite early literacy skills but also the quality, or how adults read to children. Children who are read to early and often succeed not just because they are exposed to books, but also because the experience of sharing books with adults reflects their engagement in the process, the particular strategies of parents and other adults, and children's interpersonal relationships with adults.[38]

As mentioned earlier, *shared reading* refers to the interaction between adults and children while reading books. Specifically, we define *shared reading* as the interactive sharing of a book between an adult and a child, particularly with the active involvement and engagement of both in a conversation that focuses on a book's words, pictures, and story or content.[39] So shared reading is more than simply reading a book to a child; instead, shared reading is reading a book *with* a child and having the child be part of the process. In shared book reading, adults read the text with the child, point out words, talk about words that may not be familiar to the child, and have the child express what he or she thinks is going on in the book by looking at the pictures. Shared book reading is one of the most important activities that adults can do with children to help get them ready to read.[40] Studies have found that shared book reading predicts children's vocabulary, and in turn, children's vocabulary predicts their phonological awareness and reading comprehension. Moreover, parent reports of shared reading in kindergarten have predicted children's reports of reading for pleasure in the fourth grade.[41]

A report of the National Early Literacy Panel noted that interventions and programs that use shared reading have the biggest impact on oral language outcomes. The effect is statistically significant, falling in the "upper limits of the moderate range,"[42] and consistent with that found in other studies. The report states that there is evidence indicating that shared reading contributes to the development of print awareness, as well as reading, writing, and spelling.[43]

Some researchers believe that the most significant aspect of shared reading is not readily apparent until children are in elementary school: "it is not until older elementary school students acquire the ability to decode text fluently that their receptive language skills can 'exert their full influence.'"[44] In other words, the tests that are given to young children to assess their reading skills might not accurately reflect the real impact of shared reading on the children's abilities to read and understand texts.

WRITING

The Russian psychologist Lev Vygotsky proposed that drawing and writing are precursors of reading. He stated that when children draw or scribble on paper, they use symbols as a way to express ideas and thoughts.[45] Indeed, it is now believed that reading and writing develop concurrently, each with its own developmental stages (for a graphic on the stages of writing, see www.wiu.edu/itlc/ws/ws1/docs/Stages_of_%20ChildWrit.pdf).

Writing is not as easy as it looks! Writing involves the ability to think and the coordination to be able to simultaneously make relatively small marks on paper. Children have to be able to hold a writing instrument and make small lines and circles, not just the wide circles and scribbles of very young children. Fine or small motor activities, such as grasping toys, playing with playdough, stringing beads, buttoning or zipping clothing, eating with utensils, opening and closing containers, and doing fingerplays all help develop children's finger and hand dexterity and coordination. Large motor activities such as stretching, crawling, running, hopping, throwing, and playing catch help children orient their bodies in space and support the larger movement of writing across the page and from top to bottom.

Research indicates that very young children are curious about writing and how it works before they are able to print letters or understand the relationship between letters, writing, and sound (known as the alphabetic principle).[46] Research has also explained both the process and the importance of children mastering the skill of writing. Babies begin to acquire skills for writing as they grasp and manipulate toys. Toddlers scribble without meaning, but there is still a lot going on in the scribbling stage. In addition to becoming more adept at holding and controlling writing instruments, toddlers experience the cause and effect between their movements and the marks on the page, thus developing eye-hand coordination. They also learn to manipulate the speed, force, and direction of the lines they make.

Usually, children make vertical lines first, then horizontal ones, then circular ones. They often start with open strokes that go on continuously. As their coordination improves, they progress to more closed strokes that have a beginning and an end. These closed strokes later turn into shapes and drawings, and then symbols that will later become letters.[47] At first the symbols may look like letters, but they are still drawn; for example, a child might draw a circle for the letter *d* and then draw a long line from the circle upward and another short line from the circle downward. To distinguish one letter from another, children need to pay attention to what makes letters different rather than what makes them similar. This insight begins at about two and a half years old and develops as children encounter print in their environment.[48] Eventually children move from drawing writing to using symbolic writing, which is when the marks on the paper become letters that have meaning to the writer.

Children often learn to form letters when they start school. With support and encouragement from adults, they string random letters together and match letters and their appropriate sounds. Just as early talkers use one word to communicate an entire idea ("milk" to mean "May I have some more milk, please?"), early writers use the initial consonant of a word to represent the entire word. For many children, learning to write their first name is the entryway to discovering letters and letter names and the sounds they represent. Soon after, children realize that writing is a system made up of symbols. This is an enormous step, because they are then able to use letters to make words to express their ideas.

PLAYING

Play is important first and foremost because it is internally motivated, meaning that it is based on a child's own interests and steeped in what he or she already knows. Young children learn best when they are building on what they know, when adults build on their interests, and when they are exposed to new facts and ideas in a social context. Symbolic and dramatic or pretend play, in particular, support children's language and early literacy development. Through this kind of play children develop higher-level thinking and language, use their imaginations, incorporate problem solving, and practice self-regulating (i.e., the ability to control one's own behavior).

What Is Play?

A simple definition of play is activities that one engages in for enjoyment and recreation. In the context of early childhood education, play takes on a number of characteristics that distinguish it from simply having a good time. Here we define *play* more specifically as having the following characteristics:

- enjoyment and pleasure around the activity
- active engagement—the child's deep involvement and active interest
- internal motivation—the source of the activity comes from the child's intrinsic desire
- freedom from external rules—rules are agreed on by children or are implicitly understood
- attention to process rather than product (i.e., the value is in the journey, not the destination)
- element of pretend or fantasy, such as a make-believe world to experiment with limits, roles, and power

Some people distinguish between *play* and *facilitated play*, or play that includes direction from adults. Just as the way children are read to supports different aspects of language development, so does the manner in which children and adults interact in a play environment. The key to keeping play playful is to follow the child's lead.

Kinds of Play

The progression of play over different developmental levels has been observed and categorized in several ways. Here we briefly summarize the ways play has been analyzed in the early childhood literature, addressing stages of play, types of play, and levels of play. It should be noted that children differ widely in their experience with play, the extent to which their play is supported, and their individual development.

The stages of play view play in terms of social development and interaction with others:

1. **Solitary play:** A child plays alone and has limited interaction with other children; infants are able to focus on one object at a time.
2. **Spectator play:** Children observe other children playing around them and have brief interactions with them.
3. **Parallel play:** Two or more children play in the same space; they play side by side but with little interaction; children have a sense of "me" and "mine" and will claim toys.
4. **Associative play:** Children begin to play together in a loosely organized way; conversation happens around toys but not toward one goal; one child may emerge as a leader or organizer of play; and children develop friendships and preferences for playing.
5. **Cooperative play:** Children exchange ideas around toys and/or materials; there are loosely constructed rules, and children have roles in the play; children gain social and communication skills, and they are more likely to share.[49]

Types of play refer to play in terms of cognitive development and the understanding of concepts. The following types of play overlap in play environments and over different ages:

Sensorimotor play: Most associated with infancy, this is play that involves tactile movement, sound, and visual experiences.

Functional play: Children associate an object with an action, such as putting a toy telephone to their ear.

Exploratory or practice play: Children repeat new physical and mental skills until they master them, such as jumping, drawing, counting objects, or pounding and kneading dough; they repeat the actions in order to become capable (which is different from exploration, in which children repeat actions to discover the properties of materials).

Constructive play: Children create a product, such as structures or artwork; this involves problem solving, imagination, and fine motor skills.

Dramatic play: Children act out stories, play house or doctor, or role-play different situations; this play supports narrative skills and the understanding of story structure.

Symbolic play: Children transform an object into other objects (a block becomes a telephone).

Games: Children play games, which involve specific rules; children become more competitive as they grow older.

Levels of play frame play in terms of complexity and a child's maturity. The following are sequential levels of play:

1. **Chaotic, out-of-control play:** Children do not play safely, and they may be hurtful to others physically or emotionally.[50]
2. **Simplistic, repetitive play:** Toddlers often play repetitively, imitating an action they have seen adults do but without adding anything to it. Children may change roles, but the scenario and dialogue remain the same.[51]
3. **Productive, high-level play:** Children cooperate to create or enact interesting scenarios, and they build or make items to enhance what they are playing out. Children share and build on one another's ideas.[52]

Adult participation in children's play can move play to a higher level. It is important that adults participate while still following the children's interests and lead. In all play, adults have the opportunity to use the children's interests and to follow their lead while intentionally adding early literacy elements and increasing children's level of language and imagination.

This summary of the early literacy components and the ways that the five practices can support early literacy is the basis for sharing information with adults in

Symbolic Play

There are several developmental stages of symbolic play. The first stage is when there is no element of pretending. For example, a baby puts a cup to his mouth to drink—the baby is using the object for its intended purpose. In the next stage, even if there is no liquid in the cup, toddlers pretend to drink, but they still use the cup for its original purpose. The toddler might then pretend by including another person or object (e.g., feeding a teddy bear). The pretending develops further when children make up a situation that they act out in sequence (making a cake by pretending to mix batter, pour it into a pan, and put it in the oven) or reenact an event and announce what they are going do before they pretend to do it.

Symbolic play is particularly powerful because the underlying conceptual thinking that takes place in symbolic play (i.e., that one thing can represent another) is also present in early literacy. For example, when a child pretends that a block is a telephone, she sees the block as a symbol for or representation of a telephone. She knows it is not the real phone, but she uses the block to represent the phone. In the same way, a picture of an apple is not the real apple; it represents the apple or is a symbol for a real apple. This symbolic play correlates to early literacy; for example, the text of the word *apple* is not the real apple but represents an apple.

the storytime setting. In the following chapters we look at specific ways to incorporate early literacy information into storytimes.

NOTES

1. Scott Paris, "Reinterpreting the Development of Reading Skills," *Reading Research Quarterly* 40 (2005): 184–202.

2. David Sousa, *How the Brain Learns to Read* (Thousand Oaks, CA: Corwin Press, 2005), 15.

3. Reading Horizons, "Reading Strategies: What Is Decoding," www.readinghorizons .com/reading-strategies/what-is-decoding.aspx.

4. National Reading Panel, *Teaching Children to Read: An Evidence-Based Assessment of the Scientific Research Literature on Reading and Its Implications for Reading Instruction* (Washington, DC: National Institute of Child Health and Human Development, 2000), 13.

5. Anne E. Cunningham and Jamie Zibulsky, "Tell Me a Story: Examining the Benefits of Shared Reading," in *Handbook of Early Literacy Research*, vol. 3, ed. Susan B. Neuman and David Dickinson (New York: Guilford Press, 2011), 405.

6. Kathleen Paciga, Jessica Hoffman, and William Teale, "The National Early Literacy Panel and Preschool Literacy Instruction: Green Lights, Caution Lights, and Red Lights," *Young Children*, November 2011, 55.

7. David Dickinson, Roberta Golinkoff, Kathy Hirsh-Pasek, Susan Neuman, and Peg Burchinal, "The Language of Emergent Literacy: A Response to the National Institute for Literacy Report on Early Literacy," January 12, 2009, http://nieer.org/pdf/ CommentaryOnNELPreport.pdf.

8. Adapted from National Institute for Literacy, *Learning to Talk and Listen: An Oral Language Resource for Early Childhood Caregivers* (Washington, DC: National Institute for Literacy, 2009), 14, http://lincs.ed.gov/publications/pdf/LearningtoTalk andListen.pdf.

9. Heather Bortfeld, James L. Morgan, Roberta Michnick Golinkoff, and Karen Rathbun, "Mommy and Me: Familiar Names Help Launch Babies into Speech-Stream Segmentation," *Psychological Science* 16, no. 4 (2005): 298–304, www.ncbi.nlm.nih.gov/pmc/ articles/PMC2981583/pdf/nihms249912.pdf.

10. Betty Hart and Todd R. Risley, *Meaningful Differences in the Everyday Experience of Young American Children* (Baltimore: Paul H. Brookes, 1995).

11. Sousa, *How the Brain Learns to Read*, 14.

12. Beth Phillips, Jeanine Clancy-Menchetti, and Christopher Lonigan, "Successful Phonological Awareness Instruction with Preschool Children," *Topics in Early Childhood Special Education* 28, no. 1 (2008): 3–17.

13. Laura M. Justice and Khara L. Pence, with Angela R. Beckman, Lori E. Skibbe, and Alice K. Wiggins, *Scaffolding with Storybooks: A Guide for Enhancing Young Children's Language and Literacy Achievement* (Newark, DE: International Reading Association, 2005), 13.

14. Shayne B. Piasta, Laura M. Justice, Anita S. McGinty, and Joan N. Kaderavek, "Increasing Young Children's Contact with Print during Shared Reading: Longitudinal Effects on Literacy Achievement," *Child Development* 83, no. 3 (2012): 817.

15. Sousa, *How the Brain Learns to Read*, 36.

16. Scott G. Paris, "Developmental Differences in Early Reading Skills," in *Handbook of Early Literacy Research*, vol. 3, ed. Susan B. Neuman and David Dickinson (New York: Guilford Press, 2011), 237.

17. Connie Juel, "The Impact of Early School Experiences on Initial Reading," in *Handbook of Early Literacy Research*, vol. 2, ed. David Dickinson and Susan B. Neuman (New York: Guilford Press, 2006), 414.

18. Justin Harris, Robert Michnick, and Kathy Hirsh-Pasek, "Lessons from the Crib for the Classroom: How Children Really Learn Vocabulary," in *Handbook of Early Literacy Research*, vol. 3, ed. Susan B. Neuman and David Dickinson (New York: Guilford Press, 2011), 57.

19. National Center on Accessing the General Curriculum, *Curriculum Enhancement Report: Background Knowledge* (Washington, DC: U.S. Office of Special Education Programs), 1–3, http://aim.cast.org/sites/aim.cast.org/files/ncac_BKNov3.pdf.

20. Catherine Snow, David Dickinson, and Patton Tabors, "The Home-School Study of Language and Literacy Development," www.gse.harvard.edu/~pild/homeschoolstudy.htm.

21. Hart and Risley, *Meaningful Differences*.

22. Lauren Barton and Holly Brophy-Herb, "Developmental Foundations for Language and Literacy from Birth to Three Years," in *Learning to Read the World: Language and Literacy in the First Three Years*, ed. Sharon Rosenkoetter and Joanne Knapp-Philo (Washington, DC: Zero to Three, 2006), 24.

23. Meredith L. Rowe and Susan Goldin-Meadow, "Differences in Early Gesture Explain SES Disparities in Child Vocabulary Size at School Entry," *Science* 323, no. 5916 (2009): 951–53.

24. Hart and Risley, *Meaningful Differences*.

25. Todd Risley, interview, www.childrenofthecode.org/interviews/risley.htm.

26. Ibid.

27. Hart and Risley, *Meaningful Differences*, 155.

28. Kathleen A. Roskos, Patton O. Tabors, and Lisa A. Lenhart, *Oral Language and Literacy: Talking, Reading, and Writing*, 2nd ed. (Newark, NJ: National Reading Association, 2009), 34.

29. David Dickinson, Julie Griffith, Roberta Golinkoff, and Kathy Hirsh-Pasek, "How Reading Books Fosters Language Development around the World," *Child Development Research* (2012), www.hindawi.com/journals/cdr/2012/602807/.

30. Roskos et al., *Oral Language and Literacy*, 46.

31. Robert Pianta, Karen La Paro, and Bridget Hamre, *Classroom Assessment Scoring System Manual: Pre-K* (Baltimore: Paul H. Brookes, 2008), 104.

32. Richard Anderson et al., *Becoming a Nation of Readers: The Report of the Commission on Reading* (Champaign: University of Illinois, 1985), 23.

33. Monique Sénéchal, "A Model of the Concurrent and Longitudinal Relations between Home Literacy and Child Outcomes," in *Handbook of Early Literacy Research*, vol. 3, ed. Susan B. Neuman and David Dickinson (New York: Guilford Press, 2011), 180.

34. Monique Sénéchal, "Reading Books to Young Children: What It Does and Does Not Do," *Literacy Development and Enhancement across Orthographies and Cultures*,

ed. D. Aram and O. Korat (New York: Springer Science and Business Media, 2010), 119–20.

35. Tanya Christ and X. Christine Wang, "Bridging the Vocabulary Gap: What the Research Tells Us about Vocabulary Instruction in Early Childhood," *Young Children*, July 2010, 86.

36. Bankstreet College of Education, *Bankstreet College's Guide to Literacy for Volunteers and Tutors*, http://bankstreet.edu/literacy-guide/glossary-reading-terms.

37. Sénéchal, "Model of the Concurrent and Longitudinal Relations," 182.

38. Cunningham and Zibulsky, "Tell Me a Story," 409.

39. Helen Ezell and Laura Justice, *Shared Storybook Reading: Building Young Children's Language and Emergent Literacy Skills* (Baltimore: Paul H. Brookes, 2005), 2.

40. Cunningham and Zibulsky, "Tell Me a Story," 397.

41. Sénéchal, "Reading Books to Young Children," 120.

42. Cunningham and Zibulsky, "Tell Me a Story," 406.

43. Ibid.

44. Ibid., 404.

45. Roskos et al., *Oral Language and Literacy*, 59.

46. Dorit Aram and Iris Levin, "Home Support of Children in the Writing Process: Contributions to Early Literacy," in *Handbook of Early Literacy Research*, vol. 3, ed. Susan B. Neuman and David Dickinson (New York: Guilford Press, 2011), 190.

47. Jennifer Hallissy, *The Write Start: A Guide to Nurturing Writing at Every Stage, from Scribbling to Forming Letters and Writing Stories* (Boston: Shambhala Publications, 2010), 12.

48. Susan B. Neuman, "Literacy Development for Infants and Toddlers," in *Learning to Read the World: Language and Literacy in the First Three Years*, ed. Sharon Rosenkoetter and Joanne Knapp-Philo (Washington, DC: Zero to Three, 2006), 278.

49. Gretchen Owocki, *Literacy through Play* (Portsmouth, NH: Heinemann, 1999), 12–13.

50. Gaye Gronlund, *Developmentally Appropriate Play: Guiding Young Children to a Higher Level* (St. Paul, MN: Redleaf Press, 2010), 18.

51. Ibid., 20.

52. Ibid., 24.

chapter 2

Early Literacy and Your Storytimes

IN THIS CHAPTER WE ILLUSTRATE HOW TO INCORPORATE EARLY LITERACY COMPO-
nents and practices into storytimes. Subsequent chapters help storytime presenters articulate these connections to the parents and caregivers so that they see the
relationship between the storytime activities and later reading, thereby encouraging parents and caregivers to continue activities at home or in child-care settings.

You will note that there is overlap between the early literacy components and
the practices as we apply them to our storytimes. For examples of how the components and the practices support each other, see web extra 2.1, at www.alaeditions
.org/webextras.

Applying the Early Literacy Components in Storytimes

PHONOLOGICAL AWARENESS

Hearing the smaller sounds in words can be easily and seamlessly highlighted
through books as well as rhymes, songs, and fingerplays. Animal sounds, environmental sounds (e.g., cars honking), pointing out the beginning sound of a word,
alliteration, clapping syllables, and helping children recognize and play with
rhyming words (e.g., in books, poems, songs, fingerplays, nursery rhymes) all support phonological awareness at different stages of children's development. As we

sing, we can point out that singing slows down language and that we often hear a different note for each syllable. Using shakers and musical instruments with music supports the rhythm of language.

PRINT CONVENTIONS AND AWARENESS

Children focus much more on the pictures than on the text of a book. Simply running your finger under the title or under repeated phrases helps children focus on the text. Running your finger under the words on a page helps children understand that the direction of print, and reading, in English is top to bottom and left to right. Some books lend themselves easily to pointing out print—books with fonts that emphasize how words might be said (loudly, softly, with a certain emotion, or reflecting a certain kind of movement), books with signs or writing as part of the story, and books that use callouts to show who is speaking. Pointing out the author and title each time we introduce a book is also part of supporting print awareness. For younger children, we can help parents understand that young children may chew on books or bat at them as they try to turn pages, but this is part of the development of print awareness. When out and about, adults can point out street signs and store marquees and logos to children of all ages. As parents and caregivers point this out in the books they share with children, they are supporting early literacy and particularly print awareness.

LETTER KNOWLEDGE

To help build children's letter knowledge, it's important to remember that letters are abstract concepts, and particularly in English, they don't consistently correspond to a particular sound. Because of this, rather than doing "letter" storytimes in which a letter is a theme, it's best to talk about letters by organizing storytime around topics of interest to children (e.g., trucks, babies, dinosaurs) and then talking about the letter in the context of the theme. Children often learn the letters in their names before other letters, so using name tags or a sign-in list for them to write (or scribble) their names is another way to incorporate letter knowledge.

The first step of letter knowledge is shapes. We talk about shapes as we read a shape book or share a fingerplay on shapes, but we can also notice shapes in illustrations, find shapes in the environment, and provide shape magnets and puzzles to play with after storytime. Another beginning concept for letter knowledge is noticing what is alike and different. Matching games on a flannelboard, talking about similarities and differences in an illustration, and comparing how one character looks in two different illustrations are all supportive of building letter knowledge in storytimes.

VOCABULARY

While the language of books can be quite rich and is fertile ground for introducing children to unfamiliar words, it is also important to note that books for our youngest children are often not language rich but rather have only one or two words per page. In this situation we want to take the opportunity to encourage adults to use the books as conversation starters, as a catalyst for talking about something they remember, to tell a story, or to share information, which will enhance a young child's vocabulary. We can also point out words in nursery rhymes that children may not be familiar with, use props to provide explanation or to point out distinctions (e.g., shovel and trowel), or show children pictures of things that might be new to them.

With preschool children in particular it has been found that actually explaining words, rather than just allowing children to guess possible meanings of the word, is helpful in developing a strong vocabulary. There is no need to interrupt a book to do this, and we need not explain every unfamiliar word. We can explain words before starting the book or come back to a word or two following the reading of the book. Strategies such as relating a new word to one children already know, having young children act out a word, or using props to introduce children to something that might be unfamiliar are all good ways to support vocabulary.

BACKGROUND KNOWLEDGE

Background knowledge, or children's prior knowledge, covers a wide range of areas. Coming to storytimes at the library, in and of itself, adds to children's general knowledge: What is a library? What do we do in the library? What is a storytime? What do we do in storytime?

There are many opportunities to broaden children's background knowledge through the use of books and other materials. Exposing children to various types of books shows them that books have different purposes. In books, for example, they find stories, factual information (e.g., about cars or animals), concepts (e.g., colors, the alphabet), and poetry.

Children see library staff reading in ways that are both similar to and different from ways others may share books. This is true for adults as well. In storytimes, the way we share books and model and encourage parents and caregivers to share books with their children can support conceptual thinking. Asking open-ended questions that cannot be answered with yes or no and having children predict or problem solve while discussing books support abstract thinking, which supports later comprehension while reading.

Books can explain things and get children thinking about concepts and ideas. In storytime there is not time to find out what each child knows about a topic or a story, but we can model for parents and caregivers the ways they can elicit from their children what they know about a topic or story. We can encourage parents and caregivers to add what they know to help develop their children's thinking. We can help children learn more by choosing informational books for storytime that are rich in vocabulary and content and then encouraging adults to borrow similar books to read at home with their children.

A book picture walk—talking about what the book is about and then eliciting what children know or might guess about the story or book—is one way to stimulate children's background knowledge. By bringing children's knowledge to the fore, we help increase their understanding of their world. Through books children can learn about things that do not exist in their own environment. When they are exposed to a variety of stories, children learn both the language of story and the structure of story: that stories have a beginning, a middle, and an end; that there may be a repeated phrase or action; that there may be certain patterns (e.g., things in threes), that there is a problem that is then resolved.

Applying the Five Practices to Storytimes

TALKING

Given the critical importance of language development and its relationship to learning about and understanding the written word, library programs should include parents and caregivers and their children from infancy. Babies and toddlers need language to be successful. Parents and caregivers do not always know about language development and their role in it with respect to the youngest children, and yet the most language growth occurs at very young ages. The significance of the amount and kind of talk between adults and infants and toddlers cannot be overestimated.

Library staff can share the message of language stimulation for young children as they do programs both in and outside of the library. When we create storytimes and library programs, we should be aware of the importance of using and defining a wide range of words. We should use new words multiple times and encourage program participants, both adults and children, to use them as well. We should not assume that adults have large vocabularies and know what all words are. By including definitions of words in storytime, we are supplying both adults and children with new words.

As noted in chapter 1, it is easier to read a word you know than one you don't. Children cannot know too many words! Children need to hear all different kinds of words, especially new and sophisticated words, in conversations and natural situations. Often our one-on-one interactions with children in a library setting take place just before or just after storytime. When we are aware of how we can encourage communication, we can best respond to each child's needs.

Adults' rich language talk is one way to build vocabulary and background knowledge. It is equally important to allow children opportunities to speak, to share what they know, to ask questions, and to wonder aloud. A storytime setting does not usually lend itself to this kind of individual turn taking, though. Asking questions will most probably elicit responses from those children who are most verbal. But we can support interactive talking by encouraging less verbal children to talk by first saying what we expect. For example, in a preschool storytime, you might say, "When I am done reading this book, I am going to ask you what happened to [a certain character]." Pair up children and adults and then ask them to share a response to your question or activity with their partner. In addition, we can model asking open-ended questions. Even though we cannot hear the responses of each child, we can point out to parents the importance of the child's verbal participation in conversations to later comprehension.

The way adults talk with children can also support vocabulary. As already noted, when we define words and help clarify words and meaning, and add details to conversations, children gain a deeper understanding of the meaning of words. For less verbal children, adults can ask questions, pause and then give answers, repeat a word or two and build on it, all while making sure to build on the interests of the child and to affirm the child's efforts. With infants and young toddlers, we use gestures or props and act out words to help children understand them. Although one-on-one talking with each child is not feasible in a storytime setting, we can offer parents ideas for ways to support vocabulary development as they talk with their children at home.

The book picture walk and dialogic reading are other ways of encouraging adults to interact with a child around a book (see chapter 1).

You might decide to create more opportunities for children to talk by adding or incorporating a time for reading together or book sharing. During this time, children choose a book from a table or basket and adults and children share the book together. The storytime presenter can demonstrate a way to encourage talk around a picture in a book, and then ask parents or caregivers and children to practice it. For example, pick a picture and have children tell about something they remember related to the picture, ask them to tell what is happening in the picture, add at least one new word to what the child says, or strive for five interactions on one page ("strive for five" means keeping the conversation interchange going five times, but remember that all five interactions don't have to be questions; they can be acknowledgments of what the child said or adults' addition of a bit of information or a memory).

In addition, encourage rich talk through the use of compelling themes, or those that nourish children's curiosity, humor, and imagination. While exploring themes, opportunities arise to think aloud, thus exposing the children to new ideas and vocabulary. Make sure that you incorporate into storytime informational books targeting ages two and up; this will allow you to talk about a variety of topics while building on children's interests and curiosity and developing vocabulary and background knowledge. As Nell K. Duke, codirector of the Literacy Research Center at Michigan State University, has noted, parents talk more and encourage children to talk more when sharing informational books rather than storybooks. However, both storybooks and informational books are important.[1]

When we model the use of picture books and informational texts, we encourage children's development of language and syntax. Books contain more "rare" words than typical adult speech, and they also use unusual sentence structures—from long sentences to distinctive styles of writing (e.g., "said he" rather than the more standard "he said"). Furthermore, activities that engage children in storytelling, such as repeating words or phrases and retelling the story using flannelboards, props, or puppets, are enjoyable ways to develop the expressive part of language. Acting out what we read is an important first step toward developing reading comprehension skills.

In storytimes, we should model talking *with* children, not just *to* them—and we should urge parents and caregivers to do the same. In addition to supporting a child's social and emotional development, this kind of interaction is best for helping language grow. Language blossoms when adults talk with children, encourage them to use their background knowledge to articulate responses to questions, and then add to what children say. Vocabulary grows when adults and children wonder together about what might happen or what could be. This approach supports children's thinking skills, narrative skills, and vocabularies.

Adults have an opportunity to build children's vocabulary and background knowledge when they talk with children as they play together. When we offer informal playtime after storytime, we encourage children to develop more complex verbal interactions. Not surprisingly, children are more likely to learn words that have to do with events and things that they are familiar with. Playing school, making lists, and engaging in dramatic play all contribute to their vocabulary development and background knowledge; we can use these opportunities to follow their lead and build on what they already know.

While vocabulary development and background knowledge can be strongly supported by talking, so can each of the early literacy skills. For example, we emphasize the fact that words rhyme by talking about two words that rhyme, thereby supporting phonological awareness; we point to a word on a page and talk about how the size of the font means we should say it loudly, thereby supporting print conventions and awareness; when we start a book we might mention that it is one of our favorite books and what we like about it, thereby supporting print motivation. The richness of talking is powerful, and talking directs attention to the various elements of language.

We should have fun with language. Take advantage of every opportunity to talk with the young children with whom you come in contact in storytime.

SINGING

We have long been promoters of song and rhyme as part of storytimes. Especially at the preschool level, songs are often used as activity fillers. Singing songs is not only enjoyable for children but also helps their phonological awareness, or ability to hear the smaller sounds in words. Singing slows down language, and most songs have a different note for each syllable. Younger children learn the cadence of language in songs and hear language slowed down so that they can hear word sounds more clearly.

As pointed out in chapter 1, phonological awareness progresses from hearing sounds to recognizing sounds to making sounds. Singing songs is on the first level of hearing. When we point out the rhyming words or clap out the syllables of words as we sing, we help children and model for parents ways that singing can support higher levels of phonological awareness. When we ask children to fill in the second in a set of rhyming words or ask them for a word that rhymes with a word we give, they are producing the rhyme, which is more difficult. In addition, songs are a great way to play with and emphasize the sounds that start words and rhymes in words. We provide specific examples in our sample storytimes in part 2.

READING

The techniques we use with talking often overlap with reading. How we share books with children is as important as the act of sharing books with children. Sharing the same book in a variety of ways, with repeated readings at home or in a child-care setting, helps young children become comfortable with books and their contents, and to learn something each time the book is shared. Because repeated readings of books, especially when adults have children say new words, help children increase their vocabulary, we should encourage parents to reread books, to talk about new words, and to encourage children to say new words, but without overwhelming children or turning the reading experience into a lesson. Even though it is not feasible for us to read the same book several times in a storytime or to have every child repeat new words, we can model these behaviors and encourage parents and caregivers to continue these activities at home or at child-care centers.

In a book picture walk, we talk about the illustrations. With shared reading, the words of the text come into play. Children may repeat a phrase or fill in rhyming words used in the text. And when we have the attention of the children, we may simply treat them to a continuous reading of a book. All of these ways of sharing books contribute to different aspects of early literacy development. Shared book reading motivates children to learn how to read, which is great news for librarians!

If you provide handouts to support activities in storytime, we recommend including a connection to early literacy (see chapter 11, "Storytime Extras"). In addition to providing adults with a list of songs and books that were used in storytime, handouts can encourage adults to actively participate in helping their children develop an early literacy component in enjoyable ways. It is this element of intentionality that is a key difference between early literacy enhanced storytimes and more traditional storytimes.

We can point out to adults that reading takes place with more than just books. Adults read when they go through the mail, look at newspapers, gather information from a website, or read a recipe. Even if we do not have the opportunity to show these situations during storytime, we can be sure to convey this information to parents and caregivers at the end of storytime verbally or through handouts.

WRITING

Of the five practices, writing is perhaps the most difficult one to incorporate into storytimes. But writing is motivating and empowering for children. Can you remember when you (or a young child in your life) discovered the magic in writing words of your own choosing?

We lovers of the written word should do whatever we can to encourage children's ability to put thoughts onto paper. Encouraging children to express their thoughts in this manner is one way to help them and their caregivers see just how much we value and respect their ideas and their words. We understand how intimately writing and reading are intertwined, and we want young children to go to school ready to read and to write! When we incorporate writing into our storytimes, we show parents that we value it as greatly as we do reading.

We can incorporate writing into storytimes by asking children to write their names on name tags or a sign-in sheet (or mural paper or a whiteboard) when they arrive. Some children might scribble their names, others might draw a picture of themselves, and others might write letters in varying degrees of legibility.

Doing fingerplays and other activities that help children coordinate their body movements supports their coordination for later writing. You can also build writing into craft activities or include it take-home activities on handouts. We show children how important writing is when we do story dictations and use graphs and charts to organize information we have learned in storytime. If it is not feasible to include these activities at the end of or just after storytime, we can certainly suggest to parents that they do them at home and demonstrate ways to make the activities easier for them to do with their children. (These and other methods of incorporating writing are further explored in chapters 7–9 and 11).

PLAYING

During storytime we are playful in what we do, and we make book sharing and activities enjoyable. However, being playful is not the same as engaging children in play. One kind of play that can be included in storytimes is dramatic play. When we encourage children to repeat phrases or actions as part of a story, have children take different parts to act out a story, or offer a handout for props or puppets to encourage them to retell or act out the story at home, we are encouraging dramatic play. Adults can also do these dramatic play activities at home.

At storytime we can offer suggestions to parents about play and help them support higher-level play in their preschoolers, point out that play encourages strong language because it employs symbolic thinking, and offer ways to incorporate print into play activities. We can also encourage through our own actions the use of new vocabulary words and sentence structures when we play with children.

Some libraries offer playtime following storytime in the storytime area or in the children's area. This is a wonderful way to incorporate play into storytime programs, especially when we can create and support a language-rich environment. Language-rich environments, though, are dependent on both materials and personal interaction. We should include toys that encourage children's active participation and learning, and we can put out books to play with as well.

Children are more likely to engage in language-rich play when toys, puppets, or props cluster around a theme or the retelling of a particular story, so we can rotate toys and realia to match the storytime theme. This clustering gives children some structure around which to build language in a more purposeful and focused way, which actually makes it easier for them to interact and play than when playing with a larger number of miscellaneous groupings.

Make sure that you have a variety of toys for this kind of playtime. For infants and toddlers, who think more concretely, having objects that represent real things helps their play. For example, a toy phone, a barn with farm animals, and plastic food with pots and dinnerware allow for talk and play around those topics. In addition, manipulatives like shape sorters, simple knob puzzles, and building blocks are also appropriate. Preschoolers can turn those blocks into pretend props of any sort—the only limitation is their own imagination. For preschoolers, toys that can be used in different ways or that allow for open-ended exploration (e.g., blocks, clay, pipe cleaners) make for more language-rich play. If possible, incorporate signs, labels, and writing into the playtime activities and environment.

The interactions of library staff and parents and caregivers around the children's play also affect the richness of the children's experience. There are times, of course, when children can be left to explore. However, putting words to what children are doing, offering information they might not know, and encouraging more complex scenarios while following the child's lead all support a more language-rich environment.

By understanding different kinds of play, we can not only enrich children's play but also model and articulate to parents and caregivers ways that they can enrich their children's play at home or in the child-care setting.

NOTE

1. Nell K. Duke, *Information Books in Early Childhood*, 2003, p. 1, http://journal.naeyc .org/btj/200303/InformationBooks.pdf.

chapter 3

English–Language Learners in Storytimes

CHILDREN COME INTO THE LIBRARY AND OUR STORYTIMES WITH DIVERSE CULTURAL and linguistic backgrounds. Their experiences with the English language are as varied as the countries from which they come. Some come to us fully immersed in American culture and language. Others may appear with their adults, all with virtually no understanding of English, but possessing a wealth of background knowledge in their home language. Still others might have few language skills in any language at all. Regardless of children's backgrounds, we want them to enjoy our storytimes, to learn, and to feel welcome. Research into how children learn a second language can help shed some light on what we librarians can do to help. Numerous studies acknowledge the following about English-language learners (ELLs):

- Children who are literate in their native language have an advantage in learning English.
- Phonological awareness transfers between languages.
- Phonics instruction, combined with exposure to reading materials in multiple genres, helps ELLs learn how to read.
- ELLs need more vocabulary instruction than their native-English-speaking peers. They are more likely than their classmates to lack the background knowledge in English needed to understand texts.[1]

Compelling research done by Lily Wong-Fillmore and others explains the following:[2]

- Native-language literacy is critical because language and thought are so closely tied. When children have a strong command of their native language, this helps them understand and label abstract concepts like ideas and feelings.
- Children who are not yet five years old usually have not firmly established command of their language. Learning a second language may result in these children losing their first language rather than adding a new one.
- Some children lose their first language because of pressure from society at large to speak English.
- Once the second language is acquired children can transfer the complexity of their first language to the new language.
- Children with partial mastery of two languages may mix them instead of using them as two separate, fully developed languages.
- Children's relationships with their families, who may not be fluent in English, can be seriously damaged if children become unable to communicate with family members.

Although many parents become concerned when children mix languages, it is not uncommon for young bilinguals to *code switch,* or to use multiple languages in the same thought or conversation. By the age of three, most children have learned to distinguish among the languages they know and have figured out how to use them appropriately.[3]

Bilingualism is complex, but bilingual children and adults have certain advantages, including the following:[4]

Communication: wider networks; dual-language literacy; and metalinguistic awareness, or a better understanding of how language works

Cultural: broader and deeper sense of cultures, two worlds of language for experiencing things, experiencing less racism and more tolerance

Cognitive: brain plasticity, as well as improved memory and thinking abilities

Character: increased self-esteem, security in one's identity

Curriculum: increased achievement and ability to learn a third or more languages

Financial: more job opportunities and other economic benefits

Research has indicated that children who are bilingual from birth learn both languages in the same pattern or sequence as monolingual children. Recently, researchers at the University of Washington used measures of electrical brain responses to compare so-called monolingual infants, from homes in which one language was spoken, to bilingual infants, exposed to two languages. The researchers found that at six months, monolingual infants could discriminate between phonetic sounds, whether they were uttered in the language they were used to hearing or in another language not spoken in their homes. By ten to twelve months, however, monolingual babies were no longer detecting sounds in the second language, only in the language they usually heard. The researchers characterized this as "neural commitment," in which the infant brain wires itself to understand one language and its sounds. In contrast, the bilingual infants followed a different developmental trajectory. At six to nine months, children did not detect differences in phonetic sounds in either language, but when children were older—between ten and twelve months—they were able to discriminate sounds in both. "What the study demonstrates is that the variability in bilingual babies' experience keeps them open," according to Dr. Patricia Kuhl, codirector of the Institute for Learning and Brain Sciences at the University of Washington and an author of the study. "They do not show the perceptual narrowing as soon as monolingual babies do. It's another piece of evidence that what you experience shapes the brain." The learning of language—and the effects on the brain of the language we hear—may begin even earlier than six months of age.[5]

There is much variation in how quickly an individual can learn a second language. Young children seem to have an easier time than adults in learning a second language because the language they are learning is less difficult in cognitive terms. In fact, children learn to speak a second language quickly and often with nativelike pronunciation. This conversational fluency is known as basic interpersonal communication skills. However, problems arise when we consider children proficient in a language when they demonstrate good basic interpersonal communication skills or social skills in a language. Higher-level thinking in a second language is known as cognitive academic language proficiency. Young adults and adolescents are better at acquiring this type of language in their second language. This kind of proficiency takes five to seven years to attain, but if children have no prior schooling or no support in native-language development, it may take them seven to nine years to catch up to their peers.[6]

Bilingual children continue to use both languages as long as they perceive that both have value in society. They seem to forget new languages more quickly than adults, replacing their new language with their old one.[7]

Just as there is a sequence in learning how to speak a first language, so is there a sequence in acquiring a second language. In the first stage, children use one language in play. When they realize that that language doesn't get them the hoped-for response, they stop using it with people who don't understand that language.[8]

In the next stage, children become silent because they are observing and listening in an effort to understand the new language and the verbal cues that go with it. This period can last for a month or two up to six months, when children begin to try out the new language by using telegraphic and formulaic speech, using one or two words to convey an entire sentence, and using whole phrases that the child has memorized but without fully understanding their meaning.

Once children understand the basic rules of the second language, they can use those rules to master the language. In this period, children sound more like native speakers, and they can use two different kinds of language—social and academic. Social English is used informally and is mostly spoken. It requires a smaller vocabulary because it has simple, short sentence structures. Social English is used with friends and adults in play and in relaxed situations. Academic English takes longer to acquire than informal English. It requires a larger vocabulary and longer, more complex sentences.[9]

Regardless of the language spoken, children learn letter knowledge through activities that focus on shapes, things that are alike and different, and letter recognition. They can increase phonological awareness along with the sounds that make up words and how letters are related to those sounds. Both of these skills are important to English-language learners.[10] Moreover, print awareness develops as children's vocabularies grow. When you introduce books in different languages, children will see the different forms that written languages assume.[11]

Making Storytimes ELL-Friendly

Knowing the sequence of how children acquire a new language can help us work with ELLs in a more thoughtful and sensitive way. Children who do not speak in storytime may be in the silent phase of absorbing language, but they might be chatterboxes in their native language. Realizing that ELL children need to learn many new words in English reminds us to point out words that native English language speakers might know but that are less familiar to ELL children and their families.

Most librarians in the United States are monolingual speakers of English, which raises the question of how we can support research-based best practices. At the Public Library Association's biennial conference in Minneapolis in March 2008, Dr. Lillian Duran, who conducted a study comparing language and literacy development of children in a bilingual classroom to those in a monolingual English program, suggested some strategies that librarians can use in her workshop "Supporting Early Literacy in Young English Language Learners." For example, Duran recommends that librarians keep languages separate, such as by holding a Mandarin Chinese storytime rather than a bilingual Mandarin-English storytime. When we do hold bilingual programs, Duran suggests that the language other than English be read first, giving it the honor of first place rather than implying that it is an afterthought. Not just stories but all storytime activities should provide children and accompanying adults with the opportunity to engage in literacy-related activities.

In addition, Duran suggests using multicultural rhymes, fingerplays, and music. Parents can help lead these parts of storytime. Such activities help children develop the ability to hear rhyme and alliteration. She also suggests summarizing the main points in the second language when using a bilingual book. According to Duran, young bilingual children need to hear the formal "book" language of their first language. Many English-language-learner children have fewer opportunities to do this in their first language than English-speaking children.

Another recommendation is that libraries send parents home with literacy activities they can do with their young children—reading is not the only literacy activity adults can do with them.

Duran reported that homemade books with pictures of families and their communities have been shown to increase children's receptive language. Parents also tend to ask more *W* questions when they share this kind of book with their children.

In her presentation, Duran also suggested that libraries consciously include images of people from various cultures in their buildings and handouts. When librarians speak with families, we need to convey the message that native-language literacy is important and that we support this effort by providing library materials in their native languages. Bilingual books often reflect people of different cultures and present great multicultural stories and families, so consider using them even if you read only the English.

Some libraries have had success holding storytimes in multiple languages, especially by partnering with bilingual community members who can do storytimes as a stand-alone program or with bilingual presenters alongside the librarian. We can invite parents to share songs and rhymes from their native cultures and languages during storytime as well.

Publicizing a family storytime as an English-language-learner storytime can sometimes draw in families who would not otherwise come to the library. The use of props and stories, rhymes and songs with repetitive phrases, and the incorporation of actions, makes storytime easier for all participants.

When you set up displays of books, make sure to include books in other languages or bilingual books, if available. Showcasing them lets parents know that the library has more than just English books, and attendees may tell others in the community as well. When offering handouts, try to have them available in the languages spoken in your community. For example, the Reading Tip Sheet offered by Reading Rockets in eleven languages is available at www.readingrockets.org/article/18935/. Most important, efforts to include speakers of languages other than English enrich everyone's library experience.

NOTES

1. Suzanne Irujo, "What Does Research Tell Us about Teaching Reading to English Language Learners?" *Reading Rockets*, 2007, www.readingrockets.org/article/19757/.

2. Rebecca Novick, *Developmentally Appropriate and Culturally Responsive Education* (Washington, DC: Office of Educational Research Improvement, 1996), 72–73.

3. California Department of Education, *Preschool English Learners: Principles and Practices to Promote Language, Literacy, and Learning; A Resource Guide*, 2nd ed. (Sacramento: California Department of Education, 2009), 46, www.cde.ca.gov/sp/cd/re/documents/psenglearnersed2.pdf.

4. Ibid., 35.

5. Adrian Garcia-Sierra, Maritza Rivera-Gaxiola, Cherie R. Percaccio, Barbara T. Conboy, Harriett Romo, Lindsay Klarman, Sophia Ortiz, and Patricia K. Kuhl, "Bilingual Language Learning: An ERP Study Relating Early Brain Responses to Speech, Language Input, and Later Word Production," *Journal of Phonetics* 39, no. 4 (2011): 546–57.

6. Virginia Collier, *Acquiring a Second Language for School in Directions in Language and Education* (Washington, DC: National Clearinghouse for Bilingual Education, 1995), 5.

7. Beverly A. Clark, "First- and Second-Language Acquisition in Early Childhood," Early Childhood and Parent Collaborative, 183, http://ceep.crc.uiuc.edu/pubs/katzsym/clark-b.html.

8. California Department of Education, *Preschool English Learners*, 56.

9. Ibid., 47–51.

10. Patton O. Tabors, *One Child, Two Languages*, 2nd ed. (Baltimore: Paul H. Brookes, 2008), 118.

11. Ibid., 123.

chapter 4

Screen Time
and Storytime

ADVICE ON HOW MUCH EXPOSURE TO VISUAL MEDIA, OR "SCREEN TIME," IS APPROPRI-
ate for young children is of one voice—adults are discouraged from allowing their
children under the age of two to spend time in front of screens.[1] The position taken
by the National Academy of Pediatrics is rooted in what is known about how children learn and how they acquire language: the interaction between adults and
children give children the language they need to understand their world. Given
this, it seems only logical that we librarians would heed their advice and not use
screens with our youngest patrons.

In spite of the recommendations of pediatricians, on any given day in the
United States, 47 percent of babies between the ages of zero and one watch television or DVDs for an average of almost two hours. The average time for children
younger than two to be read to is twenty-three minutes. Almost one-third of children younger than age two have a television in their bedroom.[2]

Another issue of concern is "secondhand" television, or background screen
time. This occurs when adults may or may not be watching a program while a
DVD or television show is on the screen. Studies show that the background media
distracts adults and decreases adult-child interaction. Infant vocabulary growth is
directly related to the amount of time that parents spend speaking to infants. Parents with media on in the background spend less time talking with their children.[3]

What, then, of children older than age two? Studies on high-quality educational television programs indicate that children can and do learn from them, as well as from newer technologies like smart phones and other handheld, portable devices. Children need to connect with people to learn, but given the interactive nature of some e-books and programs for use with computers and smart phones, won't children be learning from them, too?

There is evidence that young children learn from applications (or apps), which are activities downloaded from the Internet onto a mobile device. Apps based on the PBS shows *Martha Speaks* and *Super Why* helped children between the ages of three and seven increase their vocabularies, with five-year-olds gaining the most. Apparently, the five-year-olds were developmentally ready to learn new words and were less likely than older children to already know them.[4]

A recent study in the journal *Pediatrics* explored the impact of watching a fast-paced television program on four-year-olds' executive function, or the ability to delay gratification and to pay attention to a task. The study found the following:

> Watching a 9-minute episode of a fast-paced television cartoon immediately impaired young children's [executive function] relative to watching an educational television show or drawing. [Those children] scored significantly worse than the others, despite being equal in attention at the outset. This result is consistent with others showing long-term negative associations between entertainment television and attention.[5]

What's a librarian to do? We often look to our colleagues in the field of early childhood development for research-based recommendations. In January 2012, the National Association for the Education of Young Children and the Fred Rogers Center for Early Learning and Children's Media at Saint Vincent College adopted a position statement on media use and young children: *Technology and Interactive Media as Tools in Early Childhood Programs Serving Children from Birth through Age 8.*[6] The statement offers some suggestions that might help inform decisions on how to use, or not to use, technology in storytime. It urges that technology be used with children in an intentional way, as a tool to facilitate young children's learning. When technology is used with children, it must be developmentally appropriate and culturally sensitive, engaging children in an active and hands-on manner, with the content being the focus of the activity, not the technology itself. The position paper also affirms concerns raised by public health researchers on the impact of screen time on children's development and health, including correlations between time spent in front of screens and childhood obesity. It also cautions that use of technology needs to be equitable, that all children, including those with special needs, have the opportunity to play and explore with it.

In a research study done by the Joan Ganz Cooney Center comparing parent-child co-reading on print, basic, and enhanced e-book platforms, it was found that in conversations between parents and preschool children around the printed book and the basic e-book, similar levels of content related actions occurred (e.g., labeling, pointing, and verbal elaboration of story features).[7] Enhanced e-books, with more bells and whistles, drew out fewer content-related actions. Both basic and enhanced e-books prompted more noncontent-related actions (e.g., behavior, device-focused talk) than did print books. The increased content verbalization with print books can lead to improved vocabulary and overall language development. The study also found that across all formats, children could explain a critical element in the story, but those who read e-books recalled significantly fewer narrative details than those who read the print version of the same story. Finally, the study found that while print books were more advantageous for literacy building, e-books, particularly enhanced e-books, were more advantageous for engaging children and prompting physical interaction. Thus, e-books have value for their ability to prompt less motivated readers to engage when those readers might otherwise avoid books altogether.

The digital world is changing rapidly. There is a dearth of research on what kind of impact digital content has on young children older than age two. We suggest that librarians consider the following when deciding if and how to use screens in their storytimes:

Educational DVDs and websites contain a lot of good content on science and social studies that can add to children's background knowledge while introducing or reinforcing vocabulary and other early literacy components.

Children need to know that books aren't the only kind of media where they can find information.

Young children and adults need to learn about digital literacy and about what quality apps and e-books look like.

If using e-books or other technology, demonstrate how the adult interaction makes a difference in children's understanding, as well as how the adult interaction enhances children's experience with the electronic book.

Children are very attracted to media, but what if screens, and not traditional books, become the main attraction? What if the first question children ask in storytime is, "When are we going to use the iPad?" or "What movie will we see today?"

Ask yourself the following questions: What kind of impact will the use of digital media have on social interactions among adults and children in storytime? What might we do to model responsible use of media? Is not using it and explaining why we don't use it a good thing to do? What part of our storytime will we drop to accommodate this new addition? What will we not do anymore? How will children's language and imaginations grow as a result of adopting technology?

If you offer stories in different modes (e.g., storytelling, books, e-books), ask adults to notice children's reactions. What elements make a difference in the way children interacted with a story? How might that affect their own sharing of stories and information with their children?

Ultimately, it is up to each of us to decide how to handle technology in storytime. We hope that more research on the impact of technology on young children will be done, which should help inform our decision making. In the meantime, we know that the absence of screens has not been negative for generations of children who have attended our storytimes.

NOTES

1. Council on Communications and Media, American Academy of Pediatrics, "Media Use by Children Younger Than Two Years," *Pediatrics: Official Journal of the American Academy of Pediatrics*, October 17, 2011, 1.

2. Victoria Rideout, *Zero to Eight: Children's Media Use in America: A Common Sense Media Research Study* (San Francisco: Common Sense Media, 2011), 11.

3. Council on Communications and Media, "Media Use by Children," 4.

4. Cynthia Chiong and Carly Shuler, *Learning: Is There an App for That? Investigations of Young Children's Usage and Learning with Mobile Devices and Apps* (New York: Joan Ganz Cooney Center, Sesame Street Workshop, 2010), 18, http://dmlcentral.net/resources/4496.

5. Angeline S. Lillard and Jennifer Peterson, "The Immediate Impact of Different Types of Television on Young Children's Executive Function," *Pediatrics: Official Journal of the American Academy of Pediatrics*, September 12, 2011, 4.

6. National Association for the Education of Young Children and Fred Rogers Center for Early Learning and Children's Media at Saint Vincent College, *Technology and Interactive Media as Tools in Early Childhood Programs Serving Children from Birth through Age 8,* 2012, www.naeyc.org/files/naeyc/file/positions/PS_technology _WEB2.pdf.

7. Cynthia Chiong, Jinny Ree, and Lori Takeuchi, "Print Books vs. E-books: Comparing Parent-Child Co-reading on Print, Basic, and Enhanced E-book Platforms," May 15, 2012, pp. 1–5, www.joanganzcooneycenter.org/publication/quickreport-print-books -vs-e-books/.

chapter 5

Using Informational Books with Young Children

BECAUSE CHILDREN ARE NATURALLY INTERESTED IN EXPLORING AND MAKING SENSE of their world, it seems only fitting that we adults would use informational texts in our work with them. We define factual or informational books as having the following traits:[1]

- They have a primary focus on teaching children information about the world around them.
- They are usually written by someone with knowledge and authority about a subject.
- They usually include diagrams or photographs.
- The text explores cause and effect or compare and contrast.
- The book uses headings and has an index.
- The book employs a particular writing style, such as the use of generic nouns and timeless verbs.

Libraries often shelve factual books with general nonfiction titles, and some libraries have a separate "easy nonfiction" section. We use the terms *informational books* or *factual books* because *nonfiction* includes more than just factual books, such as folklore and poetry. Most early learning standards use the term *informational text* rather than *factual text* or *factual books*.

The use of informational books helps children learn that books and reading are ways of getting and communicating information. It is also beneficial for them to see that informational books are read differently than narratives. For example, we often read children's informational books in a nonlinear way, dipping in and out of them, and sometimes using an index.[2] The fact that books serve many purposes is related to how books work, and it is part of children's background knowledge.

Some children have a marked preference for informational books, and research indicates that it is developmentally appropriate to use such books with children.[3] In fact, informational books are an excellent way to help children develop content knowledge—a subdivision of background knowledge—which is so crucial to being a good reader; research suggests that children in kindergarten develop content knowledge from informational books that were read to them.[4]

Because research has shown that children's preferences and attitudes toward different kinds of books are influenced by how their adults use and discuss them, it is important for children to be exposed to informational texts.[5] Also, researchers have learned that young children who are exposed to informational texts have an increased ability to read and write informational texts later on in school.[6] Hands-on experiences that used both realia and science experiments have been shown to help children learn new words. The combination of dialogic reading of informational books with hands-on activities can help young children understand scientific processes as well as providing them with necessary context and language to help them more completely understand scientific processes.[7]

Researcher Nell Duke describes one study of adult-child interactions in a Head Start classroom that showed that mothers who read informational books with their children introduced more vocabulary words and asked more questions than when reading narrative texts.[8]

Other research has shown that exposure to language with higher levels of cognitive demand has a positive effect both on children's ability to use higher-level language themselves and on their later literacy.[9] In one study that looked at pairs of parents and preschool children sharing informational books and storybooks, there were some similarities in the way the books were shared but also some important differences. Those pairs who tended to talk more did so with both types of books. However, when reading informational books, parents used on average more than twice as many utterances as with storybooks and allowed children to use almost twice as many utterances. Parents used higher-level words and concepts (making inferences and recalling information presented earlier; making text-to-life comparisons, or relating to the child's experiences; and making text-to-text comparisons, or recalling other books) as compared with lower-level vocabulary builders such as labeling and describing objects.[10]

Other research has indicated that young children can learn scientific names for complex ideas.[11] Further research needs to be done on what preschool children learn from books that combine story and fact. It seems that preschoolers have difficulty discerning fact and narrative, so adults may need to make distinctions clear.

Storytime presenters should include informational books in storytimes for children age two and up, even if the book is not read from cover to cover. We should promote informational books to adults who are looking for interesting titles to share with their children. Especially for preschoolers, scientific knowledge should be part of their experience as they interact with the world. Adult mediation is critical in this respect—children need someone who can teach them scientific terminology and provide them with guidance while helping them work through a question.

Storytime presenters can show adults how to use informational books by incorporating them into storytimes and creating activities to help children deepen and broaden their understanding of their world. We can incorporate into storytimes opportunities for children to ask their own questions about what they see and hear. When adults respond with additional information, include new vocabulary words, or explain words, they help children become better readers when they are older because they are increasing their vocabularies, as well as their content and background knowledge, which are absolutely essential to children's academic success.

We often use picture books or themes in storytime that incorporate the basics of social studies, which is defined as "the integrated study of the social sciences and humanities to promote civil competence."[12] These topics include the development of individuals and their relationships to family, how individuals are alike and different, and what people need and want. Stories about families, how children grow, and the work people do are part of this. Themes involving people from different parts of the world and how we are alike and different, as well as maps and stories about neighborhoods and transportation, pertain to social studies, too. Moreover, understanding money, the difference between needing and wanting something, and how to make a difference in a community all fall into this category. Also, ideas about what is fair and how to make decisions and the relationship between decisions and consequences are part of social studies.[13]

In this book, though, we focus more on science and math than on social studies for several reasons. The first is that ECRR2 includes science and math as one of the parent-child workshops, and we feel that librarians would appreciate more information on these two topics to become more comfortable with the content. Second, for many of us it is easy to create storytimes using social science concepts, but we find math and science more challenging. In addition, there is a big push in education to encourage children to become involved in science, technology, engineering, and mathematics (STEM; for more information, see the website of the STEM Education Coalition, at www.stemedcoalition.org). Last, using science and math in storytime opens up a whole new world of possibilities for those of us who have not been exploring these topics.

Using books to help children learn about language and literacy is natural for many children's library staff. Our libraries are full of narrative storybooks that are rich in language and imagery that feed children's and adults' imaginations and intellects. Although one goal of public libraries is to create an environment for lifelong learning, public libraries are not often viewed as places that support development of children's math and science skills and other content areas. How can we explore these areas in storytime, and why should we?

Research abounds about the importance of encouraging young children's exposure to and interest in science and math. Most embrace the concept that explorations of science and math capitalize on young children's innate interest in and curiosity about the world around them and their keen ability to observe, even from infancy. In addition, children's natural interest in science can be the foundation for developing early literacy skills; after all, language and literacy deal with knowledge.[14] Science, which connects to cooking, life sciences, and art, is rich in language and presents opportunities for meaningful language-based interactions.[15]

Many resource books explain how to hold programs using very specific picture books tied to explicit concepts or content. Our approach is to share basic science and math concepts and then demonstrate how to use those concepts as part of storytime. We believe that this will help library staff understand concepts and begin to understand how flexible and enjoyable using these concepts can be as part of storytime.

Science Knowledge and Concepts

There are three areas in which young children need to achieve in science: content, processes, and attitudes. Content is the body of knowledge about the world; processes include predicting, making a hypothesis, observing, classifying, experimenting, and communicating; and specific attitudes that are important to scientific inquiry include curiosity about the world and a desire to experiment, to challenge theories, and to share ideas.[16]

Some scientific explorations can be conducted right in storytime. Other activities are better suited for after storytime or for adults to do with their children at home. Here we suggest ways storytimes can include science knowledge and concepts without changing the basic storytime structure and purpose. Explorations of science will vary greatly depending on the ages and developmental stages of the children, much in the same way that language-based activities are used with different groups of children.

Clearly, children's ability to participate in scientific activities will vary depending on their age and language ability. For example, an eighteen-month-old will react differently to a rock than an older child will. An older child can talk about the rock—that it is heavy and rough, where rocks are found—whereas the younger child might just look at it and touch it while we provide the descriptive words. When very young children observe things, they use all of their senses, but children need to have vocabulary words to help them explain what they observe.[17]

The beginnings of understanding scientific concepts can be seen even in infants. At about eight months old, babies have acquired an understanding of object permanence, or the realization that just because something is not immediately visible does not mean that it no longer exists. Before six months of age, if a ball is rolled passed an infant, he does not turn to go after it—the ball doesn't exist if he can't see it. But at around eight months old, babies will go look for the ball that passes them by.[18]

Another scientific concept that babies can learn is cause and effect. At first, babies hear the sound of a rattle that they shake in their hand, but they have no idea that they are causing the sound. Later, babies realize that if they move an arm, they can make the noise of the rattle. Babies often enjoy repeating an action in order to get the same response from an object, like shaking a rattle—this is called secondary circular response. In storytime when we use shakers, for example, we encourage the development of these skills.[19]

Older children enjoy searching for hidden objects and playing hide-and-seek. Around eighteen months old, children are able to experiment with objects. They experiment with shape boxes (seeing which shapes can fit into which holes) and stacking or nesting toys (which sizes fit inside other sizes). When children do an action and then modify it to see what will happen, this behavior is called tertiary circular response.[20]

Two-year-olds' observation skills are different from those of younger toddlers—they can visualize events and keep mental images of objects that they can remember, and they can try out what they have seen happen. They enjoy playing with props and toys that encourage this kind of activity.[21]

Classification is closely tied to observation and is a basic requirement to be able to think logically; it also helps children make sense of their world. Young children can put objects in groups but without being able to explain how they organized the collection. By the time they are in preschool, they are able to classify things by one characteristic. Adults need to help children learn the vocabulary to describe attributes of size, like *big*, *small*, and *tall*. This ability develops over time through different stages of childhood.[22] In storytime we might classify objects related to our themes. For example, in a storytime on shoes, we can classify footwear in groups by tie shoes, sneakers, or other attributes. If a storytime theme includes animals, we might provide a matching activity such as sorting adult and baby animals. Classifying also involves quantity, as well as comparing things on the basis of size, weight, length, volume, time, or temperature.

Measuring involves being able to quantify observations. Measurement-based activities can be used to teach children the vocabulary associated with measurement. In early childhood, measurements can be done using nonstandard instruments, such as body parts like feet and fingers. Weight can be explored using things like crayons and paper clips.[23]

Just as young children communicate thoughts and feelings through language, so can they express and clarify their thoughts about scientific events, as well as think and reason. By thinking and talking about their experiences with science, they begin to understand scientific phenomena. Children need continual exposure to new words and the opportunity to use those words. So in addition to using words, we can help children to understand how to communicate using graphs and charts and pictures. We can encourage them to share their ideas through their own drawing and writing.[24]

Prediction is based on prior knowledge and observation, which children use to figure out future events. To be successful at predicting, children need to have a lot of background knowledge, because predictions are based on information that children already possess.[25] During storytime we can help children develop this skill when we ask open-ended questions in a book picture walk. For example, asking, "What do you think will happen?" helps children develop this skill.

Inference is the use of logic to come to conclusions or to make assumptions based on what one has observed. It is similar to prediction in that both are based on observations, but inference involves looking at what happened in the past, whereas prediction deals with the future.[26] In storytime we make a lot of inferences based on pictures, and we can ask, "What do you think is happening here?" rather than "What do you think will happen?"

In storytime we can mention facts, the information part of science. But young children learn best by actively participating in investigative experiences—the process part of science. By doing science, children learn science. Through these experiences and by explaining scientific concepts and activities to parents and caregivers, we can help children learn that they can make discoveries about their world through investigation. They also come to understand that science is not about knowing the right answer.[27] Integrating hands-on science activities with informational texts helps children learn scientific concepts while also learning the words they need to talk about those concepts. They learn more effectively and don't develop misconceptions when the two are combined.[28]

What, then, are the most important skills for young children to learn around science and math? How can we use math and science concepts to enrich our storytimes? For content, we can look to the standards advocated by the National Association of Math Teachers, the National Science Teachers Association, and the National Association for the Education of Young Children. These standards are also noted in many state early learning standards, and in the child outcomes for Head Start and other programs.

The following sections discuss aspects of scientific learning as set forth in the early learning standards adopted by many states.

SCIENTIFIC KNOWLEDGE

There are two categories of scientific knowledge: *content* and *scientific process.* In terms of early literacy these are most directly tied to vocabulary and background knowledge, especially to conceptual thinking and narrative skills. The *content* category comprises several specific areas:

> **Characteristics of living things:** Understanding and having information about living things, their habitats, interrelationships, and interdependencies (life science), including the plant and animal kingdoms (and humans), where species live, and how they are connected through sharing the earth and its resources. In discussing these concepts, we can ask questions like, "Where do frogs go in the winter?" and "How does a caterpillar change?"
>
> **Knowledge of physical properties of objects and materials:** Understanding physical properties by observing and manipulating common objects and materials (physical science). This area provides the opportunity to talk about what things are made of and the properties of different things. We might ask, "Does it float or sink?" and "Where does water go when it evaporates?"
>
> **Tools and technology:** Using tools and technology to perform tasks (design technology). Children need the opportunity to try out the tools of science and exploration, like using implements to measure length and weight. We might ask, "Who has the biggest feet?" or "Can you measure something using paper clips?"
>
> **Scientific knowledge:** Understanding and having information about the earth and living things, including their relationships and interdependencies (earth and space science). This area deals with information about the solar system and the universe, as well as how the earth changes over time, weather, seasons, and time of day. We might ask, "What happens to trees in the fall?"

Scientific processes are those processes through which children apply and test their scientific knowledge, including making sensory observations, asking questions, and collecting and analyzing data. When we ask children to predict what will happen next, we encourage the development of scientific inquiry. Doing a book picture walk and asking, "What do you think is happening here?" helps with these skills. Scientific content and/or processes can be incorporated into any storytime. By asking ourselves certain questions, we can make links to basic scientific concepts, and we can then use those concepts to broaden our book sharing and supportive activities. At the same time, we are encouraging and helping parents to become aware of how they can explore scientific concepts. We relate the importance of scientific activities to early literacy when we talk about content knowledge, pre-diction, hypotheses, abstract ideas, and the meanings of vocabulary words.

Mathematical Knowledge and Concepts

Most librarians have a love of the written word, but this might not be true of numbers. Whether or not we are comfortable with math and mathematical con-cepts, we can become knowledgeable about helping children make the connec-tions between math and their world. Mathematical knowledge and concepts are part of children's discovery, and books, activities, and the language that goes with them expands their knowledge, which in turn piques and satisfies their natural curiosity.

Many of us incorporate numeracy in our storytimes, such as using fingerplays that count down or count out, talking about where things are located in space (words that express spatial relationships), and playing with shapes and sizes. There is much more that we can do to help children build their vocabularies and background knowledge in mathematics, such as intentionally focusing on some key mathematical concepts and activities. This not only is beneficial to children but also is an enormous amount of fun. In so doing, we also help parents and caregivers add to their children's knowledge in enjoyable ways.

Over the past twenty-five years, research has shown that almost from birth to the age of five, young children have everyday knowledge about mathematics—ideas about quantities like more and less, taking away (subtraction), sizes, shapes, patterns, position, and location. These ideas develop in a child's everyday world, usually with no direct instruction. We can see that young children are sponta-neously interested in mathematical ideas by the way they play with blocks (which tower is higher) and make patterns and shapes.[29]

Young children need to learn how to think mathematically. Children begin with the rote saying of numbers, then one-to-one correspondence (one plate for each person who is eating), and then counting the number of people and the num-ber of spoons needed. Research indicates that young children can be competent in numerical operations, geometry and spatial relationships, measurement, data analysis, and algebraic thinking. Adults tend to underestimate both children's interest in and ability to learn mathematics.[30]

Young children need to be able to reason about numbers. For example, they need to understand that if $1 + 2 = 3$, then $2 + 1 = 3$. They need to be able to make inferences; for example, if you add something to a number, the number gets big-ger. For geometry, knowing the name of a shape is a beginning step. As children get older, they need to be able to make and analyze shapes and to understand the features that distinguish shapes. Children also need to be aware of the mathemat-ical strategies that they use and be able to talk about them. If we use words like

Tyrannosaurus rex with children, why do we hesitate to teach them words like *hexagon* or *octagon*?[31]

Other research has suggested that children understand one-to-one correspondence before they can count verbally with understanding. For example, they can match up two sets of things or point to items in a collection, labeling them with a number, even though it might be the wrong number.[32]

Young children can also make a mental match of objects to things that they can't see. For example, a young child will get two cookies for two children who are in another room, which shows an intuitive understanding of the relationship among objects.[33]

According to research, children have informal knowledge about geometry, forms, and shapes before becoming preschoolers. By the age of four, children can identify some shapes.[34]

Children exhibit a grasp of the basic elements of algebra when they play with pattern blocks, make their own patterns, or arrange items according to a rule. Sorting and organizing objects according to attributes is part of geometry and measurement skills, which are key parts of data analysis.[35]

Exposure to mathematical concepts is important because "mathematics ability upon entry to kindergarten is a strong indicator of later academic success, and in fact is even a better predictor of later success than is early reading ability."[36] Children who participate in activities that help them recognize, compare, and order objects; learn whether objects are of the same size; and use language to describe attributes (e.g., larger, smaller) are more likely to develop math proficiency in the elementary grades. Research also has indicated that young children go to school with a body of knowledge about measurements (e.g., length, weight), but they don't know how to reason about them. It has been suggested that with enough exposure to activities, young children can move into more advanced levels of reasoning than was previously thought.[37]

There is not much research on young children and data collection, but researchers have learned that children try out different strategies to solve problems. They might try one technique, like organizing a pattern by size, and then try another strategy, like sorting by shapes. The ability to try different strategies corresponds to their later proficiency in math.[38]

Part of math education is learning the language of mathematics. Through talking and play, adults have opportunities to use words needed to think mathematically—words for numbers and the language of geometry (shapes) and words for quantity (e.g., *more*, *less*). Children learn about the relationship between symbols and ideas when adults use charts and graphs. As children talk about how they reason using math, they are developing their communication skills. They are also becoming aware of their own thought process, or how they think.[39]

State standards describe math content in a variety of ways, but most include the same basic principles. Mathematical standards developed by the National Council of Teachers of Mathematics can be divided into two groups: process and content. Process standards involve how we use math, whereas concepts deal explicitly with developing a knowledge base and understanding. In other words, process standards help us explore the mathematical concepts that young children need. The process standards include the following:

Problem solving: guessing, estimating, asking for help
Reasoning and proof: how to solve a problem
Representation: using graphs and pictures
Communication: using the language of mathematics
Connections: applying math in different situations

Content standards include the following:

Numbers and operations: counting and beginning addition and subtraction
Geometry and spatial sense: knowing shapes and words that relate to position
Algebra, functions, and patterns: using patterns, understanding changes in quantity and size
Comparison and measurement: comparing objects using words like *more* and using words describing quantities (e.g., *long, tall*)
Time and sequence: developing an understanding of the concept of time, especially in terms of daily routines, and putting objects and events in sequence
Problem solving using data analysis, statistics, and probability: collecting and sorting objects to answer questions, keeping track of information using lists or graphs (with adult assistance)

Science and Math During and After Storytime

We can explore mathematical processes and content material during and after storytime. These explorations serve to model mathematical thinking for adults as well as children. We are also adding to children's body of knowledge about their world, to their background knowledge, which is a key component of early literacy. It is important to remember that our math explorations with young children need to be appropriate for their age and interests.

Programs for children and families that feature science and math concepts, activities, and book sharing can be stand-alone family programs. The same concepts and activities can be done in a family program setting or in programs for school-age children. Here, though, we focus on the storytime setting.

We believe that every storytime offers the opportunity to explore an aspect of science or math. We do not, however, urge that this take place during every storytime. Rather, we can think of science and math as opening up an expanded world of possible storytime activities. It's important to remember that when exploring how science or math might apply to storytime, we still should start with books and other storytime elements rather than beginning with the scientific or math principle.

Table 5.1 presents some questions that you can use as a guide in planning storytimes that include scientific content and/or processes (for more examples of ways to include scientific content and processes as part of storytimes, see chapter 9, "Sample Storytimes for Preschoolers," and chapter 11, "Storytime Extras").

Table 5.1

Storytime Planning Guide—Questions for Science Concepts

CATEGORY	QUESTIONS
Scientific knowledge: All areas	Which informational books will you use to explore a concept?
	What can you bring in to physically show the children something about the topic?
	What are the vocabulary words that you need to better understand the concepts, and how will you teach those words?
	Which images will you use to ask, "What do you observe?"
	Can you make a prediction?
	What can you sort or classify by characteristics?
	How can you communicate what you observe or predict? A chart or graph?
	Is there an activity that you can do after storytime related to this concept?
	Can models be used that represent real objects?
	Is there scale, or comparisons to be made, like size and distance?
	How are patterns and relationships explored, as in properties of materials, or things that are alike or different?
Additional questions for living things	Is a system explored (parts of the human body, or an ecosystem)?
	What changes can you notice over time by observing and recording how living things grow?
	How do you know if something is alive?
	How is this the same as or different from another thing of a similar or dissimilar kind?
	How is diversity alike in living organisms or seeds explored?

Storytime Planning Guide—Questions for Science Concepts (continued)

Additional questions for physical properties	What are things made of?
	What elements in the story can you explore through movement or sound (physics) or their composition (chemistry)?
	Are there variations in the properties of things, like colors and sounds?
	Can you kick, push, pull, or drop something?
	Will something dissolve, sink, float, or change its state (liquid, gas, solid)?
Additional questions for tools and technology	What kind of equipment might you use? Magnifying glass? Ruler? Scale? Pen and paper?
	What can you build with _____?
	How might you make this differently?
	How can you encourage children to look at a situation from various perspectives and then come up with alternative solutions?
	Can you ask the question, what if there were no _____?
	How are structure and function in plants, animals, tools, and utensils used in the story?
Additional questions for scientific knowledge	Does the book explore a relationship between or among living things and the earth?
	How do the concepts relate to the place where the children live?
	How do things change over time (e.g., seasons, growing)?
	Are cause and effect explored? Other phenomena (e.g., shadows, gravity)?

Storytime Planning Guide—Questions for Science Concepts (continued)

Scientific inquiry	What do you observe or notice?
	
	Hypothesis
	    - Can you make a hypothesis, using "if . . . then" to describe action in the story?
	    - Is there a sequence of events?
	    - Can you use the phrases "What if?" or "How could we?"
	
	Prediction
	    - What do the children think about what is happening?
	    - What information from the story can help them determine what is going to happen?
	
	Testing predictions
	    - Try out what you think will happen.
	
	Record observations
	    - Can you make a chart or graph?
	    - Can children draw a picture?
	
	Conclusion
	    - What happened? Why do you think it turned out this way?

Additional questions for data collection	What can you compare and/or classify in the story?
	    - Are there differences in size, distance, weight, or quantity?
	    - What can be measured using nonstandard items like crayons or shoes as well as standard units of measurement (e.g., rulers)?
	    - How are things alike or the same?
	    - How are things different?
	    - Are there patterns?
	
	What can you sort into categories according to their shared attributes (things that are alike)?
	    - Can you put these comparisons into a graph or a chart?
	
	Can the children explain what is going on? (Why?)
	
	Can you help the children make a Venn diagram to illustrate characteristics?
	
	Can the children draw what they saw, even if they don't do so accurately?

Many of the suggested activities that follow are best done after storytime. You may want to demonstrate or start off an activity that parents can continue at home with their children. Remember to model the use of rich talk and other strategies such as thinking aloud as you puzzle out possible solutions to the problems posed in the activities. The following sections provide general suggestions for use in various storytimes. The activities support both science concepts and early literacy components.

SIMPLE SCIENCE EXPERIMENTS

Libraries have many good books that include information on how to do simple science experiments. These books are found in a variety of places, including compilations of science experiments and in the subject area relating to the topic you wish to explore. Make sure that you can give a basic explanation of the scientific phenomenon before doing the experiment, just in case a child asks, "Why?" Books with simple science experiments usually provide the answer to these questions along with the instructions.

The sample experiments that follow include an explanation of which early literacy components and practices are connected with each experiment, as well as a suggested topic. A basic experiment should always include the steps of the scientific method: observation, hypothesis, prediction, experimentation, and conclusion. Some easy science investigations, suitable for after storytime, include the following:

> **Magnets:** Which elements or items are attracted to magnets?
> **Gravity:** Which items when dropped from the same height hit the floor first?
> **Weight:** Which objects weigh more?
> **Friction:** Which objects will go down an incline faster?
> **Chemistry:** What happens when you add salt to vinegar? Baking soda to vinegar?

Other experiments, such as exploring evaporation by covering a cup of water with plastic, could be started in the library and continued at home or at a childcare center and reported on at a later storytime.

Sample Experiments

Early literacy connections: Vocabulary, background knowledge (narrative skills), talking, playing

Scientific concept: Scientific inquiry

Use with: Books dealing with natural phenomena, a storytime theme, or when you have discussed making predictions

What you say:

Float or sink: Which items float? Which ones sink? (boat theme)

Sound: What happens to the sound you make when tapping on a container if you fill up the container? (noise or quiet theme)

Light and shadow: How do shadows move and change when you shift the direction of the light? (night, moon, sun, or seasons theme)

Color: What happens when you mix the primary colors of red, yellow, and blue? (color theme)

Sorting and Classifying: Making a Chart

Early literacy connections: Letter knowledge (alike and different); background knowledge (conceptual thinking), talking, writing

Scientific concept: Scientific inquiry (recording observations)

Use with: Any storytime that deals with like things—animals, dinosaurs, foods, characteristics of clothing or shoes

What you do: Think about what items have in common (e.g., size, shape, color, texture), and sort and classify them by one or multiple traits. Once you decide how you will sort the collection, create a chart to help organize the collection (figure 5.1 shows a chart for sorting animals by whether or not they have fur or feathers).

What you need: paper and pen, dry-erase board (to make the chart)

What you say: "We are going to make a chart that is going to help us sort and organize (*a category of items*) by whether or not it has (*a certain characteristic*)."

Figure 5.1

FEATHERS	FUR	TOTAL

Sorting and Classifying: Making a Bar Graph

Early literacy connections: Background knowledge, talking, writing

Scientific concept: Scientific inquiry (recording observations), data collection (organizing information and understanding a visual representation of it)

Use with: Objects or pictures of things that you are sorting by one attribute

What you do: Fill in the corresponding number associated with the graph. After you have a chart, you can make a bar graph with graph paper or by drawing one yourself, or you can fill in the graph to record the data (see figure 5.2). This is another way for children to compare the attribute you are using for sorting.

What you say: "Let's see which group has the most items in it by sorting them by (*the characteristics you have selected*)."

Figure 5.2

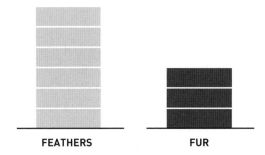

FEATHERS   FUR

Solving Problems with Technology

Early literacy connections: Background knowledge (conceptual thinking), talking
Scientific concept: Scientific knowledge (tools and technology, and using tools)
Use with: Books in which a problem is solved, or books about construction or food
What you need: A collection of items, depending on the problem you want to solve
What you do:

- to eat food (without forks or spoons)—make playdough into shapes, or use sticks (as chopsticks or spears)
- to move something without carrying it in your hands—use magnets, paper cups, straws, tape, paper, and paper clips (attach items to a magnet, or roll things on top of straws)
- to hold paper together—paper, lengths of wire or string, pieces of playdough (to make a paper clip, tie the paper together, fold the paper, or stick it together)

What you say: "It is fun to think about how to use things differently. I have put some things on the table in front of you. It is up to you to figure out how to use them to (*solve the problem*)."

Environments: Can It Live Here?

Early literacy connections: Vocabulary, background knowledge, talking, reading
Scientific concept: Scientific knowledge (relationships among living things)
Use with: Pictures of animals, habitats, clothing and its purpose, people in different countries

What you need: Pictures of animals identified with particular places (e.g., polar bears, lions, dolphins) and their respective habitats, pictures of people in clothes particular to a season or region, pictures of the habitats you are discussing.

What you do: Hand out pictures of the animals or people, and place the picture of the habitat on a flannelboard or other similar board.

What you say: "We are going to look at the pictures you have and figure out which place it would live and why. We can read parts of books to help us learn more about the habitat or the animal."

How High Can It Go?

Early literacy connections: Background knowledge, vocabulary
Scientific concept: Physical properties
Use with: Books about construction or buildings
What you need: Boxes of various sizes or blocks
What you do: Set up the boxes in groups that include many different sizes.
What you say: "You are going to build a tower. How high can you build it before it falls down?"

What Is It a Part Of?

Early literacy connections: Background knowledge (content knowledge), vocabulary, talking, writing
Scientific concept: Scientific knowledge (living things and systems)
Use with: Theme of body parts
What you need: One piece of paper per person (or to trace a child's entire body, butcher paper or art paper by the roll), crayons or washable markers
What you do: Have each child place one hand on a piece of paper. Adults (or children, if they are able) trace around each child's open hand. Label the different parts of the hand: thumb, index finger, middle finger, ring finger, and pinkie. Also use words like *palm*, *heel*, *wrist*, *knuckle*, *nail*, *cuticle*, and *vein*. With large pieces of paper, like mural paper, you can do the same thing tracing the whole body.
What you say: "(*Pointing to one of the fingers*) What is this finger called? That's right, your thumb. (*Pointing to a knuckle*) Do you know what this is called? Did you know that your foot has a heel, and your hand does, too, right above your wrist? You can press down on things very hard with the heel of your hand." Make sure to explain how the hand is connected to the rest of our bodies and how the parts of our bodies all work together because they are connected.

SIMPLE MATHEMATICAL CONCEPTS

Tables 5.2 and 5.3 list some guiding questions that point out mathematical concepts that you can integrate into storytime or do after storytime. You may want to demonstrate or start an activity that parents can continue at home with children. There is quite a bit of crossover between math and science when it comes to concepts of measurement and graphing.

Table 5.2

Storytime Planning Guide—Questions for Math Process Concepts

CATEGORY	QUESTIONS
Problem solving	Can you guess about a math-related event in the story? Is there something that you can estimate?
Reasoning and proof	How did you reach the conclusion that you reached? What thought process did you and the children use to reach your conclusion? Can you think aloud to show the children how you reason?
Representation	Can you and the children create a visual to explain a mathematical concept by making a picture or designing a graph? Can you use objects to demonstrate your point (e.g., sorting buttons into groups to show them that 2 + 3= 5)?
Communication	What math-related vocabulary words can you help the children learn? Can you talk about fractions (e.g., one-half)?
Connections	How can you and the children use math in situations other than the one represented in the book?

Table 5.3
Storytime Planning Guide—Questions for Math Content Concepts

CATEGORY	QUESTIONS

Numbers and operations	What can you count?
	     - How many are there?
	     - Counting with numerals (e.g., 1, 2) and words (e.g., one, two)
	 When separating or sorting, which has more? Which has less?
	 What happens if you add another one or take one away?
	 How can you rearrange objects or people to show the children how addition and subtraction work?

Geometry and spatial sense	What shapes can you identify in the book? What does it "look like" using geometry? (E.g., Which one has a triangle shape in it?) What words will you use to describe what the shapes look like, including three-dimensional shapes? What goes up, under, over, around? Can you use positional words, for example, *next to*, *in front of*, and *behind*?

Algebra, functions, and patterns	What patterns are there in events or language?
	     - Can you clap or move to a pattern?
	     - Are there visual patterns?
	     - Can you use a pattern to guess what will happen next?
	     - What sequence of events can you describe?
	 Has the quantity or size of something changed?

Comparison and measurement	What tools can you use to determine the following:
	- How big is it?
	- How do we measure it?
	- How much does it weigh?
	- How much can it hold?
	What happens if you add or take away something?
	Can you use vocabulary words of comparison like *more than*, *bigger than*, and *heavier than*?
	What can you describe that has attributes like long, short, tall, cold, and heavy?
	Can you compare two or more objects by height or length?
	What can you measure using standard and nonstandard tools?
	What objects can you bring in to sort and match?
	Can you guess how much or how many there are of something?
	What can you do to explain how time has passed?
Data collection and analysis	Can you chart something using a graph, bar, or pie chart?
	How can things be sorted and classified?
	What can you keep track of over time that is related to your environment?

The following sample activities provide some general ideas that you can use in various storytimes. These activities support both math concepts and early literacy components.

Counting, Adding and Subtracting, More and Less, and Patterns

Early literacy connections: Vocabulary, background knowledge

Math concept: Content (mathematical functions)

Use with: Any book that has patterns of any kind (visual, aural, narrative), themes of sharing or taking turns

What you need: Dozens of the same thing in different colors (e.g., milk caps, poker chips, colored paper clips, crayons, pieces of paper cut into shapes), or you can use paint and cookie cutters to make patterns. After one person makes a pattern, switch cookie cutters so another person can match it.

What you do: Show children how patterns work, how quantities don't change when they are moved, the concepts of more and less, and the concepts of addition and subtraction. Hand out enough items to each child or pairs of children so that they can move their pieces along with you.

What you say: Explain the concept that you are exploring. For example:

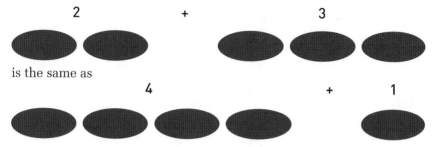

is the same as

Can you match this pattern? What comes next?

Shapes

Early literacy connections: Letter knowledge, vocabulary, talking, writing

Math concept: Content (geometry)

Use with: Any book exploring shapes or sizes

What you need: Shapes cut out ahead of time, paper, glue

What you do: Hand out a variety of shapes and a large piece of paper and glue

What you say: "(*Before handing them out*) This is a (*name of shape*). It always has (*number*) sides (*or whatever its characteristics are*). We are going to make pictures with the shapes." (See figure 5.3.)

Figure 5.3

Measuring

Early literacy connections: Vocabulary, background knowledge, talking, writing
Math concept: Content (measurement)
Scientific concept: Scientific knowledge (tools and technology, and using tools)
Use with: Things that grow over time, comparative sizes and weights (e.g., big and bigger, heavy and heavier), volume
What you need: Paper and marker to record data, appropriate tool (e.g., ruler, measuring tape, scale, cups of various sizes), or you can use a nontraditional but standard-sized thing, like a pencil, to measure (but be sure to explain why you use that thing to measure).
What you do: Measure or weigh
What you say: "We are going to see which (*person, item*) is the (*tallest, longest, heaviest, one that holds the most*) by (*measuring, weighing*) it. We are going to use this tool to figure it out."

Estimation—Guess How Many

Early literacy connections: Background knowledge (conceptual thinking), talking, writing
Math concept: Mathematical process (problem solving)
Use with: Books about quantities or that require making an estimation (e.g., "Who do you think has more?")
What you need: Clear containers of various sizes filled with objects of different sizes (no more than ten objects), paper and pencil for children and adults to guess
What you say: "Take a look at these containers. Guess how many (*objects*) there are in each one. After storytime we are going to count them to find out."

Counting Out

Early literacy connections: Singing
Math concept: Content (numbers and operations)
Use with: Any theme with which the song fits
What you need: Song lyrics, puppets or other objects (or you can use your fingers)—some song suggestions include the following: "Five Little Monkeys Jumping on the Bed," "Five Green and Speckled Frogs," and "Five Little Pumpkins."
What you say: "We are going to sing a song that starts with (*object*). One by one they are going to go away, until we are left with none!"

NOTES

1. Nell K. Duke, "Reading to Learn from the Very Beginning: Information Books in Early Childhood," *Young Children*, March 2003, 1, http://journal.naeyc.org/btj/200303/ InformationBooks.pdf.

2. Ibid., 4.

3. Ibid., 1.

4. Ibid., 3.

5. Cynthia B. Leung, "Preschoolers' Acquisition of Scientific Vocabulary through Repeated Read-Aloud Events, Retellings, and Hands-On Science Activities," *Reading Psychology* 29 (2008): 169.

6. Ibid.

7. Ibid., 170.

8. Duke, "Reading to Learn from the Very Beginning," 3.

9. Lisa Price, Anne van Kleeck, and Carl Huberty, "Talk during Book Sharing between Parents and Preschool Children: A Comparison between Storybook and Expository Book Conditions," *Reading Research Quarterly* 44, no. 2 (2009): 171–94.

10. Ibid., 189.

11. Leung, "Preschoolers' Acquisition of Scientific Vocabulary," 190.

12. National Council for the Social Studies, "About National Council for the Social Studies," www.ncss.org/about.

13. Vermont Center for the Book, *Mother Goose Cares about Social Studies* (Chester: Vermont Center for the Book, 2005), 12–15.

14. Kathleen Conezion and Lucia French, "Science in the Preschool Classroom: Capitalizing on Children's Fascination with the Everyday World to Foster Language and Literacy Development," *Young Children*, September 2002, 16.

15. Ibid., 17–18.

16. Ruth Wilson, "Promoting the Development of Scientific Thinking," *Early Childhood News*, 2, www.earlychildhoodnews.com/earlychildhood/article_view .aspx?ArticleId=409.

17. Ithel Jones, Vickie E. Lake, and Miranda Lin, "Early Childhood Science Process Skills: Social and Developmental Considerations," in *Contemporary Perspectives on Science and Technology in Early Childhood Education*, ed. Olivia N. Saracho and Bernard Spodek (Charlotte, NC: Information Age Publishing, 2008), 21.

18. Ibid., 21–22.

19. Ibid., 21.

20. Ibid., 22.

21. Ibid., 22–23.

22. Ibid., 20–21.

23. Ibid., 24.

24. Ibid., 24–25.

25. bid., 26–27.

26. Ibid., 28.

27. Wilson, "Promoting the Development of Scientific Thinking," 1.

28. Leung, "Preschoolers' Acquisition of Scientific Vocabulary," 189–90.

29. Herbert P. Ginsburg, Joon Sun Lee, and Judi Stevenson Boyd, "Mathematics Education for Young Children: What It Is and How to Promote It," *Social Policy Report: Giving Child and Youth Development Knowledge Away* 22, no. 1 (2008): 3–4.

30. Ibid., 6.

31. Ibid.

32. Kimberly Brenneman, Judi Stevenson-Boyd, and Ellen C. Frede, "Math and Science in Preschool: Polices and Practice" (Preschool Policy Brief, March 2009, no. 19, National Institute for Early Education Research, New Brunswick, NJ), 2.

33. Ibid.

34. Susan B. Neuman and Kathleen Roskos, *Nurturing Knowledge* (New York: Scholastic, 2007), 107.

35. Brenneman et al., "Math and Science in Preschool," 3.

36. Ginsburg et al., "Mathematics Education for Young Children," 3.

37. Neuman and Roskos, *Nurturing Knowledge*, 107–8.

38. Ibid., 109.

39. Brenneman et al., "Math and Science in Preschool," 4.

Part II

Doing It

chapter 6

Preparing for Early Literacy Enhanced Storytimes

Using Components, Practices, and Asides

THIS CHAPTER SERVES AS A GUIDE TO HELP YOU PLAN AND PRESENT STORYTIMES THAT incorporate early literacy practices, early literacy components, and research information into your storytimes. In the next three chapters, you will find storytimes for infants and toddlers, two- and three-year-olds, and three- to five-year-olds, which you can use as is or as a jumping-off point for creating your own storytimes. Our aim in this part of the book is to demonstrate how to convey early literacy research to parents and caregivers in a storytime context.

An early literacy enhanced storytime is a traditional storytime with three tips, or research-based asides, about early literacy that are aimed at adults. We are intentional about the ways that we support early literacy in storytimes. This intentionality includes articulating to adults the connection between what we do in storytimes and later reading. In addition, we articulate ways parents and caregivers can continue supporting early literacy even after storytime is over. We do all this while still keeping the fun in storytime. We are, in fact, showing enjoyable ways that we and parents and caregivers can and do support early literacy.

The early literacy enhanced storytime highlights one early literacy component and includes three asides or tips, a sentence or two lasting about thirty seconds each, directed at adults.

Storytimes are already full of early literacy and offer opportunities to highlight all five early literacy components (i.e., phonological awareness, print conventions and awareness, letter knowledge, vocabulary, and background knowledge), but we highlight or explain only one early literacy component through the use of early literacy tips or asides. This method keeps the information from becoming too overwhelming during storytime. We also don't want the information we share to detract from storytime itself. Because the asides are short and focused on one early literacy component, adults have enough information to take with them to continue to support that component even after storytime is over. The asides take place in the beginning, middle, and end of storytime. There are three different kinds of asides:

> **Explain:** Points out and defines or explains the early literacy component that is being highlighted for that storytime. It may give information about a practice. This is basically a short introduction both to the aspect of early literacy and to what you will point out in storytime (for a clip of an explain aside, see www.youtube.com/watch?v=4BCe-jSoR2M).
>
> **Example:** Highlights an example of the component or practice that is part of storytime and its connection to early literacy and/or later reading. Using one of the elements of storytime (e.g., song, book, fingerplay, flannelboard), the aside points out a specific instance of how what we are doing supports early literacy and later reading (for a clip of an example aside, see www.youtube.com/watch?v=HDxHMKchQiE and www.you tube.com/watch?v=A3g0oWiaPsQ).
>
> **Empower:** Usually at or near the end of storytime, this aside suggests how to continue supporting the highlighted aspect of early literacy at home or in the child-care setting. For example, articulating ways that writing or playing can support early literacy at home or at the child-care center might be easier than including these practices during storytime (for a clip of an empower aside, see www.youtube.com/watch?v=HJ89U lCTzWo).

There are several ways to convey early literacy information to adults during storytime. While the first edition of ECRR articulated the names of the skills and then showed activities that supported them, the second edition leads with the five practices—singing, talking, reading, writing, and playing—and connects those practices to early literacy and later reading. It places less emphasis on the names and definitions of the early literacy components. However, we have found that naming and explaining the early literacy components helps parents learn more about early literacy and actually motivates them to continue activities at home.

What Makes an Effective Early Literacy Aside?

Whether leading with the early literacy component or with the practice, the aside should be an "effective" one. An effective aside provides a research-based reason for why or how an activity (e.g., repeating a phrase, asking open-ended questions) or practice (e.g., singing, talking, reading, writing, playing) supports an early literacy component (e.g., phonological awareness, print conventions and awareness, letter knowledge, vocabulary, background knowledge—with or without use of those terms) or reading skill (e.g., decoding or comprehension) (for a video clip of effective and ineffective asides, see www.youtube.com/watch?v=kvnbeBcdFaI). Think, "Reason and result." Whether or not you use the name of the early literacy component, you must explain the term to connect it to later reading. (The text in square brackets below indicates optional text to use if you do choose to use the terminology of early literacy.)

Explain Aside

Ineffective aside: "Today I'll show you some ways that phonological awareness can help your child with later reading." (This aside is ineffective because there is no explanation of phonological awareness and/or how it supports later reading.)

Effective aside—Leading with the component: "Our early literacy tip of the day today is on being able to hear the smaller sounds in words. [This is called phonological awareness.] Researchers have found this skill to be important in learning to read because it helps children sound out words when they learn to read. Today I'll point out some activities with rhyming words, which you'll be able to do at home as well."

Effective aside—Leading with the practice: "Singing slows down language so children can hear the smaller sounds in words. This will help them later sound out words when they learn to read. Today I will show you some examples of this."

Effective aside—Leading with the practice: "When we sing songs with children, they often hear a different note for each syllable. This helps them hear the smaller sounds in words. [This skill is called phonological awareness, one of the early literacy skills that researchers say is important for later reading.] Keep this in mind when we are singing during storytime today."

Example Aside

Ineffective aside: "When we read books with children, they hear different words from the ones they hear in regular conversation." (This is ineffective because there is no indication of how knowing more words supports vocabulary or helps with comprehension.)

Effective aside—Leading with the component: "Books have three times as many rare words than we use in conversation with young children, words they would hardly ever hear in daily conversation. Reading books with unfamiliar or rare words helps children develop larger vocabularies, which will help them understand what they read later."

Effective aside—Leading with the practice: "When we read books with children, they hear different words from the ones they hear in regular conversation. The more words children know, the easier it is for them to understand what they read when they learn to read. Did you notice how many interesting words there were in this story?"

Empower Aside

Ineffective aside: "When you are out and about with your child, make sure you talk about the signs you see." (This is ineffective because there is no mention of how the activity supports an early literacy component or later reading.)

Effective aside—Leading with the component: "When you and your child are doing errands, point out the signs you see. Knowing that print has meaning and that print is everywhere will help your child get ready to read. [This skill is called print awareness.]"

Effective aside—Leading with the practice: "When you talk with your children about the labels on containers or signs you see, they learn that print has meaning, [which is part of print awareness,] which is a skill that children need to get ready to read. You can enrich their understanding by talking about shared experiences related to the labels and signs."

It is important for you to choose the approach that best suits your participants. You may choose to use different approaches in different storytimes. Whichever approach you decide on, each aside must be an effective one.

In both the sample storytimes in part 2 and the storytime extras in part 3, you will notice some extension activities. An extension activity is an addition or adaptation to the storytime that emphasizes the skill being highlighted. Including the extension activity makes it easier for children to learn the early literacy component and for adults to make the connection between the book or activity and the component. For example, you might add an activity that emphasizes the component, such as a song that emphasizes rhyming words for phonological awareness. The extension might be subtle, like running your finger under the words as you read them for print awareness, or very noticeable, like taping a letter to the floor for children to trace or walk on for letter knowledge.

Role of the Storytime Presenter

In an early literacy enhanced storytime, the storytime presenter is less of a presenter or entertainer and more of a facilitator or catalyst who encourages interaction between the adults and children. Some elements of storytime will more fully encourage participation not only by the children and between you and children but also between children and the adults who accompany them. Here is a list of things that you may decide to include in your early literacy enhanced storytime to encourage adults to interact with children:

- name tags for children and adults
- signs on the walls, such as "Everyone participates!" "Encourage your child to participate by participating yourself," and "Be present with your child: turn off cell phones, no texting!"
- flip charts or posters of rhymes and songs, to allow everyone to look up and follow the words all together while having their hands free to do the actions to the songs
- a handout reviewing the early literacy activities during storytime that includes a sentence or two that makes the connection between the activity and early literacy and/or later reading
- a handout with songs or rhymes for parents that you provide at the beginning of storytime so they can do them at storytime and at home
- an activity that encourages parent-child interaction (e.g., song, rhyme, craft, game)
- props, flannelboard pieces, or puppets for each person at storytime to help retell a story
- handouts related to storytime content given out at the end of storytime to encourage interactions at home or elsewhere

In the early literacy enhanced storytime, we encourage adults to attend storytime. While adults accompany the youngest children to storytime, children sometimes attend preschool storytimes on their own. Adults, though, will be better able to support their children when they are with them and participate in storytimes; thus, we highly recommend that they attend. To set the tone for this, you might want to modify the title of your programming by including a subtitle that indicates that storytime is based on early literacy research. Always thank parents for bringing their children to storytime and helping them pay attention.

If adults absolutely refuse to attend or cannot attend, take advantage of the time in which they drop off and pick up their children to talk about early literacy. Invite them in to participate in the craft or activity time and talk with them then. Make sure to have a handout for them that describes what you have done during storytime and why. Adults are most likely to use the information on the handouts when you have talked about it with them.

When adults are included in storytime, the question might arise of how to keep their attention, since many adults use storytime as a social time and may become a distraction. Being clear about expectations before and during the storytime is key but is sometimes not sufficient. By giving adults a role in storytime for at least some of the activities, we send a signal that they are also supporting their children's language development and that their participation is important.

Here are a couple of examples of simple ways to give adults a role to play. Take the action rhyme "The Itsy Bitsy Spider." There are several ways to do the actions to this rhyme (see sample storytimes). One way to involve adults in this rhyme is to have the child be the spider and to have the adult play the other parts:

> The itsy bitsy spider (*child uses fingers to climb up adult's arm*)
> Climbed up the water spout (*adult holds arm in* L *shape while child's fingers climb up*)
> Down came the rain (*adult flutters fingers like rain*)
> And washed the spider out (*child places his or her hand behind back*).
> Out came the sun (*adult makes circle above head*)
> And dried up all the rain
> And the itsy bitsy spider (*child uses fingers to climb up adult's arm*)
> Climbed up the spout again (*adult holds arm in* L *shape while child's fingers climb up*)

By making the action rhyme interactive, you make it enjoyable for both adults and children. If an adult has more than one child, there's no problem—three spiders can climb up the "water spout."

Many books have repeated phrases. For example, the book *Too Much Noise*, by Ann McGovern (Sandpiper Books, 1992), repeats the phrase "'Too noisy,' said Peter," as well as the sounds that the animals make. One way to encourage participation with this book is to have everyone say the sounds of the animals and the phrase "'Too noisy,' said Peter." Another way to make it more interactive and to give adults a role is to have children make the sounds of the animals and to have adults say, "'Too noisy,' said Peter." Not only is this more engaging; it actually reflects the meaning of the story.

ECRR2 particularly emphasizes the importance of informational books and talking about facts with young children. Science and math are the two factual topics addressed, but informational books on any and all topics can be included in storytime. As noted in chapter 5, parents talk more and allow their children to talk more when they share informational books with them. They also use a higher level of vocabulary. Some children prefer factual books to storybooks. We advocate that all storytimes for children age two and up should include at least one informational book. You need not read the whole book, and you can also use magazines with factual articles on topics. Children should be exposed to informational books, and adults should know of their specific value. Our sample storytimes reflect this approach.

Handouts

We want adults to continue to support their children's early literacy development in enjoyable ways. Add early literacy tips presented at storytime to handouts; these make a nice transition to the empower aside. Handouts may include the book titles, songs, and fingerplays used during storytime and/or puppet or craft patterns and ideas for activities for adults and their children to do together. The addition of information about early literacy reminds adults of the connection between an enjoyable activity and later literacy. When a child attends storytime without a parent, the take-home sheet serves as a way to connect children's learning to their home, and it gives parents important early literacy information. When the handout includes a pattern or an activity for adults and children to do together, adults are more likely to take home the handouts and read them. Understanding the connection between the storytime activities and how they support early literacy and later reading is a motivating factor for adults to continue these activities once storytime is over.

There are numerous ways to incorporate early literacy information and activities into handouts to encourage adults to continue to support early literacy in enjoyable ways even after storytime is over. Here are some tips for handouts that support early literacy:

- They relate directly to or build on something that took place in the storytime.
- They incorporate an early literacy component and connect it to the handout activity.
- They are not too overwhelming.
- They emphasize the importance of adult-child interaction and of adults and children doing something together.
- They include an activity or a craft—remember to emphasize that talking about the process is as important as getting to the finished product.
- They are more than a coloring sheet—if you start with a coloring sheet, be sure to add ideas to make it more interactive, such as turning the picture into a puppet, having adults and children talk about the drawing, and having the child tell a story about what is happening in the picture and having the adult write it down.

As you end your storytime and pass out the handout, mention the activity on the handout, which can make a seamless lead into your empower aside. Here are some handouts we've developed along with suggestions for using them:

Hickory Dickory Dock (www.earlylit.net/storytimeshare/wp-content/ uploads/2012/05/hickorydickorydockfbhnd.doc): Say the rhyme "Hickory Dickory Dock." Use the pattern on the handout to make flannelboard pieces. After saying the rhyme and doing it on the flannelboard, play a game in which you put the mouse in different positions in relation to the clock to indicate spatial relationships using prepositions like *above*, *below*, *behind*, *next to*, and *underneath*. Your example aside can relate this activity to learning words for positions, which develops vocabulary and later comprehension.

Winter Clothes (www.earlylit.net/storytimeshare/wp-content/uploads/ 2012/05/winterclothespractices.pdf): This handout includes a game to play that uses spatial prepositions and explains how they support vocabulary. You can see how the practices and components support each other: a direct connection is made between the practice of playing and the early literacy component of vocabulary.

Old Macdonald Had a Farm (www.earlylit.net/storytimeshare/wp-content/ uploads/2012/05/oldmacdhand.doc): Here is a drawing activity for farm animals related to the song "Old Macdonald Had a Farm"—it uses phonological awareness and singing in the early literacy tip. Younger children can draw or scribble animals.

Making activity cards for nursery rhymes and other storytime activities is one way to help parents and caregivers continue the activity at home (see web extra 6.1 at www.alaeditions.org/webextras). If you give one card to each child for parents or caregivers, they can take it home to use with their families. Each handout is a card the size of a quarter sheet of paper. You might want to punch a hole in the upper left corner and give adults a ring to put the cards on. Over time, parents and caregivers will gather a terrific collection of nursery rhymes and ready-to-use activities.

Sample Storytimes

Chapters 7–9 provide fifteen sample storytimes: five for infants and toddlers, five for two- and three-year-olds, and five for preschoolers. The five sample storytimes for infants and toddlers are purposefully repetitious. These storytimes have been prepared as if you were presenting all five in a series. Repetition is important for preschoolers, but even more important for babies from birth to age two. About two-thirds of the items are repeated in each storytime. Some items from the first storytime are skipped over for new items, and then we come back to them during the last couple of weeks. Sometimes you'll get requests for a favorite—never turn them down! Children need repetition to learn. There are some that use the same rhymes and songs in every single program. Children need repetition, but they also need variety. Their brains tune into things that are new as well.

In the sample storytimes for two- and three-year-olds and for preschoolers, we offer some different options for opening and closing songs, but we recommend keeping the same opening and closing songs so that children and adults feel comfortable and so that they become a cue for what comes next.

If the age breakdowns used here are not the ones you use for your storytimes or if your storytimes are for all ages, feel free to mix and match elements from any of the storytimes! You know your group best. The asides are targeted to the age level noted. If you have a mixed group, it is good to mention to parents whether an activity is more appropriate for older or younger children in your group. For example, eighteen-month-olds cannot make a rhyme, but they can sing a song or make animal sounds, which also supports phonological awareness.

Each sample storytime has suggestions for activities to support early literacy components. These offer opportunities for you to model support for early literacy and to informally talk about them as adults and children are doing the activities together.

Even though we hope you get some good ideas from these sample storytimes, it is more important that you become familiar with how to adapt the storytimes that you already use and feel comfortable with as a basis for making your own early literacy enhanced storytimes. Your storytimes are already full of early literacy! Now you will also articulate or point out how what you do during storytimes supports early literacy in an enjoyable way. In doing so, you will also be pointing out ways the adults can support children's early literacy development outside storytimes. Chapter 10 addresses building your own early literacy enhanced storytime.

chapter 7

Sample Storytimes for Infants and Toddlers

1. Animals Big and Small

STORYTIME INTRODUCTION

Hello, one and all. My name is (*your name*). I am so glad to see you all here today at storytime. We encourage you all to participate and to do the rhymes and songs with your children. You know your children best, so if they are not in the mood, don't force them, but do encourage them. Sometimes when they see you joining in, they will, too. We expect a fair amount of chaos during storytime, but if your child becomes disruptive, please take him or her out and join us again when your child has settled down. Let's start with our opening song.

OPENING SONG

Acka Backa Soda Cracker

(You can find the tune at http://wiki.kcls.org/
tellmeastory/index.php/Acka_Backa_Soda_Cracker.)

Use the first set of motions for babies, the second set for toddlers.

Acka backa soda cracker
  (*Rock baby back and forth. / Toddler rocks back and forth.*)
Acka backa boo
Acka backa soda cracker

We'll sing a song or two.
>   (*Bounce baby. / Toddler opens hands on each side of mouth.*)
Acka backa soda cracker
>   (*Rock baby back and forth. Toddler rocks back and forth.*)
Acka backa boo
Acka backa soda cracker
Up goes you. (*Raise baby up. / Toddler puts hands above head or stands up.*)

Acka backa soda cracker
>   (*Rock baby back and forth. / Toddler rocks back and forth.*)
Acka backa boo
Acka backa soda cracker
I love you. (*Hug baby. / Hug toddler.*)

EARLY LITERACY ASIDE: EXPLAIN

Adults, our early literacy tip today is on letter knowledge. Researchers have found that children first recognize letters by their shapes! Today I'll point out some ways you can support letter knowledge as you talk about shapes. At this early age our children's brains are wired for learning! Let's do our first bouncing rhyme.

ACTION RHYME
Trot, Trot to Boston
Trot, trot to Boston. Trot, trot to Lynn.
>   (*Child on lap facing you; bounce child up and down.*)
Look out, Baby, you're going to fall in!
>   (*Open your legs and let the child down.*)
Trot, trot to Boston. Trot, trot to Dover. (*Sway child side to side.*)
Look out, Baby, you're going to turn over! (*Stay over to one side.*)
Trot, trot to Boston. Trot, trot to Lyme. (*Bounce child up and down.*)
Look out, Baby, let's bounce another time! (*Give the child a big bounce.*)

Repeat.

BIG BOOK

I Love Animals, by Flora McDonnell (Candlewick, 1996)
Let's read this book all together. The babies won't be able to see the pictures, but they love hearing the sound of your voice. Encourage your children to make the sounds of the animals. Listen to all the interesting words in this book!

Take time with each page to indicate the meanings of words through the sound of your voice and/or your actions. Encourage toddlers to imitate you.

SHAKERS

Hand out shakers.

Yes, Sir, That's My Baby

(You can find the tune on the CD *Baby Face: Activities for Infants and Toddlers*, by Georgiana Stewart [Kimbo Educational, 1983]. Full lyrics by Gus Kahn and Walter Donaldson are at http://rickynelson.com/lyrics/yessirthatsmybaby.html; you can hear and download Rick Nelson's more rock-and-roll version at www.rhapsody.com/#artist/rick-nelson/album/more-songs-by-rickyricky-is-21/track/yes-sir-thats-my-baby.)

As you shake the shakers, recite the following lyrics:

> Yes, sir, that's my baby
> No, sir, I don't mean maybe
> Yes, sir, that's my baby now

Now shake those shakers high. Shake them low. Shake them fast. Shake them slow. Shake them to the front of you. Now to the back. Over your shoulder, and to the side.

Good! Let's do another song with shakers. This one is called "Sodeo." You'll hear it say in the song, "To the front, to the back, to the seesaw side." Just follow the rhythm.

Sodeo

(From the CD *More Singable Songs*, by Raffi [Rounder, 1996].)

Collect shakers.

SIGN LANGUAGE

Today I'd like to teach you the sign in American Sign Language for "spider." First, I'll show you a picture of a spider. See the legs? A spider crawls. Let's see you crawl.

OK, here's what the sign looks like (*make the sign; you can see a video clip of the sign for "spider" by searching the website ASL Pro, at www.aslpro.com/cgi-bin/aslpro/aslpro.cgi*). Let's do the "spider" sign all together. Good! OK, now listen for the word *spider* and keep your hands ready. We say the word as we sign it.

ACTION SONG

Itsy Bitsy Spider

(You can find the tune at www.gardenofsong.com/itsybitsy.html.)

Use the first set of motions for babies, the second set for toddlers.

> The itsy bitsy spider climbed up the water spout.
> (*Fingers crawl up baby's body. / Fingers crawl up the opposite arm.*)

Down came the rain and washed the spider out.
> (*Flutter fingers down baby's body and then side to side. / Flutter fingers downward in the air, move arms side to side.*)

Out came the sun and dried up all the rain.
> (*Circle baby's face. / Circle hands over head, then with palms up, arms move up and down again.*)

So the itsy bitsy spider climbed up the spout again.
> (*Fingers crawl up baby's body. / Move fingers up the opposite arm.*)

Repeat the song once or twice more.

ACTION SONG

Roll, Roll, Roll Your Hands

(To the tune of "Row, Row, Row Your Boat." From *Toddlers on Parade*, by Carol Hammett and Elaine Bueffel [Kimbo Educational, 1985]. Lyrics reprinted by permission of Kimbo Educational, www.kimboed.com.)

Demonstrate this song using a doll, puppet, or stuffed animal without the music. Do actions according to words in the song. Show the actions and have everyone practice: rolling hands, tapping your feet, shaking your hips. Then sing the song without the music. Now repeat, using the music for "Roll, Roll, Roll Your Hands" on the CD **Toddlers on Parade.**

Roll, roll, roll your hands
As fast as fast can be
Do it now, let me see, do it now with me

Tap, tap, tap your feet . . .
Shake, shake, shake your hips . . .
Roll, roll, roll your hands . . .

Clap when the song is done.

BALLS

Today I have some balls we can play with. Everyone feel the ball—babies, too! How does your ball feel? It might be nice and smooth. See how soft your ball is. Let's see how round feels—hug it close to you. It's a sphere, nice and round. Your arms are making a circle around the ball. Yay!

A sphere rolls. Sit down and put your leg on top of the round ball. How does that feel? Your leg might slip off because the ball keeps rolling. Let's see what colors are on your ball . . . Now let's try rolling the balls (*in adult-child pairs; if you have fewer balls, make larger groups*).

As you collect the balls, give adults the next early literacy aside.

EARLY LITERACY ASIDE: EXAMPLE

As you play with balls, blocks, or other toys with your children, talking about the different shapes as they play is one way to support letter knowledge, since children will later recognize letters by their shapes. Children learn through their senses, so talking about shapes while they are playing with them will allow them to learn new things in the way they learn best. Great! Now get ready for a bounce.

ACTION SONG

Bumping Up and Down

(From the CD *Singable Songs for the Very Young*, by Raffi [Rounder, 1996]; lyrics are available at www.metrolyrics.com/bumping-up-and-down-lyrics-raffi.html.)

Play the song.

Way to go! (*Clap together.*) Now let's see if we can find Spot, the little puppy. His mommy is looking for him.

BIG BOOK (LIFT-THE-FLAP BOOK)

Where's Spot? by Eric Hill (Penguin Putnam, 1998)

ACTION SONG

Baby's Hokey Pokey

(From the CD *Baby Face: Activities for Infants and Toddlers*,
by Georgiana Stewart [Kimbo Educational, 1983].
Lyrics reprinted by permission of Kimbo Educational, www.kimboed.com.)

Arms up, arms down, arms up
And wave them all around
Then tickle tickle wiggle giggle
Everyone knows
That's how baby's hokey pokey goes. (*Repeat.*)

Legs up, legs down, legs up
And kick them all around
Then tickle tickle wiggle giggle
Everyone knows
That's how baby's hokey pokey goes. (*Repeat.*)

Buzz, buzz, buzzzzzzzzzzz. I hear a buzzing sound! Can you make that sound? Let me hear you! Parents can make the buzzing sound to their babies. Toddlers can say, "Buzzzz" themselves. A bee makes a buzzing sound. Ready for the bees?

ACTION RHYME

The Beehive

Here is the beehive. (*Close fist.*)
Where are the bees?
Hidden away where nobody sees.
Watch as they come out of their hive. (*Extend fingers as you count.*)
One
Two
Three
Four
Five!
They're alive! (*Shake fingers or tickle child's belly.*)
BUZZZZZZZ.

Repeat once or twice.

ACTION SONG WITH FLANNELBOARD

Twinkle, Twinkle, Little Star

(You can find the tune at www.kididdles.com/lyrics/t068.html
or www.kididdles.com/lyrics/t023.html.)

You can do the actions standing or sitting. When the song is done, let each child put a felt star on the flannelboard to make a beautiful sky. You can put up a moon and one star first, to start the children off.

Twinkle, twinkle, little star (*Hands open and shut.*)
How I wonder what you are
Up above the world so high (*Raise twinkling hands.*)
Like a diamond in the sky (*Make diamond shape with fingers.*)
Twinkle, twinkle little star (*Hands open and shut.*)
How I wonder what you are

Repeat.

EARLY LITERACY ASIDE: EMPOWER

As you are talking and playing with your children throughout the day, take time to point out shapes you see as they play with their toys. As you walk or drive, you can talk about the shapes you see—signs, the wheels of cars, houses—there are shapes everywhere we go! (*If you do the take away activity below, add:*) You can draw shapes and talk about them with the bag of pudding that you can take home with you. Doing fun, informal activities like these helps children develop early letter knowledge skills.

CLOSING SONG

Acka Backa Soda Cracker

(You can find the tune at
http://wiki.kcls.org/tellmeastory/index.php/Acka_Backa_Soda_Cracker.)

Use the first set of motions for babies, the second set for toddlers.

Acka backa soda cracker
  (*Rock baby back and forth. / Toddler rocks back and forth.*)
Acka backa boo
Acka backa soda cracker
We'll sing a song or two.
  (*Bounce baby. / Toddler opens hands on each side of mouth.*)

Acka backa soda cracker
  (*Rock baby back and forth. Toddler rocks back and forth.*)
Acka backa boo
Acka backa soda cracker
Up goes you.
  (*Raise baby up. / Toddler puts hands above head or stands up.*)

Acka backa soda cracker
  (*Rock baby back and forth. / Toddler rocks back and forth.*)
Acka backa boo
Acka backa soda cracker
I love you. (*Hug baby. / Hug toddler.*)

END OF STORYTIME ACTIVITY

- *Put out board books and balls to play with. Other play items: cloth to play peek-a-boo, pots and pans for crawlers.*
- *Model ways to talk with young children, pointing out an early literacy tip to adults, such as rich talk, labeling and expanding on what child says, and modeling waiting for answer.*

TAKEAWAY

Pudding in a plastic bag: *Make these ahead of time or have the participants make at the end of storytime. Spoon some pudding into a sealable plastic bag. Children can press their fingers to leave an imprint that looks like writing. They can "write" or draw shapes or any designs or scribbles they like.*

2. Trot, Gallop, and Dance!

STORYTIME INTRODUCTION

Hello, one and all. My name is (*your name*). I am so glad to see you all here today at storytime. We encourage you all to participate and to do the rhymes and songs with your children. You know your children best, so if they are not in the mood, don't force them, but do encourage them. Sometimes when they see you joining in, they will, too. We expect a fair amount of chaos during storytime, but if your child becomes disruptive, please take him or her out and join us again when your child has settled down. Let's start with our opening song.

OPENING SONG

Acka Backa Soda Cracker

(You can find the tune at
http://wiki.kcls.org/tellmeastory/index.php/Acka_Backa_Soda_Cracker.)

Use the first set of motions for babies, the second set for toddlers.

Acka backa soda cracker
  (*Rock baby back and forth. / Toddler rocks back and forth.*)
Acka backa boo
Acka backa soda cracker
We'll sing a song or two.
  (*Bounce baby. / Toddler opens hands on each side of mouth.*)

Acka backa soda cracker
  (*Rock baby back and forth. Toddler rocks back and forth.*)
Acka backa boo
Acka backa soda cracker
Up goes you. (*Raise baby up. / Toddler puts hands above head or stands up.*)

Acka backa soda cracker
  (*Rock baby back and forth. / Toddler rocks back and forth.*)
Acka backa boo
Acka backa soda cracker
I love you. (*Hug baby. / Hug toddler.*)

EARLY LITERACY ASIDE: EXPLAIN

Reading books with your children is one of the best ways to help your child be ready to learn to read. Your children like to imitate you. Books are great conversation starters. Today, I'll point out how you can build your child's background knowledge, or what they know, by the way you talk with them as you read together. Let's have our first bouncing rhyme.

ACTION RHYME

Trot, Trot to Boston

Trot, trot to Boston. Trot, trot to Lynn.
   (*Child on lap facing you; bounce child up and down.*)
Look out, Baby, you're going to fall in!
   (*Open your legs and let the child down.*)
Trot, trot to Boston. Trot, trot to Dover. (*Sway child side to side.*)
Look out, Baby, you're going to turn over! (*Stay over to one side.*)
Trot, trot to Boston. Trot, trot to Lyme. (*Bounce child up and down.*)
Look out, Baby, let's bounce another time! (*Give the child a big bounce.*)

Repeat.

ACTION SONG

Baby's Hokey Pokey

(From the CD *Baby Face: Activities for Infants and Toddlers*, by Georgiana Stewart [Kimbo Educational, 1983]. Lyrics reprinted by permission of Kimbo Educational, www.kimboed.com.)

Arms up, arms down, arms up
And wave them all around
Then tickle tickle wiggle giggle
Everyone knows
That's how baby's hokey pokey goes. (*Repeat.*)

Legs up, legs down, legs up
And kick them all around
Then tickle tickle wiggle giggle
Everyone knows
That's how baby's hokey pokey goes. (*Repeat.*)

Here's a book with a good rhythm and an opportunity to keep your children involved with the movements.

BOOK

Jazz Baby, by Lisa Wheeler (Harcourt Children's Books, 2007)

Use movements as you go along, if you like. Use voice to suit rhythms.

Let's all stand up for some dancing to a jazz beat.

ACTION SONG

For some music with a great beat, try "Clap Your Hands" from Jazz for Kids, *by Lisa Yves (Jazz for Kids and Newsound, 2000), or use another jazz tune of your choice.*

Clap Your Hands

(From the CD *Jazz for Kids: Everybody's Boppin'*, by Lisa Yves
[Jazz for Kids and Newsound, 2000]. Lyrics reprinted by permission;
http://lisayves.com/jazz%20for%20kids.html.)

Clap your hands everybody, clap your hands
Clap your hands everybody, clap your hands
Let the music and rhythm bring you joy when you're with 'em
Clap your hands everybody, clap your hands.

Tap your toes . . .
Sing a song . . .
Do a dance . . .
Say good-bye . . .

Wonderful! Now everyone sit down for our next bounce, called "I Know a Little Pony."

ACTION RHYME

I Know a Little Pony
I know a little pony (*Bounce to the beat.*)
His name is Dapple Gray
He lives down in the meadow
Not very far away
He goes nimble, nimble, nimble
   (*Double the beat for "nimble, nimble, nimble."*)
And trot, trot, trot (*Bounce higher, but back to a slower beat.*)
And then stops and waits a bit (*Stop bouncing.*)
Gallop, gallop, gallop, hey!
   (*Bounce for each gallop and lift baby up on "hey!"*)

Repeat.

BELLS OR SHAKERS

Hand out bells or shakers. Have children practice shaking them, slowly, quickly, softly, loudly, high, and low. Shake bells or shakers to the following song.

Sodeo

(From the CD *More Singable Songs*, by Raffi [Rounder, 1996].)

Collect instruments.

ACTION RHYME

Dance Your Fingers Up

Demonstrate action on a doll for adults with infants; demonstrate for toddlers so they can do it on their own.

> Dance your fingers up, dance your fingers down.
> Dance them to the side and dance them all around.
> Dance them on our shoulders, dance them on your head.
> Dance them on your tummy, and put them all to bed!

Repeat once or twice.

BOOK

What Shall We Do with the Boo-Hoo Baby?
by Cressida Cowell (Scholastic, 2003)

When reading this book, put less emphasis on the crying and more emphasis on the sounds the animals make as they figure out what the baby wants.

Let's do a song before it's your turn to share books with your children.

ACTION SONG

Roll, Roll, Roll Your Hands

(To the tune of "Row, Row, Row Your Boat." From *Toddlers on Parade*,
by Carol Hammett and Elaine Bueffel [Kimbo Educational, 1985].
Lyrics reprinted by permission of Kimbo Educational, www.kimboed.com.)

Demonstrate this song using a doll, puppet, or stuffed animal without the music. Do actions according to words in the song. Show the actions and have everyone practice: rolling hands, tapping your feet, shaking your hips. Then sing the song without the music. Now repeat, using the music for "Roll, Roll, Roll Your Hands" on the CD Toddlers on Parade.

Roll, roll, roll your hands
As fast as fast can be
Do it now, let me see, do it now with me

Tap, tap, tap your feet . . .
Shake, shake, shake your hips . . .
Roll, roll, roll your hands . . .

Clap when the song is done.

Now it's your turn to share books with your child for a few minutes.

BOOK-SHARING TIME

Hand out a board book for each family or let families choose one from a display. While this is happening, give the next early literacy aside.

EARLY LITERACY ASIDE: EXAMPLE

Remember, reading is one of the activities that can develop prereading skills. When you read with your baby, you will notice that many books for our youngest children have very few words on each page. As you share this type of book, add information about what you see in the picture or something you know that is related to the picture. Even if your children cannot understand all you say, you are exposing them to information that later helps them understand what they read. Great! Now get ready for a bounce.

ACTION SONG
Bumping Up and Down
(From the CD *Singable Songs for the Very Young*, by Raffi [Rounder, 1996]; lyrics are available at www.metrolyrics.com/bumping-up-and-down-lyrics-raffi.html.)

Play the song.

Way to go! (*Clap together.*) Now let's see how a train moves.

ACTION RHYME
Choo-Choo Train
This is a choo-choo train (*Make a circular motion with arms.*)
Puffing down the track.
Now it's going forward. (*Make a circular motion forward.*)
Now it's going back. (*Make a circular motion backward.*)
Now the bell is ringing. (*Pretend to ring a bell.*)

Now the whistle blows. (*Cup hands to mouth and say, "Whoo-whoo."*)
What a lot of noise it makes (*Cover ears.*)
Everywhere it goes. (*Make a circular motion with arms.*)

Repeat.

SIGN LANGUAGE

Today I'd like to teach you the sign in American Sign Language for "star." Here's what the sign looks like (*make the sign; you can see a video clip of the sign for "star" by searching at the ASL Pro website, at www.aslpro.com/cgi-bin/aslpro/aslpro.cgi*). Let's do the "star" sign all together. Good! OK, now listen for the word *star* and keep your hands ready. We say the word as we sign it.

ACTION SONG WITH FLANNELBOARD

Twinkle, Twinkle, Little Star
(You can find the tune at www.kididdles.com/lyrics/t068.html or
www.kididdles.com/lyrics/t023.html.)

You can do the actions standing or sitting. When the song is done, let each child put a felt star on the flannelboard to make a beautiful sky. You can put up a moon and one star first, to start the children off.

Twinkle, twinkle, little star (*Hands open and shut.*)
How I wonder what you are
Up above the world so high (*Raise twinkling hands.*)
Like a diamond in the sky (*Make diamond shape with fingers.*)
Twinkle, twinkle little star (*Hands open and shut.*)
How I wonder what you are

Repeat.

EARLY LITERACY ASIDE: EMPOWER

You might find yourself reading the same simple board books with your child over and over again. Even though it might get boring for you, young children need lots of repetition to learn. Their brains make connections each time you share the book. To make it more interesting, you can share the book in different ways, even letting your child talk about the pictures and tell you a story. You might not understand everything your child says. Having an enjoyable time around books now goes a long way to helping them become engaged readers later.

As you read simple board books with your children, remember that you can help build your children's knowledge by using books as conversation starters.

Also, children who see their parents reading, whether it's the newspaper, magazines, recipes, instructions, or books, are more likely to become readers themselves.

CLOSING SONG

Acka Backa Soda Cracker

(You can find the tune at http://wiki.kcls.org/tellmeastory/index.php/
Acka_Backa_Soda_Cracker.)

Use the first set of motions for babies, the second set for toddlers.

Acka backa soda cracker
   (*Rock baby back and forth. / Toddler rocks back and forth.*)
Acka backa boo
Acka backa soda cracker
We'll sing a song or two.
   (*Bounce baby. / Toddler opens hands on each side of mouth.*)

Acka backa soda cracker
   (*Rock baby back and forth. Toddler rocks back and forth.*)
Acka backa boo
Acka backa soda cracker
Up goes you. (*Raise baby up. / Toddler puts hands above head or stands up.*)

Acka backa soda cracker
   (*Rock baby back and forth. / Toddler rocks back and forth.*)
Acka backa boo
Acka backa soda cracker
I love you. (*Hug baby. / Hug toddler.*)

END OF STORYTIME ACTIVITY

- *Put out animal toys and books.*
- *Model rich language, putting words to what children are doing and adding information to what children already know.*

TAKEAWAY

Make a baggie book: *Take four zip-top plastic bags and staple them together at the bottom. Cut out colored cardstock or poster board to fit inside each bag. Insert one piece in each baggie. Have catalogs or clip art or paper to draw on. Cut out pictures and slip them into the baggies, one picture on each side of the colored paper. Do not glue them down; adults can change the pictures as children learn words and talk about the pictures.*

3. Chuggin' Right Along

STORYTIME INTRODUCTION

Hello, one and all. My name is (*your name*). I am so glad to see you all here today at storytime. We encourage you all to participate and to do the rhymes and songs with your children. You know your children best, so if they are not in the mood, don't force them, but do encourage them. Sometimes when they see you joining in, they will, too. We expect a fair amount of chaos during storytime, but if your child becomes disruptive, please take him or her out and join us again when your child has settled down. Let's start with our opening song.

OPENING SONG

Acka Backa Soda Cracker

(You can find the tune at http://wiki.kcls.org/tellmeastory/index.php/
Acka_Backa_Soda_Cracker.)

Use the first set of motions for babies, the second set for toddlers.

Acka backa soda cracker
(*Rock baby back and forth. / Toddler rocks back and forth.*)
Acka backa boo
Acka backa soda cracker
We'll sing a song or two.
(*Bounce baby. / Toddler opens hands on each side of mouth.*)

Acka backa soda cracker
(*Rock baby back and forth. Toddler rocks back and forth.*)
Acka backa boo
Acka backa soda cracker
Up goes you. (*Raise baby up. / Toddler puts hands above head or stands up.*)

Acka backa soda cracker
(*Rock baby back and forth. / Toddler rocks back and forth.*)
Acka backa boo
Acka backa soda cracker
I love you. (*Hug baby. / Hug toddler.*)

EARLY LITERACY ASIDE: EXPLAIN

As you sing, talk, read, write, and play with your children every day, you can support your children's prereading (early literacy) skills even at this early age, in enjoyable ways. Help your child become comfortable with books starting now by letting them handle books. This helps children understand how books work. Knowing how to handle a book before starting school allows them to concentrate on learning how to read. This is one aspect of the skill called print awareness. I'll point out some things you can do to support it even with our youngest children. Let's have our first bouncing rhyme.

ACTION RHYME

Trot, Trot to Boston

Trot, trot to Boston. Trot, trot to Lynn.
  (*Child on lap facing you; bounce child up and down.*)
Look out, Baby, you're going to fall in!
  (*Open your legs and let the child down.*)
Trot, trot to Boston. Trot, trot to Dover. (*Sway child side to side.*)
Look out, Baby, you're going to turn over! (*Stay over to one side.*)
Trot, trot to Boston. Trot, trot to Lyme. (*Bounce child up and down.*)
Look out, Baby, let's bounce another time! (*Give the child a big bounce.*)

Repeat.

ACTION SONG

The Wheels on the Bus

(You can find the tune at www.kididdles.com/lyrics/b014.html.)

Use the first set of motions for babies, the second set for toddlers. Practice the actions with the children before starting the song.

The wheels on the bus go round and round
  (*Rock baby back and forth. / Rotate hands.*)
Round and round, round and round.
The wheels on the bus go round and round
All through the town.

The horn on the bus goes beep, beep, beep . . .
  (*Bounce baby in arms or on lap. / Fist moves to press horn three times.*)
The wipers on the bus go swish, swish, swish . . .
  (*Rock baby side to side. / Move forearms side to side.*)
The driver on the bus says, "Sit, sit, sit" . . .
  (*Bounce baby in arms or on lap. / Bounce three times.*)
The people on the bus go up and down . . .
  (*Raise and lower baby. / Sit tall and then relax.*)
The wheels on the bus go round and round . . .
  (*Rock baby back and forth. / Rotate hands.*)

SIGN LANGUAGE

Today I'd like to teach you the sign in American Sign Language for "train." Here's what the sign looks like (*make sign; you can see a video clip of the sign for "train" by searching at the ASL Pro website, at www.aslpro.com/cgi-bin/aslpro/aslpro.cgi*). Let's do the "train" sign all together. Good! OK, now listen for the word *train* and keep your hands ready. We say the word as we sign it.

BIG BOOK

Freight Train, by Donald Crews (William Morrow, 1993)

As you read the book, repeat the phrase "freight train" on several pages and use the sign for "train."

FLANNELBOARD ACTIVITY

Download the flannelboard from http://learn.tkschools.org/kfreeman/Freight%20 Train/freighttrain(C).pdf or www.earlylit.net/storytimeshare/?p=489. You may not be able to do this activity if your group is large. Choose three or four freight-train cars. Pass out flannelboard pieces to toddlers, one piece each. Put up one of the freight-train cars and describe it. You can put up your pieces and let them come up and put their pieces up at random making a train, or have them bring up the matching piece.

Let's see how a train moves.

ACTION RHYME

Choo-Choo Train

This is a choo-choo train (*Make a circular motion with arms.*)
Puffing down the track.
Now it's going forward. (*Make a circular motion forward.*)
Now it's going back. (*Make a circular motion backward.*)
Now the bell is ringing. (*Pretend to ring a bell.*)
Now the whistle blows. (*Cup hands to mouth and say, "Whoo-whoo."*)
What a lot of noise it makes (*Cover ears.*)
Everywhere it goes. (*Make a circular motion with arms.*)

Repeat.

SHAKERS

Hand out shakers.

Yes, Sir, That's My Baby

(You can find the tune on the CD *Baby Face: Activities for Infants and Toddlers*, by Georgiana Stewart [Kimbo Educational, 1983]. Full lyrics by Gus Kahn and Walter Donaldson are at http://rickynelson.com/lyrics/yessirthatsmybaby.html; you can hear and download Rick Nelson's more rock-and-roll version at www.rhapsody.com/#artist/rick-nelson/album/more-songs-by-rickyricky-is-21/track/yes-sir-thats-my-baby.)

As you shake the shakers, recite the following lyrics:

> Yes, sir, that's my baby
> No, sir, I don't mean maybe
> Yes, sir, that's my baby now

Collect shakers.

Next let's have a bounce to "I Know a Little Pony."

ACTION RHYME

I Know a Little Pony

> I know a little pony (*Bounce to the beat.*)
> His name is Dapple Gray.
> He lives down in the meadow
> Not very far away.
> He goes nimble, nimble, nimble
>   (*Double the beat for "nimble, nimble, nimble."*)
> And trot, trot, trot (*Bounce higher, but back to a slower beat.*)
> And then stops and waits a bit (*Stop bouncing.*)
> Gallop, gallop, gallop, hey!
>   (*Bounce for each gallop and lift baby up on "hey!"*)

Repeat.

ACTION RHYME

Dance Your Fingers Up

Demonstrate action on a doll for adults with infants; demonstrate for toddlers so they can do it on their own.

> Dance your fingers up, dance your fingers down.
> Dance them to the side and dance them all around.

Dance them on our shoulders, dance them on your head.
Dance them on your tummy, and put them all to bed!

Repeat once or twice.

Now it's your turn to share books with your child for a few minutes.

BOOK-SHARING TIME

Hand out a board book for each family or let families choose one from a display.

EARLY LITERACY ASIDE: EXAMPLE

As you read books with your babies and toddlers, encourage them to explore the book with you. Your babies may bat at or hit the pages. They are trying to turn the pages. For your toddler, start with the book upside down and see if they try to turn it right side up. Encouraging your toddler to turn the pages also helps him or her develop print awareness, or how to handle a book.

ACTION SONG

Baby's Hokey Pokey

(From the CD *Baby Face: Activities for Infants and Toddlers*,
by Georgiana Stewart [Kimbo Educational, 1983].
Lyrics reprinted by permission of Kimbo Educational, www.kimboed.com.)

Arms up, arms down, arms up
And wave them all around
Then tickle tickle wiggle giggle
Everyone knows
That's how baby's hokey pokey goes. (*Repeat.*)

Legs up, legs down, legs up
And kick them all around
Then tickle tickle wiggle giggle
Everyone knows
That's how baby's hokey pokey goes. (*Repeat.*)

Great! Now get ready for a bounce. This is one of our favorites.

ACTION SONG

Bumping Up and Down

(From the CD *Singable Songs for the Very Young*, by Raffi [Rounder, 1996]; lyrics are
available at www.metrolyrics.com/bumping-up-and-down-lyrics-raffi.html.)

Play the song.

Way to go! (*Clap together.*)

ACTION SONG

Put Your Little Foot

(From the CD *Baby Face: Activities for Infants and Toddlers*,
by Georgiana Stewart [Kimbo Educational, 1983].
Lyrics reprinted by permission of Kimbo Educational, www.kimboed.com.)

Put your little foot, put your little foot,
Put your little foot right there. (*Repeat two lines.*)

And we'll all stamp our feet.
Yes, we'll all stamp our feet. (*Repeat two lines.*)

Put your little foot, put your little foot,
Put your little foot right there. (*Repeat two lines.*)

Round and round we will go,
Tippy tippy tip toe. (*Repeat two lines.*)

Repeat the whole song.

EARLY LITERACY ASIDE: EMPOWER

As you talk about the pictures in books with your children at home, it is helpful
to take the time to show them the real item, if possible, as you point to the picture.
This is a key part of print awareness—the picture is not the real item; it *represents*
the real item. Later they will learn this with the text of words as well. I have a
display of books you and your children might enjoy together. Now let's do our
closing song.

CLOSING SONG

Acka Backa Soda Cracker

(You can find the tune at http://wiki.kcls.org/tellmeastory/index.php/
Acka_Backa_Soda_Cracker.)

Use the first set of motions for babies, the second set for toddlers.

Acka backa soda cracker
  (*Rock baby back and forth. / Toddler rocks back and forth.*)
Acka backa boo
Acka backa soda cracker
We'll sing a song or two.
  (*Bounce baby. / Toddler opens hands on each side of mouth.*)

Acka backa soda cracker (*Rock baby back and forth. Toddler rocks back
  and forth.*)
Acka backa boo
Acka backa soda cracker
Up goes you. (*Raise baby up. / Toddler puts hands above head or stands up.*)

Acka backa soda cracker (*Rock baby back and forth. / Toddler rocks back
  and forth.*)
Acka backa boo
Acka backa soda cracker
I love you. (*Hug baby. / Hug toddler.*)

END OF STORYTIME ACTIVITY

- *Put out flannelboard pieces of train cars for children to play with.*
- *Put out trucks and other things that go or blocks to make things that go.*
- *Have cutouts of stop signs, railroad crossings, construction signs, and so on, to show ways to support print awareness.*

4. Nature All Around Us

STORYTIME INTRODUCTION

Hello, one and all. My name is (*your name*). I am so glad to see you all here today at storytime. We encourage you all to participate and to do the rhymes and songs with your children. You know your children best, so if they are not in the mood, don't force them, but do encourage them. Sometimes when they see you joining in, they will, too. We expect a fair amount of chaos during storytime, but if your child becomes disruptive, please take him or her out and join us again when your child has settled down. Let's start with our opening song.

OPENING SONG

Acka Backa Soda Cracker

(You can find the tune at http://wiki.kcls.org/tellmeastory/index.php/
Acka_Backa_Soda_Cracker.)

Use the first set of motions for babies, the second set for toddlers.

Acka backa soda cracker
  (*Rock baby back and forth. / Toddler rocks back and forth.*)
Acka backa boo
Acka backa soda cracker
We'll sing a song or two.
  (*Bounce baby. / Toddler opens hands on each side of mouth.*)

Acka backa soda cracker
  (*Rock baby back and forth. Toddler rocks back and forth.*)
Acka backa boo
Acka backa soda cracker
Up goes you. (*Raise baby up. / Toddler puts hands above head or stands up.*)

Acka backa soda cracker
  (*Rock baby back and forth. / Toddler rocks back and forth.*)
Acka backa boo
Acka backa soda cracker
I love you. (*Hug baby. / Hug toddler.*)

EARLY LITERACY ASIDE: EXPLAIN

Hearing the smaller sounds in words, also called phonological awareness, is a key factor in children being able to sound out words when they learn to read. Even from infancy they listen to the lilt and rhythm of the languages they hear to help them figure out which sounds have meanings as words. When we talk, sing, read, write, and play with our children, we are helping them get ready to read.

ACTION RHYME WITH FLANNELBOARD OR STICK PUPPETS (Optional)

Rub-a-Dub-Dub

Rub-a-dub-dub, three men in a tub
And who do you think they be?
The butcher, the baker, the candlestick maker
They all set out to sea.

Repeat.

Rub-a-Dub-Dub and You

(Courtesy of Amy Alapati, Montgomery County [MD] Public Libraries.)

Rub-a-dub-dub, three kids in a tub,
And who do you think they be?
There's Simon, and Nathan,
And then there's Sophia,
Paddling out to sea!

Repeat with each child's name. If there are too many children then have each adult say the name of his or her child and family members' names if needed.

EARLY LITERACY ASIDE: EXAMPLE

Babies are trying to figure out where words begin and end in all the words they are hearing you say. At about four to six months old, babies recognize their names. In fact, using your child's name becomes a signal to help him or her identify words. So, by saying your child's name first, your child tunes in longer to the upcoming word for longer than if there is no familiar word before it. So by saying, "Kevin, blanket, here is your blanket," you help your child tune in to the word *blanket*. Your child's name becomes an anchor in a sea of words. Isn't it amazing how young children learn language!

ACTION RHYME

Trot, Trot to Boston

Trot, trot to Boston. Trot, trot to Lynn.
 (*Child on lap facing you; bounce child up and down.*)
Look out, Baby, you're going to fall in!
 (*Open your legs and let the child down.*)
Trot, trot to Boston. Trot, trot to Dover. (*Sway child side to side.*)

Look out, Baby, you're going to turn over! (*Stay over to one side.*)
Trot, trot to Boston. Trot, trot to Lyme. (*Bounce child up and down.*)
Look out, Baby, let's bounce another time! (*Give the child a big bounce.*)

Repeat.

SHAKERS

Shake the shakers to a variety of fast and slow songs on the CD Jim Gill Sings Do Re Mi on His Toe Leg Knee *(Jim Gill Music, 1999).*

ACTION SONG

Roll, Roll, Roll Your Hands

(To the tune of "Row, Row, Row Your Boat." From *Toddlers on Parade*,
by Carol Hammett and Elaine Bueffel [Kimbo Educational, 1985].
Lyrics reprinted by permission of Kimbo Educational, www.kimboed.com.)

Demonstrate using a doll, puppet, or stuffed animal without the music. Do actions according to words in song. Show the actions and have everyone practice: rolling hands—your hands are going in a circle! Tap your feet, shake your hips. Then sing the song without the music. Now repeat, using the music for "Roll, Roll, Roll Your Hands" on the CD Toddlers on Parade.

Roll, roll, roll your hands
As fast as fast can be
Do it now, let me see
Do it now with me

Tap, tap, tap your feet . . .
Shake, shake, shake your hips . . .
Roll, roll, roll your hands . . .

Clap when the song is done.

SIGN LANGUAGE

Today I'd like to teach you the signs in American Sign Language for "I love you." Here are what the signs look like (*make the signs; you can see a video clip of the signs for "I love you" by searching the ASL Pro website, at www.aslpro.com/ cgi-bin/aslpro/aslpro.cgi*). Let's all do the signs for "I love you" together. Good! OK, now listen for the words "I love you" and keep your hands ready. We say the words as we sign them.

BIG BOOK

I Love You, Sun, I Love You, Moon, **by Karen Pandell (Penguin Putnam, 1994)**

Point to the words as you read them to help everyone read together.

Parents, your little ones love the sound of your voice, so read the words even if your children are too young to see the pictures. (*Come back to the night-sky page.*) Look at the night sky—all the stars. Our next rhyme has stars, too.

ACTION SONG

Twinkle, Twinkle Little Star
(You can find the tune at www.kididdles.com/lyrics/t068.html or
www.kididdles.com/lyrics/t023.html.)

You can do the actions while standing or sitting.

Twinkle, twinkle, little star (*Hands open and shut.*)
How I wonder what you are
Up above the world so high (*Raise twinkling hands.*)
Like a diamond in the sky (*Make diamond shape with fingers.*)
Twinkle, twinkle little star (*Hands open and shut.*)
How I wonder what you are

Repeat.

ACTION SONG

Itsy Bitsy Spider
(You can find the tune at www.gardenofsong.com/itsybitsy.html.)

Use the first set of motions for babies, the second set for toddlers.

The itsy bitsy spider climbed up the water spout.
(*Fingers crawl up baby's body. / Fingers crawl up the opposite arm.*)
Down came the rain and washed the spider out.
(*Flutter fingers down baby's body and then side to side. / Flutter fingers downward in the air, move arms side to side.*)
Out came the sun and dried up all the rain.
(*Circle baby's face. / Circle hands over head, then with palms up, arms move up and down again.*)
So the itsy bitsy spider climbed up the spout again.
(*Fingers crawl up baby's body. / Move fingers up the opposite arm.*)

Repeat once or twice more.

SONG

Rain, Rain, Go Away

Rain, rain, go away,
Come again another day.

Repeat twice.

In our next book, let's see how much baby loves rain. There are so many things baby loves.

BOOK

Baby Loves, by Michael Lawrence (Dorling Kindersley, 1999)

Read the book.

Baby loved a kitty, too. (*If you have kittens on a flannelboard or as stick puppets for the rhyme below:*) Look at these kittens sleeping on a chair. There are five of them. We can count them—one, two, three, four, five.

RHYME

You can use flannelboard or stick puppets with this rhyme.

Five Little Kittens

Five little kittens sleeping on a chair,
One rolled off, leaving four there.
Four little kittens, one climbed a tree
To look in a bird's nest; then there were three.
Three little kittens wondering what to do,
One saw a mouse; then there were two.
Two little kittens having lots of fun,
One chased a ball; then there was one.
One little kitten with fur soft as silk
Was left all alone to drink a dish of milk.

Repeat.

ACTION SONG

Reach for the Ceiling

(From the CD *Toddlers on Parade*, by Carol Hammett and Elaine Bueffel [Kimbo Educational, 1985]. Lyrics reprinted by permission of Kimbo Educational, www.kimboed.com.)

Reach for the ceiling; touch the floor.
Stand up again; let's do some more.
Touch your head; then your knees.

Up to your shoulders, if you please.
Reach for the ceiling; touch the floor.
That's all now; there isn't any more.

Repeat.

EARLY LITERACY ASIDE: EMPOWER

Parents, listening to and singing songs that you enjoy with your children also helps them hear the smaller sounds in words. Singing slows down language and has often has different notes for different syllables, and so enjoyable, too!

CLOSING SONG

Acka Backa Soda Cracker

(You can find the tune at http://wiki.kcls.org/tellmeastory/index.php/
Acka_Backa_Soda_Cracker.)

Use the first set of motions for babies, the second set for toddlers.

Acka backa soda cracker
  (*Rock baby back and forth. / Toddler rocks back and forth.*)
Acka backa boo
Acka backa soda cracker
We'll sing a song or two.
  (*Bounce baby. / Toddler opens hands on each side of mouth.*)

Acka backa soda cracker
  (*Rock baby back and forth. Toddler rocks back and forth.*)
Acka backa boo
Acka backa soda cracker
Up goes you. (*Raise baby up. / Toddler puts hands above head or stands up.*)

Acka backa soda cracker
  (*Rock baby back and forth. / Toddler rocks back and forth.*)
Acka backa boo
Acka backa soda cracker
I love you. (*Hug baby. / Hug toddler.*)

END OF STORYTIME ACTIVITY

Pass out scarves to each person (adults and children). Toddlers wave them themselves, imitating you—high, low, throw, and pick up. Adults with babies wave scarves, and babies follow the scarves' motions. Model talking about what the children are doing with their scarves. Play with scarves to the tune of "A-Tisket, A-Tasket," from Miss Ella's Playhouse, *by Ella Fitzgerald (Verve, 2008).*

5. All Wet

STORYTIME INTRODUCTION

Hello, one and all. My name is (*your name*). I am so glad to see you all here today at storytime. We encourage you all to participate and to do the rhymes and songs with your children. You know your children best, so if they are not in the mood, don't force them, but do encourage them. Sometimes when they see you joining in, they will, too. We expect a fair amount of chaos during storytime but if your child becomes disruptive, please take him or her out and join us again when your child has settled down. Let's start with our opening song.

OPENING SONG

Acka Backa Soda Cracker
(You can find the tune at http://wiki.kcls.org/tellmeastory/index.php/
Acka_Backa_Soda_Cracker.)

Use the first set of motions for babies, the second set for toddlers.

Acka backa soda cracker
  (*Rock baby back and forth. / Toddler rocks back and forth.*)
Acka backa boo
Acka backa soda cracker
We'll sing a song or two.
  (*Bounce baby. / Toddler opens hands on each side of mouth.*)

Acka backa soda cracker
  (*Rock baby back and forth. Toddler rocks back and forth.*)
Acka backa boo
Acka backa soda cracker
Up goes you. (*Raise baby up. / Toddler puts hands above head or stands up.*)

Acka backa soda cracker
  (*Rock baby back and forth. / Toddler rocks back and forth.*)
Acka backa boo
Acka backa soda cracker
I love you. (*Hug baby. / Hug toddler.*)

EARLY LITERACY ASIDE: EXPLAIN

Having a good vocabulary, or knowing the meanings of words, is critical to your children being able to understand what they will later read. Young children understand the meanings of words not just from what you say but also by watching your facial expressions and your gestures, and by listening to the tone of your voice. I'll point out ways you can support vocabulary development in today's storytime. As you spend time with your children, when you sing, talk, read, write, and play with them, you are helping develop their prereading (early literacy) skills.

ACTION RHYME

Trot, Trot to Boston

Trot, trot to Boston. Trot, trot to Lynn.
   (*Child on lap facing you; bounce child up and down.*)
Look out, Baby, you're going to fall in!
   (*Open your legs and let the child down.*)
Trot, trot to Boston. Trot, trot to Dover. (*Sway child side to side.*)
Look out, Baby, you're going to turn over! (*Stay over to one side.*)
Trot, trot to Boston. Trot, trot to Lyme. (*Bounce child up and down.*)
Look out, Baby, let's bounce another time! (*Give the child a big bounce.*)

Repeat.

ACTION RHYME WITH FLANNELBOARD OR STICK PUPPETS (Optional)

Rub-a-Dub-Dub

Rub-a-dub-dub; three men in a tub
And who do you think they be?
The butcher, the baker, the candlestick maker
They all set out to sea.

Repeat.

Rub-a-Dub-Dub and You

(Courtesy of Amy Alapati, Montgomery County [MD] Public Libraries.)

Rub-a-dub-dub; three kids in a tub,
And who do you think they be?
There's Simon, and Nathan,
And then there's Sophia,
Paddling out to sea!

Repeat with each child's name. If there are too many children then have each adult say the name of his or her child and family members' names if needed.

SONG

Cleano

(From the CD *Woody's 20 Grow-Big Songs*,
by Woody Guthrie and Arlo Guthrie [Warner Brothers, 1992].)

Play the song.

This big book, *Itsy Bitsy Spider*, by Iza Trapani, also comes in board-book form.

BOOK

Itsy Bitsy Spider, by Iza Trapani (Scholastic, 1993)

I am showing you *Itsy Bitsy Spider* in book form, but it is also a rhyme. Today I'd like to teach you the sign in American Sign Language for "rain." Then, when you hear the word *rain*, we'll all do the sign together. Here's what the sign looks like (*make the sign; you can see a video clip of the sign for "rain" by searching the ASL Pro website, at www.aslpro.com/cgi-bin/aslpro/aslpro.cgi*). Let's do the "rain" sign all together. Good! OK, now listen for the word *rain* and keep your hands ready. We say the word as we sign it. Just as with talking, repetition is what helps children learn and remember—whether it is the spoken word or the sign that is being repeated.

During the reading of Itsy Bitsy Spider, *describe and talk about what is happening in several of the pictures. You can do this as you read the book, or you can come back to pages of your choice to talk about the pictures.*

EARLY LITERACY ASIDE: EXAMPLE

As you read books, say more than just the words on the page. You can use a picture and a word on the page as conversation starters. You can tell a story, something you know about the object, or anything you know or remember. You are building your child's vocabulary by talking with them and exposing them to lots of information and many different words. In their second year of life, children learn between eight and ten words a day.

ACTION SONG

Itsy Bitsy Spider

(You can find the tune at www.gardenofsong.com/itsybitsy.html.)

Use the first set of motions for babies, the second set for toddlers.

The itsy bitsy spider climbed up the water spout.
   (*Fingers crawl up baby's body. / Fingers crawl up the opposite arm.*)
Down came the rain and washed the spider out.
   (*Flutter fingers down baby's body and then side to side. / Flutter fingers*

downward in the air, move arms side to side.)

Out came the sun and dried up all the rain.

(Circle baby's face. / Circle hands over head, then with palms up, arms move up and down again.)

So the itsy bitsy spider climbed up the spout again.

(Fingers crawl up baby's body. / Move fingers up the opposite arm.)

Repeat once or twice more.

PLAYING: BUBBLES

Blow bubbles together, and have children try to catch them.

Hello, Bubble

(To the tune of "Frère Jacques," available at www.kididdles.com/lyrics/f010.html; lyrics from "Storytime Openings and Closings Compilation," by Olivia Spicer, PUBYAC electronic discussion list, December 2, 2004.)

Hello, bubble; hello, bubble
Come and land, come and land
Right in the middle, right in the middle
Of my hand! Of my hand!

Good-Bye, Bubble

(To the tune of "Frère Jacques")

Good-bye, bubble; good-bye, bubble
Time to go, time to go
You can help me; you can help me.
With a blow! With a blow!

Here comes another song with the word *rain* in it, so keep your hands ready to sign.

SONG

It's Raining

(You can find the tune at www.kididdles.com/lyrics/i028.html.)

It's raining, it's pouring
The old man is snoring
He went to bed and he bumped his head
And didn't get up till the morning

Repeat.

Here's a book about a bunny who has some fun even when it rains. Once again, listen to sign for the word *rain*!

BOOK

Bunny Fun, by Sarah Weeks (Harcourt Children's Books, 2008)

Read the book. After reading the first rainy-day page, you can sing the following song. If you decide to shorten the book by skipping some pages in the middle (read through "underneath the bed" or through "slippery socks" and then start again with "Ha-ha . . . cha-cha . . ." and end with "Look, Bunny! Sunny day!"), then let parents know that young children may not sit for a whole book, but as they get into the habit of listening, they will sit for longer and longer periods and work their way up to a whole book.

SONG

Rain, Rain, Go Away

Rain, rain, go away,
Come again another day.
Little Bunny wants to play.

Repeat.

Bunny and Mouse got all wet and dirty in the puddles. Let's have a washing song. Clap along to this rhyme.

ACTION RHYME

Splish, Splash, Splosh

(From the CD *It's Play School*, by Peter Mapleson and Robyn Mapleson [Mushroom Music Pty. Ltd., 1999]. Lyrics reprinted by permission; www.cduniverse.com/productinfo.asp?pid=7952655.)

Splish, splash, splosh, I'm having a wash,
Splosh, splash, splish, I'm wet as a fish.
Soap on my body, shampoo in my hair,
Scrub-a-dub-dub, now I'm clean everywhere.
Splish! Splash! Splish! Splash! Splosh!
I'm having a wash!

STORY WITH FLANNELBOARD OR PROPS

Fill the Tub with Water

(To the cadence of "Brown Bear, Brown Bear, What Do You See?" by Amy Alapati and Virginia Krute, Montgomery County [MD] Public Libraries; flannelboard pieces available at www.earlylit.net/storytimeshare/wp-content/uploads/2012/06/filltubwaterFB1.doc.)

You can shorten this according to the attention span of your group.

Fill the tub with water, what do you see?
  I see bubbles floating in the bathtub sea.
Fill the tub with water, what do you see?
  I see a washcloth floating in the bathtub sea.
Fill the tub with water, what do you see?
  I see a cake of soap floating in the bathtub sea.
Fill the tub with water, what do you see?
  I see a shampoo bottle floating in the bathtub sea.
Fill the tub with water, what do you see?
  I see a little boat floating in the bathtub sea.
Fill the tub with water, what do you see?
  I see a pouring cup floating in the bathtub sea.
Fill the tub with water, what do you see?
  I see a toy shark floating in the bathtub sea.
Fill the tub with water, what do you see?
  I see some swim goggles floating in the bathtub sea.
Fill the tub with water, what do you see?
  I see a watering can floating in the bathtub sea.
Fill the tub with water, what do you see?
  I see a rubber ducky floating in the bathtub sea.
Fill the tub with water, what do you see?
  I see a nice, clean baby splashing in the bathtub sea.

RHYME WITH FLANNELBOARD OR PROPS

Baby's Bath

(By Amy Alapati and Virginia Krute, Montgomery County [MD] Public Libraries; flannelboard pieces available at www.earlylit.net/storytimeshare/wp-content/uploads/2012/06/babybathFB.doc.)

Baby's ready for a bath.
Here's the baby's tub.
Here's the baby's washcloth.
Rub-a-dub-a-dub.

Here's the baby's cake of soap,
And here's the towel to dry,
And here's the baby's cradle,
Rock-a-baby-bye.

EARLY LITERACY ASIDE: EMPOWER

After our closing song, we are going to put out bubbles for you and your children to play with together. Here and at home children learn through play. It is good for them to explore on their own, but they also learn from you. Describing what your child is doing as he or she is doing it, mentioning colors, size, using some words your child does not yet know, helps your child develop vocabulary while having fun exploring. The time you take to talk with your child now makes a big difference in helping your child be ready to learn to read when he or she gets to school. Vocabulary is key to understanding what you are reading!

CLOSING SONG

Acka Backa Soda Cracker

(You can find the tune at http://wiki.kcls.org/tellmeastory/index.php/
Acka_Backa_Soda_Cracker.)

Use the first set of motions for babies, the second set for toddlers.

Acka backa soda cracker
   (*Rock baby back and forth. / Toddler rocks back and forth.*)
Acka backa boo
Acka backa soda cracker
We'll sing a song or two.
   (*Bounce baby. / Toddler opens hands on each side of mouth.*)

Acka backa soda cracker (*Rock baby back and forth. Toddler rocks back and forth.*)
Acka backa boo
Acka backa soda cracker
Up goes you. (*Raise baby up. / Toddler puts hands above head or stands up.*)

Acka backa soda cracker
   (*Rock baby back and forth. / Toddler rocks back and forth.*)
Acka backa boo
Acka backa soda cracker
I love you. (*Hug baby. / Hug toddler.*)

END OF STORYTIME ACTIVITY

- *Blow bubbles.*
- *Model adding new words while talking about bubbles and playing with them; for example, talk about size, colors in the light, blowing forcefully and softly, reaching, catching, and popping bubbles.*

Thanks to Amy Alapati and Virginia Krute (Montgomery County [MD] Public Library) and Susie Heimbach (New York Public Library).

chapter 8

Sample Storytimes for Two- and Three-Year-Olds

1. On the Move

STORYTIME INTRODUCTION

Hello, one and all. My name is (*your name*). I am so glad to see you all here today at storytime. We encourage you all to participate as we share books, rhymes, songs, and more with your children. You know your children best, so if they are not in the mood, don't force them, but do encourage them. Sometimes when they see you joining in, they will, too. We expect a fair amount of chaos during storytime, but if your child becomes disruptive, please take him or her out and join us again when your child has settled down. Let's start with our opening song.

OPENING SONG

Hello, Children

(To the tune of "Good Night Ladies," available at www.youtube.com/watch?v=2uuuAyHnLf4; lyrics by Jennifer Wharton, PUBYAC electronic discussion list, September 28, 2010.)

Ask three children their names (or their parent can tell you the child's name).

Hello, Scarlett; hello, Tyler; hello, Lucia,
It's nice to see you here.

Then move on to the next three children's names. Finish with names of the adults.

EARLY LITERACY ASIDE: EXPLAIN

Our early literacy tip for today is on phonological awareness, the ability to hear and play with the smaller sounds in words. This is the skill children use that later helps them sound out words when they learn to read. You help them by talking about all kinds of sounds that they hear around them.

THEME TALK

Our storytime today is on moving around. Sometimes we move around easily, and sometimes we get stuck! Several of our books today are about trucks. Before our first book, let's learn the sign for "truck." The American Sign Language sign for "truck" looks like this (*make the sign; you can see a video clip of the sign for "truck" by searching the ASL Pro website, at www.aslpro.com/cgi-bin/aslpro/ aslpro.cgi*). OK, let's see everyone make the sign for "truck." Good! Now, when we come to the word *truck* in our books today, you can make the sign for "truck"!

BOOK

Red Truck, **by Kersten Hamilton,**
illustrated by Valeria Petrone (Viking Juvenile, 2008)
Our first story is called *Red Truck*, by Kersten Hamilton and illustrated by Valeria Petrone. Look at this truck on the cover. It's a special kind of truck—a tow truck. Let me hear you say that, "tow truck." A bit louder, everyone . . .

There is a hook at the end of a chain at the back of this tow truck. It's used to pull cars or other vehicles out when they are stuck or can't move. Let's see what happens in this story.

Read the book. Children can make the sign for "truck" each time you say it. As you come to the sound words throughout the book, have the children and adults chime in. Clap at the end for "red truck."

EARLY LITERACY ASIDE: EXAMPLE

We just made the sounds that the tow truck was making. Making animal sounds, listening for and talking about sounds around the house, like a telephone or door-bell—all of these are first steps to sounding out words.

INFORMATIONAL BOOK

Tow Trucks, **by Teri DeGezelle (Capstone Press, 2006)**
Our next book is a true book. The name of it is *Tow Trucks*, by Teri DeGezelle. Let's look at some of these photographs of tow trucks and what they are doing.

Choose a few pages to share. Use some of the special words such as boom, *which is used to lift trucks that have tipped over or a wheel lift to raise the front wheels of the car.*

ACTION SONG

The Wheels on the Truck

(To the tune of "The Wheels on the Bus," available at www.kididdles.com/lyrics/b014.html)

> The wheels on the truck go round and round,
>> (*Roll hands around each other.*)
> Round and round, round and round.
> The wheels on the truck go round and round
> All through the town.
>
> The horn on the truck goes honk, honk, honk . . .
>> (*Slap palm in front of you, honking a horn.*)
> The hook on the truck lifts up the bus . . . (*Pick up something heavy.*)
> The worker tells the driver how to back it up . . .
>> (*Put your thumb back over your shoulder.*)
> The engine in the truck goes vroom, vroom, vroom . . .
>> (*Move fists in circles quickly.*)
> The bus on the truck bumps up and down . . . (*Bodies up and down.*)

SONG WITH FLANNELBOARD

Hickory Dickory Dock

(Adapted from www.earlylit.net/storytimeshare/wp-content/uploads/2012/05/
hickorydickorydockfbhnd.doc; you can find the tune at www.songsforteaching.com/
nurseryrhymes/hickorydickorydock2kind.php.)

First, do the rhyme on the flannelboard without the motions. Begin by raising one arm and bending it at the elbow.

> Hickory dickory dock (*Sway arm back and forth.*)
> The mouse ran up the clock
>> (*Crawl fingers of other hand up arm toward hand.*)
> The clock struck one (*Hold up pointer finger of bent arm.*)
> The mouse ran down (*Crawl fingers down arm toward elbow.*)
> Hickory dickory dock. (*Sway arm back and forth.*)

Repeat once or twice more, using actions instead of the flannelboard. For more active adult interaction after you have done all the actions, do them again in partners: the adult is the clock and holds one arm up, bent at the elbow. The child is the mouse and does the actions on the adult's arm.

BOOK

***Stuck in the Mud*, by Jane Clark, illustrated by Garry Parsons (Walker Children's Books, 2008)**

In our next story, it looks like a little chick is stuck in the mud. Lots of animals try to get the chick out. The animals push and pull over and over again. Let's see you all push. (*Push forward with hands.*) OK! Now let's see you all pull. (*Pull as if you were holding something and pulling it back.*) Let's put those motions together—push and pull, push and pull. Good!

As I read the book you can do these motions each time you hear the words. Let's see what happens now in this book called *Stuck in the Mud*, by Jane Clark, with illustrations by Garry Parsons.

Read the book and encourage children and adults to say the sounds of the animals and to use motions as described above. At the end, Chick wants the other animals to join her playing in the mud.

Now, let's have a stretch and we'll all move together, using different parts of our bodies. I am going to tell you and show you how we are going to move our body parts. If I say we are moving slowly, move slowly. (*Show them how. Include putting your foot in and trying to pull it out—it's stuck!*)

ACTION SONG

The Hokey Pokey

(For a toddler version, see the CD *It's Toddler Time*, by Carol Hammett
and Elaine Bueffel [Kimbo Educational, 1982]. For a faster pace, go to
www.karaoke-version.com/mp3-backingtrack/ray-anthony/hokey-pokey.html.)

If it is too hard to do the hokey pokey in a circle, you can just have everyone stand up and do it in adult-child pairs facing each other.

You put your right hand in
You take your right hand out
You put your right hand in
And shake it all about
You do the hokey pokey and you turn yourself around.
That's what it's all about.

You put your left hand in . . .
You put your right foot in . . .
You put your left foot in . . .
You put your backside in . . .
You put your head in . . .
You put your whole self in . . .

EARLY LITERACY ASIDE: EMPOWER

Whether you are taking a walk, driving around, or in your home, talking about and making the sounds of different things is a great way to help children listen to and identify sounds. This is the same type of skill they will later need for sounding out words when they read. I also have some books on display that you can take home that encourage children to make sounds for different animals or things.

Thank you for coming to the library today. I'm looking forward to seeing you all again next time.

CLOSING SONG

Storytime Is Over Now
(To the tune of "London Bridge Is Falling Down,"
available at www.kididdles.com/lyrics/l037.html)

Storytime is over now, over now, over now.
Storytime is over now.
See you next time.

END OF STORYTIME ACTIVITY

Assemble a variety of items, some heavier than others, like a ball and a rock. Try to use items that families would have in their homes. Also, choose some objects that are light and easy to carry, and others that might be light but more awkward to hold.

Tow trucks carry heavy things. Let's try to see which of these items are heavy and which are light. Which ones weigh more? Which ones are easy to carry and which ones are hard to carry? Which is easier to carry, a book or a ball? Which items are too heavy to pick up?

Let adults know that doing activities that expand their children's experiences related to what they have read is one way to help them learn to think and to understand.

ALTERNATE BOOKS

Choo Choo Clickety Clack, by Margaret Mayo (Orchard, 2008)
Giant Pop-Out Vehicles (Chronicle Books, 2007)
Jazz Baby, by Carole Weatherford (Harcourt Children's Books, 2007)
Preschool to the Rescue, by Judy Sierra (Harcourt Children's Books, 2001)
Tip Tip Dig Dig, by Emma Garcia (Boxer Books, 2007)
Where's My Truck? by Karen Beaumont (Dial Books, 2011)

2. Happy, Sad, Angry, Glad

STORYTIME INTRODUCTION

Hello, one and all. My name is (*your name*). I am so glad to see you all here today at storytime. We encourage you all to participate as we share books, rhymes, songs, and more with your children. You know your children best, so if they are not in the mood, don't force them, but do encourage them. Sometimes when they see you joining in, they will, too. We expect a fair amount of chaos during storytime, but if your child becomes disruptive, please take him or her out and join us again when your child has settled down. Let's start with our opening song.

OPENING SONG

Say Hello

(To the tune of "Here We Go Round the Mulberry Bush,"
available at www.kididdles.com/lyrics/m014.html)

This is the way our hands say hello
With a clap, clap-clap, clap, clap-clap
This is the way our hands say hello
With a clap, clap-clap, clap-clap

This is the way our knees say hello
With a tap, tap-tap, tap, tap-tap.
This is the way our knees say hello
With a tap, tap-tap, tap-tap.

EARLY LITERACY ASIDE: EXPLAIN

If you like, use a puppet and sing the following words to the tune of "Pop Goes the Weasel" (you can find the tune at http://kids.niehs.nih.gov/games/songs/childrens/weaselmp3.htm).

Our early literacy tip of the day is vocabulary.
Knowing the meaning of lots of words will help children read.

At this age children are learning so many words so quickly. I'll be pointing out some ways you can help your child learn new words as you sing, talk, read, write, and play together throughout the day. The more words children know when they get to school, the easier it will be for them to both recognize words they are sounding out and understand what they read. Children learn words best as they explore the world around them.

THEME TALK

Today we're talking about different kinds of feelings. Our faces often look different depending on how we feel. Sometimes we feel happy, sad, angry, worried, or tired.

INFORMATIONAL BOOK

Lots of Feelings, by Shelley Rotner (Millbrook Press, 2003)

Let's look at this book called *Lots of Feelings*, by Shelley Rotner, and see what the faces look like. (*Talk about some of the feelings associated with the faces in the photographs.*)

SONG

Feelings

(From the CD *Getting to Know Myself*, by Hap Palmer [Educational Activities, 1972].
Lyrics reprinted by permission of Hap Palmer, © Hap-Pal Music, www.happalmer.com.)

> Sometimes I'm feeling happy and I'm wearing a smile.
> Let me show you how I look when I'm feeling happy.
> Sometimes I'm feeling sad and I'm wearing a frown.
> Let me show you how I look when I'm feeling sad.
> Oh, feelings don't always stay the same, they can change
> Sometimes I'm happy; sometimes I'm sad.
> It's OK; it's not bad.

> Sometimes I'm feeling angry and I stamp my feet.
> Let me show you how I look when I'm feeling angry.
> Sometimes I'm feeling sleepy and I have to yawn.
> Let me show you how I look when I'm feeling sleepy.
> Oh, feelings don't always stay the same, they can change
> Sometimes I'm happy; sometimes I'm sad.

> Sometimes I'm feeling funny and I have to laugh.
> Let me show you how I look when I'm feeling funny.

BOOK

Where's My Truck? by Karen Beaumont,
illustrated by David Catrow (Dial Books, 2011)

Our next book is called *Where's My Truck?* by Karen Beaumont, with illustrations by David Catrow. This boy named Tommy is worried, frustrated, and angry because he cannot find his truck, and he loves his truck!

There's a repeated phrase in this book—"I want my truck!" Let me hear you all say that—"I want my truck!" Louder . . . OK, I'll read the book and each time I point to the words, everyone together, adults and children, say, "I want my truck!" (*Read the book and run your finger under the words "I want my truck" each time.*)

EARLY LITERACY ASIDE: EXAMPLE

Using words that your children may not know as you talk with them throughout the day is one way to develop their vocabulary. Use synonyms, or a different word that means the same thing, when you talk with your child. We can be angry, mad, and furious, not to mention livid! Knowing a lot of words will help them understand what they are reading.

BOOK

Llama Llama Home with Mama, **by Anna Dewdney (Viking Juvenile, 2011)**

Talk about how it feels when you're sick. After reading the book, ask how it feels when we help someone.

MUSIC ACTIVITY

Reach for the Ceiling

(From the CD T*oddlers on Parade*, by Carol Hammett and Elaine Bueffel
[Kimbo Educational, 1985]. Lyrics reprinted by permission of Kimbo Educational,
www.kimboed.com.)

Reach for the ceiling; touch the floor.
Stand up again; let's do some more.
Touch your head; then your knees.
Up to your shoulders, if you please.
Reach for the ceiling; touch the floor.
That's all now; there isn't any more.

Now add your own actions to show feelings on your faces:
Reach for the sky; touch the floor.
Smile a big smile; let's do some more.
Touch your nose; bend your knees,
Make a sad face, if you please.
Reach for the sky; touch the floor.
That's it for now, there is no more.

Substitute in different faces and/or feelings.

BOOK WITH PROPS

***Thank You, Bear*, by Greg Foley (Viking Juvenile, 2007)**
In our next book Bear thinks he has a great present for Mouse. This is one of my favorite books. I love how Bear keeps going, in his own quiet and determined way, until he gets to Mouse. Let's see what happens in this book, *Thank You, Bear*, by Greg Foley.

Read the book using props or puppets. If you like, read it once through and then retell it with props.

Mouse was so happy that he said, "Thank you, Bear." And I thank you all for coming today.

EARLY LITERACY ASIDE: EMPOWER

As you talk and play with your children this coming week, see if you can think of ways to expand their vocabulary, to build on what they already know. You can talk about feelings and use some specific feeling words or just add new words as you play together. (*For a handout with words for feelings that you can distribute here, see web extra 8.1 at www.alaeditions.org/webextras.*) No need to quiz them—just keep it fun. The more words they know, the better readers they will be!

CLOSING SONG

Say Good-bye

(To the tune of "Here We Go Round the Mulberry Bush,"
available at www.kididdles.com/lyrics/m014.html)

This is the way our hands say good-bye
With a clap, clap-clap, clap, clap-clap.
This is the way our hands say good-bye
With a clap, clap-clap, clap-clap.

This is the way our knees say good-bye
With a tap, tap-tap, tap, tap-tap.
This is the way our knees say good-bye
With a tap, tap-tap, tap-tap.

This is the way we wave good-bye
Wave good-bye, wave good-bye
This is the way we wave good-bye
Good-bye until next time.

END OF STORYTIME ACTIVITY

- *Have a list of feelings (choose some from list at end of this storytime) to help everyone think of feelings other than happy and sad.*
- *Have some mirrors available to allow children to look in the mirror and make faces. Adults talk with the children about what the faces look like and how the child might be feeling. Adults also should make faces and talk about the related feelings. If you do not have mirrors, let adults and children make faces and guess feelings.*

ALTERNATE BOOKS

Funny Face, by Nicola Smee (Bloomsbury USA Children's, 2006)
Good Day, by Kevin Henkes (Greenwillow Books, 2007)
Pigeon Has Feelings, Too, by Mo Willems (Hyperion 2005)
Uh-Oh, by Rachel Isadora (Harcourt Children's Books, 2008)

Some Words for Feelings

Afraid	Enthusiastic	Hopeful	Moody	Silly
Angry	Envious	Hopeless	Nasty	Sleepy
Annoyed	Excited	Humiliated	Nervous	Sorry
Anxious	Exhausted	Hurt	Nice	Strong
Ashamed	Faithful	Impatient	Obnoxious	Sure
Bashful	Fearful	Important	Overwhelmed	Surprised
Beautiful	Forgiving	Innocent	Pampered	Sympathetic
Bored	Frightened	Insecure	Patient	Thoughtful
Brave	Frustrated	Inspired	Pleased	Timid
Bullied	Funny	Intimidated	Proud	Tired
Calm	Furious	Jealous	Puzzled	Tolerant
Confident	Generous	Joyful	Quarrelsome	Uncertain
Confused	Glad	Kind	Queasy	Understanding
Content	Good	Lazy	Quiet	Unforgiving
Creative	Grateful	Lively	Rambunctious	Upset
Curious	Great	Lonely	Rejected	Vain
Depressed	Greedy	Lost	Responsible	Wild
Disappointed	Grumpy	Loved	Rowdy	Worried
Discouraged	Guilty	Loving	Scared	Zany
Disgusted	Happy	Mad	Selfish	Zonked
Eager	Hateful	Mischievous	Serious	
Embarrassed	Helpful	Miserable	Shy	
Energetic	Helpless	Mixed up	Sick	

3. Animals All Around

STORYTIME INTRODUCTION

Hello, one and all. My name is (*your name*). I am so glad to see you all here today at storytime. We encourage you all to participate as we share books, rhymes, songs, and more with your children. You know your children best, so if they are not in the mood, don't force them, but do encourage them. Sometimes when they see you joining in, they will, too. We expect a fair amount of chaos during storytime, but if your child becomes disruptive, please take him or her out and join us again when your child has settled down. Let's start with our opening song.

OPENING SONG

Your Name Is

(From the CD *Songs and Games for Toddlers*, by Bob McGrath and Katharine Smithrim [Bob's Kids Music, 1998]. Lyrics reprinted by permission of Bob McGrath.)

Your name is (*child's name*), that's your name.
Your name is (*child's name*), always the same.
Your name is (*child's name*), all the time.
Your name is (*child's name*), isn't that fine.

For a small group, you can do the whole song for one child; for a larger group, put a different name in for each line of the song. For a very large group, sing the song once or twice with children's names. Then have adults sing with their own children.

EARLY LITERACY ASIDE: EXPLAIN

Today in storytime I will point out some ways that playing and talking with your children can support learning about letters. Many letters look alike, so helping children notice things that are alike and different is a first step toward helping them recognize similarities and differences in letters. Playing matching games and playing with puzzles are some ways to support letter knowledge with your children. Knowing letters will help children decode, or figure out words, once they are reading.

THEME TALK

This storytime is on the animals around us; some of them are wild and some are pets. Wild animals are ones we might see in a zoo or in nature. Pet animals are ones that some people have in their homes.

BOOK

Where's My Mom? by Julia Donaldson, illustrated by Axel Scheffler (Dial Books, 2008)

Our first book is a story about a monkey who is looking for her mother. As she tries to find her she sees lots of other animals. It's called *Where's My Mom?* by Julia Donaldson, with illustrations by Axel Scheffler.

Read the book, pointing out the pictures of the animals.

Today let's learn the American Sign Language sign for "elephant." It looks like this (*make the sign; you can see a video clip of the sign for "elephant" by searching the ASL Pro website, at www.aslpro.com/cgi-bin/aslpro/aslpro.cgi*). Now you all try it. Good! It has a long trunk. In our next song the word *elephant* is repeated. Each time you say the word *elephant*, make the sign, too. Using sign language adds the visual to the audio or hearing aspect of language. So let's sing a song about an elephant. We usually see elephants in the zoo.

SONG

One Elephant
(Adapted from "Five Little Ducks Went Out One Day."
You can find the tune at http://kids.niehs.nih.gov/lyrics/fiveducks.htm.)

One elephant went out to play
Upon a spider's web one day.
He found it such enormous fun
That he called for another elephant to come!
Elephant! Elephant! (*All call together.*)

Two elephants went out to play . . .

If you like, you can do an extension activity and have each child come over to play, one at a time, as he or she does the sign for elephant.

BOOK

Who's on the Farm? by Dorothea DePrisco (Cahners, 2002)

Our next book is a lift-the-flap book. Each flap has a picture with the word underneath. I'll lift the flap as I say the word. This book is about farm animals, and it's also a riddle book. See if you can guess the animal.

Read the book, lifting the flaps as you say the words underneath. Then pause to allow them time to guess the animal.

FLANNELBOARD ACTIVITY

You can find flannelboard pieces of baby animals at http://earlylit.net/wordpress/ wp-content/uploads/2010/04/startwk2fbbabyanimalshandout.doc, and flannelboard pieces of adult animals at http://earlylit.net/wordpress/wp-content/uploads/2010/04/ startwk1fbanimalhandout.doc. You can also use clip-art pictures of adult farm animals and their matching babies. Share the names of the adult and the baby.

    cow—calf
    horse—foal
    pig—piglet
    hen or rooster—chick
    turkey—poult
    duck—duckling
    goat—kid
    sheep—lamb
    mouse—pup
    dog—puppy
    cat—kitten

Pass out pictures of the animals—adult and baby. Have duplicates for yourself. Put up the picture of an adult animal. Ask which child(ren) have the matching adult animal and invite them to put it up on the flannelboard. Then put up the baby animal and ask the child(ren) who have that animal to come put it up. Talk about how the adult and baby look alike and different. Clap as each one comes up to put up the flannelboard piece.

EARLY LITERACY ASIDE: EXAMPLE

By talking about how adult and baby animals look alike and different, you help children notice the similarities and differences. Helping them notice similarities and differences will help them to notice differences and similarities between, for example, a lowercase *n* or *h* and an uppercase *C* and *G*. Seeing what is alike and different is a beginning step in learning letters, an important part of being able to decode, or read, words.

BOOK

Be Gentle, by Virginia Miller (Candlewick, 1997)

Our next story is about a pet kitten and a bear named Bartholomew. Bartholomew has to be very careful and very gentle when he takes care of the little kitten. Let's see what happens. The book is called *Be Gentle*, and it was written by Virginia Miller.

Read the book. If you like, you can have everyone repeat the phrase "Be gentle" and/ or "Nah." On some, if not all, pages, point out or have the children say how the kitten is feeling.

INFORMATIONAL BOOK

Backyard Birds, by Jonathan Latimer (Sandpiper Books, 1999)

This book is called *Backyard Birds*, by Jonathan Latimer. It is a bird guide and helps us know what different kinds of birds look like and what they are called. We can also learn some interesting facts about birds. Let's look at a couple of pages and see if we can find a bird that might look familiar to you. (*Choose pages to share.*)

EARLY LITERACY ASIDE: EMPOWER

As you play with your children throughout the day, there are many opportunities to talk about similarities and differences. Even when you go to the store, your child can help; for example, match a coupon to the actual item. All kinds of matching and sorting help later with letter knowledge, a skill children need to be able to read.

I look forward to seeing you all again next time. Now it's time for our closing song.

CLOSING SONG

The More We Get Together

(You can find the tune at www.kidsongs.com/lyrics/did-you-ever-see-a-lassie.html.)

The more we get together, together, together
The more we get together, the happier we'll be
For your friends are my friends and my friends are your friends
The more we get together, the happier we'll be

The more we sing together, together, together
The more we sing together, the happier we'll be
For your songs are my songs and my songs are your songs
The more we sing together, the happier we'll be

The more we read together, together, together
The more we read together, the happier we'll be
For your books are my books and my books are your books
The more we read together, the happier we'll be

The more we get together, together, together
The more we get together, the happier we'll be
For your friends are my friends and my friends are your friends
The more we get together, the happier we'll be

END OF STORYTIME ACTIVITY

- **Make-a-puzzle activity:** *Using cardstock or poster board, have child draw a picture of an animal, or whatever else they like. Adults can tell children that they will make a puzzle. Adults can cut out pictures into as many pieces as is appropriate for the child, fewer for younger child. Adults and children put the puzzle together. Be prepared to have extra paper in case children want to keep a drawing that is not cut up. Have enough paper for adults to also draw a picture and make a puzzle. Use this opportunity for adults and children to talk about what they drew, what colors they used, what shapes they see, and how their pictures are alike and different.*
- **Matching activities:** *Have a simple matching game set up for everyone to play. They can match one animal to its exact match. They can match an animal to its baby. They can sort animals according to type—number of legs, where they live, pet or wild. Provide them with a sheet that they can take home if they don't have time to stay (www.earlylit.net/storytimeshare/?p=189).*

ALTERNATE BOOKS

Doghouse, by Jan Thomas (Harcourt Children's Books, 2008)
How Do You Make a Baby Smile? by Philemon Sturges (HarperCollins, 2007)
Kitten Tale, by Eric Rohmann (Dragonfly Books, 2011)
Our Yard Is Full of Birds, by Anne Rockwell (Simon and Schuster Children's Publishing, 1992)
Please, Puppy, Please, by Spike Lee (Simon and Schuster Books for Young Readers, 2005)

4. Nice and Cozy

STORYTIME INTRODUCTION

Hello, one and all. My name is (*your name*). I am so glad to see you all here today at storytime. We encourage you all to participate as we share books, rhymes, songs, and more with your children. You know your children best, so if they are not in the mood, don't force them, but do encourage them. Sometimes when they see you joining in, they will, too. We expect a fair amount of chaos during story-time, but if your child becomes disruptive, please take him or her out and join us again when your child has settled down. Let's start with our opening song.

OPENING SONG

Here We Are Together

(To the tune of "The More We Get Together," available at www.kidsongs.com/
lyrics/did-you-ever-see-a-lassie.html; adapted from Jennifer Wharton,
PUBYAC electronic discussion list, September 28, 2010.)

Here we are together, together, together
Here we are together at the library
With Johnny and Logan and Tamika and Simon
Here we are together at the library.

Continue with the names of the children. The child or parent says the child's name and adults say their own name. Repeat until all names are said. If there are too many people to go through all the names, parents and children can fill in their names in unison (with Nathan and Mommy and Mommy and Nathan).

EARLY LITERACY ASIDE: EXPLAIN

Leading with the early literacy component: Our prereading tip of the day today is on background knowledge, which is simply what a child knows. Children are naturally curious about so many things, even things we take for granted. Talking with them about what we are doing and what we are thinking is an excellent way to support their background knowledge. Today I'll point out some things you can do to help them develop this, which will later help your children understand what they read.

Leading with the practice: Did you know that the *ways* we talk with our children make a difference in their prereading skills? When we give them time to ask questions and add information to what they already know, we help develop their knowledge, which will later help them understand what they read.

THEME TALK

Our storytime today is about feeling cozy and cared for. In our first book, a baby kangaroo is exploring the world but comes back to his mommy's pouch. Do you know what a pouch is? It's like a pocket. Baby kangaroos, called joeys, are carried by their mothers until they are too big to fit in the pouch. (Use a kangaroo puppet or stuffed animal if available, or wear an apron to demonstrate.) Do you have pockets? Yes, but yours aren't used for carrying babies, are they?

The American Sign Language sign for "pouch" looks like this (*make the sign; you can see a video clip of the sign for "pouch" by searching the ASL Pro website, at www.aslpro.com/cgi-bin/aslpro/aslpro.cgi*). OK, let's see everyone make the sign for "pouch." Good! Now, when we come to the word *pouch* in our books today, you can make the sign.

BOOK

Pouch! **by David Stein (Putnam Juvenile, 2009)**

Read the book. Have everyone do the sign for "pouch" each time Joey says "pouch." If children need more activity, allow them to hop or jump. If you like, you can retell the story with yourself wearing an apron to be the mother kangaroo and use a stuffed animal or cut out of a joey (baby kangaroo).

INFORMATIONAL BOOK

Red Kangaroo: The World's Largest Marsupial, **by Natalie Lunis (Bearport Publishing, 2010)**

I thought you might like to see some photographs of real kangaroos. Our next book is *Red Kangaroo: The World's Largest Marsupial*, by Natalie Lunis.

Show photos on pages you select. Talk about the facts about kangaroos.

EARLY LITERACY ASIDE: EXAMPLE

You'll notice that for our informational book, I didn't read it from cover to cover. I pointed out and talked about a few facts that I thought might interest the children. Sometimes, when you read and talk with them at home, individually, they ask questions themselves, which leads you to share further information. You are developing their background knowledge, which will help their comprehension!

ACTION SONG

Turn Around

(From the CD *Getting to Know Myself*, by Hap Palmer [Educational Activities, 1972]. Lyrics reprinted by permission of Hap Palmer, © Hap-Pal Music, www.happalmer.com.)

Close your eyes; open your eyes; nod your head
And turn around, turn around, turn around.

Open your mouth; close your mouth; wiggle your nose
And turn around, turn around, turn around.

Stamp your feet loudly; stamp your feet softly.
Clap your hands loudly and clap your hands very softly.
Shake your arms; shake your legs; wiggle your fingers
And turn around, turn around, turn around.

Touch your ears; scratch your back; rub your stomach
And turn around, turn around, turn around.

Stamp your feet loudly; stamp your feet softly.
Clap your hands loudly and clap your hands very softly.
Bend your arms; bend your legs; bend from your waist
And turn around, turn around, turn around.

BOOK

Hug, by Jez Alborough (Candlewick, 2009)

Our next book is *Hug*, by Jez Alborough. See how the little gorilla says "hug"? If you feel like getting a hug from your grown-up, get a hug! Yay!

Read the book, using your own words to describe what is happening in the pictures. Ask children what they see in the pictures, and give responses if necessary.

ACTIVITY

Monkey See, Monkey Do

Have everyone stand up. You do a motion and have everyone imitate you. This can also be done in pairs between adults and children. Be sure to use words to describe what you are doing.

Monkey see, monkey do,
Whatever I do, you do, too!

BOOK

Tuck Me In! **by Dean Hacohen and Sherry Scharschmidt (Candlewick, 2010)**

You can encourage participation in several ways, such as using flannelboard or stuffed animals and blanket props. Children can take turns if the group is small enough, or they can play with props after storytime. Have children say, "I do," and adults say, "Good night, baby."

EARLY LITERACY ASIDE: EMPOWER

As you read books about various topics that your children are interested in, don't hesitate to add information you know on the topic as well, even if it is not included in the book. Children learn about the world from everything you say and do. All the bits and pieces of information you share with them adds up to build their background knowledge, which will make it easier for them to later understand what they read while also satisfying their curiosity.

CLOSING SONG

Here We Are Together

(To the tune of "The More We Get Together,"
available at www.kidsongs.com/lyrics/did-you-ever-see-a-lassie.html)

Here we are together, together, together
Here we are together but now we must go
Good-bye parents and children and children and parents
Good-bye everybody, now we must go!

END OF STORYTIME ACTIVITY

Put out some informational books for parents and children to look at. Tell parents to choose a book with their child and to talk with their child to find out what he or she knows about the topic: "Children are very curious. What would they like to find out?"

ALTERNATE BOOKS

I Can Help, by David Costello (Farrar, Straus & Giroux, 2010)
Leap Back Home to Me, by Lauren Thompson (Margaret K. McElderry Books, 2011)
No Matter What, by Debi Gliori (HMH Books, 2012)
On Mother's Lap, by Ann Scott (Sandpiper Books, 1992)
Uh-Oh, Calico! by Karma Wilson (Little Simon, 2007)

5. What Grows?

STORYTIME INTRODUCTION

Hello, one and all. My name is (*your name*). I am so glad to see you all here today at storytime. We encourage you all to participate as we share books, rhymes, songs, and more with your children. You know your children best, so if they are not in the mood, don't force them, but do encourage them. Sometimes when they see you joining in, they will, too. We expect a fair amount of chaos during storytime, but if your child becomes disruptive, please take him or her out and join us again when your child has settled down. Let's start with our opening song.

OPENING RHYME

Heckedy Peckedy Bumblebee

Heckedy peckedy bumblebee, won't you say your name for me?
   (*Clap out the syllables in each name. Include adults, too. If the group is large, do a few names and then have adults and children clap out each other's names all at the same time.*)
My name is . . . (*Start by saying your name.*)
Whisper . . . (*Whisper your name.*)
Clap it . . . (*Clap your name.*)
Tap it . . . (*Tap out your name.*)
Hooray! . . . (*Say your name.*)

EARLY LITERACY ASIDE: EXPLAIN

While you talk, read, and write with your children throughout the day, you are able to help them understand that print has meaning. Helping your children understand the connection between the print we see and the words we say will help them later as they learn to read. I'll mention a few things in today's storytime that support this prereading skill, print awareness.

THEME TALK

Today our storytime is about things that grow. Can you think of some things that grow? I have some things that grow. (*Show pictures, photographs, or actual items.*) What are they?

BOOK

Big Yellow Sunflower, by Frances Barry (Candlewick, 2008)

Our first book is about a flower that grows. It's called *Big Yellow Sunflower*, by

Frances Barry. You can see how the flower starts from a seed and grows into a tall flower. (*Read the book.*)

SHAKERS

Pass out shakers or instruments. Let children experiment with playing their instruments loudly, softly, quickly, and slowly.

Everything Grows

(From the CD *Everything Grows*, by Raffi [Rounder, 1996];
words and music by Debi Pike and Raffi Cavoukian. © 1987 Homeland Publishing.
Nettwerk One Music Limited. All Rights Reserved. International Copyright Secured.
Used by permission of Music Sales Limited.)

Chorus
Everything grows and grows
Babies do
Animals too
Everything grows
Everything grows and grows
Sisters do
Brothers too
Everything grows

A blade of grass, fingers and toes
Hair on my head, a red, red rose
Everything grows, anyone knows
That's how it goes
Chorus

Food on the farm, fish in the sea
Birds in the air, leaves on the tree
Everything grows, anyone knows
That's how it goes
Yes, everything grows and grows
That's how it goes under the sun
That's how it goes under the rain
Everything grows, anyone knows
That's how it goes
Chorus

Mamas do and papas too
Everything grows

Collect shakers.

INFORMATIONAL BOOK

Do You Know Which Ones Will Grow? **by Susan Shea (Blue Apple Books, 2011)**
Many things in our world do grow, but some things do not. Here is a book that helps us think about what grows and what doesn't.

Read all of the book or select pages. Point to the words "yes" and "no." Encourage children to say the words as you point to them.

EARLY LITERACY ASIDE: EXAMPLE

Pointing to a few words or a repeated phrase in a book is one easy way to support print awareness, to help your child relate the printed word to the words we are saying. Drawing your children's attention to the text, not just the pictures, will help them focus on words later when they are learning to read.

BOOK

Farmyard Beat, **by Lindsey Craig (Knopf Books for Young Readers, 2011)**
This book has a good beat to it. You can just hear the animals dancing! (*Read the book.*)

ACTION SONG

Bunny Hop

(From the CD *Hunk-Ta-Bunk-Ta Wiggle: 12 Tunes for Toddlers*, vol. 1,
by Katherine Dines [Hunk-Ta-Bunk-Ta Music, 2007].
Lyrics reprinted by permission of Katherine Dines, copyright 2003
by Kiddie Korral Music, ASCAP, all rights reserved, www.hunktabunkta.com.)

Bunny hop, bunny hop, hop, hop, hop!
Bunny hop, bunny hop, hop, hop, hop!
Bunny hop, bunny hop, hop, hop, *stop*!
Wiggle your ears—
Wiggle your nose—
Wiggle your paws—
Wiggle your cottontail.
Bunny hop, bunny hop, hop, hop, hop!
Bunny hop, bunny hop, hop, hop, hop!
Bunny hop, bunny hop, hop, hop, *stop*!

Repeat.

BOOK

Little Green Frogs, by Frances Barry (Candlewick, 2008)
For some animals, the babies are smaller but look similar to the grown-up. For example, the baby elephant looks like a small adult elephant. But for some animals it is different. A baby frog is a tadpole before it becomes a frog. Let's see what happens.

After reading the book, guide the children to act out going from eggs (curled up) to tadpoles (stretched out long like the tadpole in the book) to froglets (say, "Let me see you bend your knees, because froglets are getting their legs"), and then to frogs (say, "Bend your elbows too and sit up like a frog!").

EARLY LITERACY ASIDE: EMPOWER

Drawing and writing with your children are great ways to help them make the connection between what we write and what we say. Have your children draw pictures and then write down what they say about them. Encourage them to write down lists or to write cards to family and friends. Pointing out what signs say is another way to develop print awareness as you talk with your children. They soon notice the signs themselves and "read" them, a first step to reading.

CLOSING SONG

Storytime Is Over Now

(To the tune of "London Bridge Is Falling Down," available at www.kididdles.com/lyrics/l037.html)

Storytime is over now, over now, over now.
Storytime is over now.
See you next time.

END OF STORYTIME ACTIVITY

- *Provide the materials for the activity suggested above in "Early Literacy Aside: Empower."*
- *Make a matching game of adult animals and their babies.*

ALTERNATE BOOKS

Animal Bop Won't Stop, with CD, by Jan Ormerod (Barron's Educational Series, 2005)

Doing the Animal Bop, with CD, by Jan Ormerod (Barron's Educational Series, 2005)

Giant Pop-Out Food (Chronicle Books, 2012)

chapter 9

Sample Storytimes for Preschoolers

As mentioned in chapter 5, "Using Informational Books with Young Children," you will see here how science and math concepts and activities can be incorporated into storytimes.

1. I Love My Storytime Shoes!

STORYTIME INTRODUCTION

Welcome to storytime. Grown-ups, please join in with your children. It is more fun when everyone participates, plus it will help you learn the words so that you can do the rhymes and songs later with your child. Please make sure that you and your child write your names on the name tags.

OPENING SONG

Welcome, Welcome, Everyone

(To the tune of "Twinkle, Twinkle, Little Star," available at www.kididdles.com/lyrics/
t068.html and www.kididdles.com/lyrics/t023.html)

Welcome, welcome, everyone.
Join me for some storytime fun.
We'll share some books and sing some songs.

Help me please and sing along.
Welcome, welcome, everyone.
Storytime has just begun!

EARLY LITERACY ASIDE: EXPLAIN

Today we are going to be looking at writing, which is one way to help your child develop letter knowledge, which means knowing that letters are different from one another and represent sounds. This is one of the five components of early literacy, which is the foundation that children need to get ready to read.

THEME TALK

Who has shoes on their feet? You do, you do, and so do I. What kinds of shoes do you have on?

Talk about the kinds of shoes the children are wearing.

We have different kinds of shoes on, don't we? We wear different shoes for different reasons. Our first book talks about this.

BOOK

Which Shoes Would You Choose? by Betsy R. Rosenthal,
illustrated by Nancy Cote (Putnam Juvenile, 2010)
Our first book is called *Which Shoes Would You Choose?* written by Betsy R. Rosenthal and illustrated by Nancy Cote.

After reading the book, split up into small groups, each with an adult. The adult needs a large piece of paper and a marker or a dry-erase board. Explain that you are going to write down each child's name in the name column. (Everyone should have a name tag you can use to copy from.) Then put an X in the column that corresponds to the kind of shoe—with laces, with Velcro, or neither. You could sort by a different attribute, like color or material. Talk about which column has the most in it. Mention each child's name: "Sylvia has tie shoes; Kyle's shoes have Velcro." Make sure you point to the first letter of each child's name, slightly emphasizing the sound.

EARLY LITERACY ASIDE: EXAMPLE

Children often learn the first letter in their names. You can help them learn how to write their names by talking with them about all of the letters that are in their names. Start with the letters in their name when teaching them the alphabet. Research indicates that children who know some letters before starting school have an easier time learning how to read.

INFORMATIONAL BOOK

Shoes, Shoes, Shoes, by Ann Morris (HarperCollins, 1998)

Our next book is called *Shoes, Shoes, Shoes*, by Ann Morris. (*Read the book.*)

ACTIVITY

One Shoe, Two Shoes

Before you recite this rhyme, explain that two of the same thing make a pair—for example, two shoes make one pair.

> One shoe, two shoes
> Three shoes, four.
> One pair, two pairs.
> How many more?

Count the shoes of the children. You can count in groups of ten or keep going. How many shoes are there? How many pairs?

ALTERNATE ACTIVITY

There Was an Old Woman Who Lived in a Shoe

Use a flannelboard or cutout of a big shoe, or an actual shoe. Instruct the children to stick their name tags on or in the big shoe. Say their names as they put them on the shoe.

> There was an old woman who lived in a shoe
> She had so many children she didn't know what to do
> She gave them some broth and a slice of bread
> And kissed them all gently and sent them to bed.

BOOK

Pete the Cat: I Love My White Shoes, by Eric Litwin (HarperCollins, 2010)

Our next book is about a cat named Pete and his shoes. It is called *Pete the Cat: I Love My White Shoes*. The words were written by Eric Litwin, and the pictures were drawn by James Dean. (*Read the book.*)

Pete's name starts with the letter *P*. What is the first letter in your name? (*You can talk about this if there is time.*)

Download Pete's song at http://harpercollinschildrens.com/feature/petethecat/audio/pete-the-cat.mp3. You can sing it after reading the book, if you like.

EARLY LITERACY ASIDE: EMPOWER

Parents, I hope you will stay after storytime to do our activity. If you can't stay, you can pick up a copy to take with you. Please encourage your child to write his or her name. It will help them decode, or figure out what a word says, once they are learning how to read. Thanks so much for coming to storytime!

CLOSING SONG

Good-bye, Good-bye, Everyone

(To the tune of "Twinkle, Twinkle, Little Star," available at www.kididdles.com/lyrics/
t068.html and www.kididdles.com/lyrics/t023.html)

Good-bye, good-bye, everyone.
Thanks for coming; we had fun.
We shared some books and sang some songs.
We read together and got along.
Thank you, thank you, everyone.
Our time to read and sing is done!

END OF STORYTIME ACTIVITY

Give each child a copy of a white shoe. Use multiple copies of shoes stapled together so children can make their own book, if you wish. Tell them they are going to make a story like Pete's. It will be called (Child's Name) the Kid: I Love My White Shoes. They can make up stories about what they are stepping in and what color their shoes become.

SCIENCE AND MATH CONCEPTS DURING STORYTIME

- *Activity with the book* Which Shoes Would You Choose? *supports science and math concepts, including recording observations, sorting, and expressing results.*
- *Counting children's shoes—math concepts (numbers)*

ALTERNATE MATH ACTIVITY

One-to-one correspondence. Have the children put all their shoes in a jumble. Remove one or three shoes. Sort them to their owners. A couple of people will be short a shoe. Talk about how each foot gets one shoe.

ALTERNATE SCIENCE ACTIVITIES

- *Why don't animals wear shoes? Go back through* Shoes, Shoes *and talk about why people wear different kinds of shoes. It depends on where they live or what their habitat is.*
- *Show pictures of different kinds of places on the earth and guess what kinds of shoes people wear. This could be a matching game, with shoes matched to different places.*

2. If You Read a Book to Children, They Are Sure to Ask for More!

STORYTIME INTRODUCTION

Hello and welcome! Thank you for bringing your child to storytime. My name is (*your name*). Please fill out a name tag for you and your child. Your children can write their own name tags if they'd like.

Make name tags. To print off cat name tags, visit www.mousecookiebooks.com/ activities/pdfs/cupcake_activities.pdf. If you are using one of the other books, make your own name tag using Pigeon images from www.hyperionbooksforchildren.com/ pigeon_drawing_instr.pdf.

Let's begin.

OPENING SONG

Let's Get Started, Everyone

(To the tune of "Twinkle, Twinkle, Little Star," available at www.kididdles.com/lyrics/
t068.html and www.kididdles.com/lyrics/t023.html)

Let's get started, everyone.
It's time for us to have some fun.
We'll read some books along the way.
We'll also talk and sing and play.
I'm happy you're here with me.
It's time to start—one, two, three!

EARLY LITERACY ASIDE: EXPLAIN

I am going share some information with you about how you can help your children get ready to read by increasing their background knowledge. Knowing about lots of different things will help them understand what they are reading once they go to school. Background knowledge includes knowing about scientific processes, one of which we will be looking at during storytime. There are lots of ways that you can help your child develop background knowledge when you spend time talking and reading together.

THEME TALK

Today we are going to be reading books about how when one thing happens it changes what happens next. Does it sound complicated? Don't worry. You'll see what I mean after we read the first book.

BOOK

If You Give a Mouse a Cookie, If You Give a Moose a Muffin,
***If You Give a Pig a Pancake* (or any other book in this series),**
by Laura Joffe Numeroff (HarperCollins)
Our first book is (*book title*), by Laura Numeroff. Let's see what kind of trouble that (*the character*) is going to get into! (*Read the book.*)

FLANNELBOARD ACTIVITY (Optional)

Use flannelboard to allow children to help retell the story.

BOOK PICTURE WALK

Show the children the front of the book. Go on a book picture walk with them (for more information, see www.earlylit.net/workshopmats/elest2/6parentpicwalk2.pdf). Ask the children what is happening, using open-ended questions. After reading the book together, intersperse the retelling of the book with the singing of this song.

SONG

If You Give a Pig a Pancake
(To the tune of "If You're Happy and You Know It,"
available at www.kididdles.com/lyrics/i007.html)

Use different words from the story to fill in the blank.

> If you give a pig a _____, he'll want more.
> If you give a pig a _____, he'll want more.
> If you give a pig a _____, then he'll surely ask for more.
> If you give a pig a _____, he'll want more.

Add as many verses as the children's interest and attention indicates.

EARLY LITERACY ASIDE: EXAMPLE

Part of science exploration is making a prediction, or making a guess based on what you already know. You can play around with this concept in lots of different ways, such as having your child look at some ingredients and then guessing what will be for dinner, or when reading a story together, stopping and asking what might happen next.

BOOK

***Don't Let the Pigeon Drive the Bus!* by Mo Willems (Hyperion Books, 2012)**
Let's see what happens if Pigeon is allowed to drive this bus. The book is called *Don't Let the Pigeon Drive the Bus!* by Mo Willems. (*Read the book.*)

What would happen if children were allowed to drive a bus? Who else shouldn't be allowed to drive a bus?

CHANT

Who Told the Pigeon He Could Drive the Bus?
(Chant to the rhythm of "Who Stole the Cookie from the Cookie Jar?")

Clap along with the words to highlight the rhythm. Take turns using each child's name as the one who told the Pigeon he could drive the bus.

Who told Pigeon he could drive the bus?
(*Child's name*) told the Pigeon he could drive the bus.
Who, me?
Yes, you.
Couldn't be.
Then who?

Continue until all of the children's names are chanted. If the group is large, break into smaller groups.

OPTIONAL ACTIVITY

Instead of putting the name tags on the children, put them in a bowl. Take turns drawing names from the bowl. Or you could make two name tags, which the children could match in case they don't know one another's names, or they can recognize first letters in one another's names. The name on the tag is the one who "told Pigeon he could drive the bus." This is especially good for child-care storytimes where children have been "reading" one another's names regularly.

INFORMATIONAL BOOK

Our next book is an informational book about how one thing leads to another in nature. It is interesting to think, what would happen if . . .

Read a book about the food chain or a cycle in nature, like water. You might also choose a factual article from a children's magazine.

EARLY LITERACY ASIDE: EMPOWER

The more we talk with our children about what we see going on around us, the more they will learn. Please stay after storytime to do a science experiment! If you are unable to stay, please pick up the handout so you can do the experiment at home.

CLOSING SONG

Let's Get Ready to Go, Everyone

(To the tune of "Twinkle, Twinkle, Little Star," available at www.kididdles.com/lyrics/
t068.html and www.kididdles.com/lyrics/t023.html)

Let's get ready to go, everyone.
We have had lots of fun.
We read some books along the way.
We also talked and sang and played.
I'm happy you were here with me.
It's time to go—one, two, three!

END OF STORYTIME ACTIVITY

- *In this case, read the Pigeon book last and leave out the request that they stay for storytime. Tell parents that writing helps children understand that print, whether written or drawn, has meaning. Ask them what else you might not want to let Pigeon do and then ask the child to draw it. Have the adults write down their words on the page or another sheet of paper. This is story dictation.*
- Draw Pigeon: *Learn how to draw Pigeon at www.pigeonpresents.com/activities/ pigeon_draw01.pdf. Give the children the finished Pigeon to make a finger puppet. Give the adults and the children time to let Pigeon ask for more things to do. For more Pigeon fun, see www.pigeonpresents.com.*
- *For links of activities related to the If You . . . series, see www.lauranumeroff .com/teachers/teacher_links.htm.*

ALTERNATE SCIENCE ACTIVITY

Magnetic or not? *For this activity you will need magnets, objects to test whether they are magnetic, a chart made up ahead of time with columns indicating the name of the objects and a column for yes and no and results, and paper and pencil to record results. Explain to the adults that you are going to predict which objects will stick to a magnet. Write down the children's guesses. Give each child a chart and a magnet. Encourage them to take the chart home to see which things are attracted to the magnets.*

ALTERNATE BOOKS

Color Zoo, by Lois Ehlert (HarperCollins, 1989) (for younger children)
If You Give a Cat a Cupcake, by Laura Joffe Numeroff (HarperCollins, 2008)
If You Give a Dog a Donut, by Laura Joffe Numeroff (Balzer and Bray, 2011)
If You Give a Pig a Party, by Laura Joffe Numeroff (HarperCollins, 2005)
Just in Case, by Judith Viorst (Atheneum Books for Young Readers, 2010) (for older children)
Where There's a Bear, There's Trouble, by Michael Catchpool (Tiger Tales, 2002) (for younger children)

3. Let's Get Moving!

STORYTIME INTRODUCTION

Hello and welcome! It's great to see so many of you again. I really appreciate that you adults stay here with your children. It is more fun for everyone to have you here and participating! If you have little one with you, please just follow along the best you can.

OPENING SONG

We Have Come to Be Together

(To the tune of "The More We Get Together," available at http://kids.niehs.nih.gov/
games/songs/childrens/morewegetmp3.htm)

We have come to be together to sing songs and read books,
To read books and sing songs.
We have come to be together,
So let us begin.

EARLY LITERACY ASIDE: EXPLAIN

Children who can hear and play with the smaller sounds in words have good phonological skills. This early literacy component is critical to helping them learn how to read because they need to hear those sounds before they can sound out words. Today we are going to look at some ways to help children develop this skill as we read some books that emphasize the sounds in words through singing and rhythm.

THEME TALK

Today we are going to be sharing books about jumping, moving, and dancing. We will play around with different beats and rhythms of words and stories.

BOOK

Rap a Tap Tap: Here's Bojangles—Think of That, **by Leo Dillon and Diane Dillon (Blue Sky Press, 2002)**
Our first book is called *Rap a Tap Tap: Here's Bojangles—Think of That*, by Leo and Diane Dillon. It is about a very famous dancer named Bill "Bojangles" Robinson. He was a tap dancer, which means that he danced with shoes that had metal pieces, called taps, on the bottoms of his shoes. When he danced, they made a really cool sound.

Read the book through once. Encourage the children to repeat the phrase "Rap a Tap Tap, think of that." Read the book again. Ask the children to clap along to the rhythm of the phrase.

Now, let's say this poem.

ACTIVITY

Dancer, Dancer

You can print the poem on paper to make it bigger so that you can point to the words as you read it. Have the children clap with the phrase while they say it. On the next reading, leave out the words and clap only.

Dancer, dancer on the street
Dancing to his own special beat
Rap-a-tap-tap, think of that!

Dancer, dancer with taps on his feet
Dancing to his own special beat
Rap-a-tap-tap, think of that!

Dancer, dancer, with moves so sweet
Dancing to his own special beat
Rap-a-tap-tap, think of that!

EARLY LITERACY ASIDE: EXAMPLE

When you talk and sing with your children, you can emphasize the rhythm of words by tapping them out. This helps the children hear how words can be broken apart or segmented. This will help them when they are puzzling out words as readers.

ACTIVITY

Let's play with the pattern rap-a-tap-tap. Let's tap our feet to this beat. Good job. Now let's change it to rap-rap-tap-tap (*the tap-tap is slower than the rap-rap*). What other patterns could we try?

BOOK

Rain Stomper, by Addie Boswell (Amazon Children's Publishing, 2008)
Our next book is about a girl who is disappointed when the weather turns bad and ruins her plans for the day. It is by Addie Boswell and is called *Rain Stomper*. (*Read the book.*)

ACTIVITY

Let's look at the book and see what kinds of things Jazmin did to get the rain to stop. She stomped . . . splashed . . . yelled . . . spun . . . shook . . . skipped.

Play a variation of the game Simon Says.

I am the Rain Stomper. When I tell you do something, I will say, "The Rain Stomper says, 'Stomp your feet.'" If I don't say, "The Rain Stomper says," then don't do what I say.

Practice the game a few times. Use words from the story and make up more if you wish!

BOOK

Saturday Night at the Dinosaur Stomp,
by Carol Diggory Shields (Candlewick, 2008)
Let's take a look at what dinosaurs did at their parties! (*Read the book.*)

ACTIVITY

Point out the names of the kinds of dinosaurs that are on the end pages. Have the children clap out one clap for every syllable in each word. For more activities related to Saturday Night at the Dinosaur Stomp, *see www.teachervision.fen.com/tv/printables/ Candlewick/SatNightDinosaurStmp_ActKit.pdf.*

INFORMATIONAL BOOK

How Animals Move, **by Pamela Dell (Capstone Press, 2006)**
(or any informational book you like on this topic)
We jump and dance on our feet. Animals and insects move differently than we do. Let's take a look at *How Animals Move*, by Pamela Dell. (*Read the book.*)

EARLY LITERACY ASIDE: EMPOWER

Have fun with your child as you play with words and their sounds and rhythms when you talk and sing together. You can have lots of fun while you help your child get ready to decode, or figure out, words. Please stay after storytime to make your own "rain stomper" baton, or take the materials with you. Who knows what else the baton might turn into!

CLOSING SONG

We Came to Be Together

(To the tune of "The More We Get Together," available at http://kids.niehs.nih.gov/games/
songs/childrens/morewegetmp3.htm)

We came to be together to sing songs and read books,
To read books and sing songs.
We came to be together.
Now storytime is done!

END OF STORYTIME ACTIVITY

*Give the children each a straw and ribbons. Tell them that they can make their own
batons, like that of the Rain Stomper, to use to tell the rain to stop.*

ALTERNATE MATH ACTIVITY

There are many ways to explore patterns—we can clap our hands and move our
bodies to make patterns. We can also draw patterns using different shapes and
colors. Patterns are a part of geometry!

*Cut out shapes of various colors ahead of time. Let each pair choose the shapes they
want to use. Have plastic bags handy so they can take their shape collections home.*

Take turns making and copying each other's patterns.

Early Literacy Aside for math activity

You can say out loud what your pattern is, by using the name of the shape or the
color. Playing with patterns in this way will help your child recognize patterns
with numbers once he or she gets to school.

ALTERNATE BOOKS

If You're Hoppy and You Know It, by April Pulley Sayre (Greenwillow
   Books, 2011) (for younger children)
Move, by Robin Page (Houghton Mifflin Books for Children, 2006) (for
   younger children)

4. Ah-Choo!

STORYTIME INTRODUCTION

Welcome to storytime. My name is (*your name*), and I am happy to see you all here today. Grown-ups, I appreciate that you have silenced your cell phones and put away all other devices so that we can all pay attention to what we are doing in storytime today!

OPENING CHANT

Let's Begin

Clap your hands in time to the beat.

> One, two, look up here. (*Point to eyes.*)
> Three, four, lend an ear. (*Cup your ear.*)
> Five, six, please sit down.
> Seven, eight, it's getting late!
> Nine, ten, let's begin.

EARLY LITERACY ASIDE: EXPLAIN

Today I am going to show you some ways you can help your children develop a large vocabulary, which is knowing the meanings of words for things and concepts. Vocabulary is a very important skill that will help your children understand what they will read. When we talk with them about the words we read, we are helping them to grow their vocabularies.

THEME TALK

In today's storytime we are going to talk about what happens when we feel sick. What do you have to do when you get sick? In our first book Bear has a cold.

BOOK

The Sniffles for Bear, by Bonny Becker (Candlewick, 2011)

Let's look at the cover or front of this book. Here is Bear. Wow, look at his snout, or nose. Here's Mouse. How does Mouse look? So who do you think has the cold in this book? Bear, that's right. Good job at looking at the picture and then figuring out or predicting what is going to happen! Our first book is called *The Sniffles for Bear*, by Bonny Becker.

When you read the book, add a definition for the words that you don't think the children know. For "gravity of my situation," add, "that means how serious his cold is." When you come to "sing mournful" songs, you could add, "or sad" to make sure the children understand.

EARLY LITERACY ASIDE: EXAMPLE

Did you notice that there are many sophisticated words in this book? Children's books have three times more "rare" words than we use in everyday conversation. Notice that most of them are understandable in context, because we know the other words in the sentence, and as I was reading, I gave some explanations of the words. Children with large vocabularies do better in school.

RHYME

I Am a Germ

Repeat the rhyme as many times as necessary. Have the words printed on a dry-erase board or whatever you use for joint viewing.

> How did Bear get a cold? He caught a cold from a germ.
> I am a germ. (*Indicate something small with thumb and index finger.*)
> I get around. (*Make a sprinkling gesture.*)
> With coughs and sniffles (*Cough and sniffle.*)
> I am found.
> Don't share me. (*Shake finger no.*)
> Just do this please. (*Plead with hands.*)
> Cover your mouth (*Cover mouth with sleeve or arm.*)
> When you sneeze!

INFORMATIONAL BOOK

***Germs Are Not for Sharing*, by Elizabeth Verdick**
(Free Spirit Publishing, 2006) (or any factual book about germs or colds)
Our next book explains what germs are. They are very tiny things that make us sick. (*Read the book.*)

SONG

This Is the Way We Cover Our Mouths

(To the tune of "Here We Go Round the Mulberry Bush,"
available at www.kididdles.com/lyrics/m014.html)

Make gestures as the lyrics indicate.

This is the way we cover our mouths,
Cover our mouths,
Cover our mouths.
This is the way we cover our mouths.
When we cough and sneeze.

This is the way we wash our hands,
Wash our hands,
Wash our hands.
This is the way we wash our hands,
To wash the germs away.

BOOK

Barnyard Song, by Rhonda Gowler Greene
(Atheneum Books for Young Readers, 2001)

*After reading the book, show children how to mix up the animal sounds with the
sounds you make when you have a cold using the following song.*

SONG

Did You Ever Hear a Horse?

(To the tune of "Did You Ever See a Lassie?"
available at www.kidsongs.com/lyrics/did-you-ever-see-a-lassie.html)

Sway in time to the song. Stand if you wish.

Did you ever hear a horse, a horse, a horse,
Did you ever hear a horse cough this way and that?
Cough, cough, neigh, cough, cough, neigh,
This way and that way and this way and that way.
Did you ever hear a horse neigh this way and that?

Did you ever hear a cow, a cow, a cow,
Did you ever hear a cow,
Moo this way and that.
Cough, cough, moo, cough, cough, moo.

Continue with as many animal noises as you wish.

BOOK

***Llama Llama Home with Mama*, by Anna Dewdney (Viking Juvenile, 2011)**
Here's another story about a friend of ours who is sick. It is called *Llama, Llama, Home with Mama*, and it is by Anna Dewdney. What do you call your mother? Mom? Mommy? Mama? (*Read the book.*)

EARLY LITERACY ASIDE: EMPOWER

There are many different ways of saying the same thing using different words, or synonyms. When you talk and read with your children you can help them get ready to read by helping them learn new words. You can add in the words they know for the ones they don't. How many ways can you say *big*? Remember, children cannot know too many words. Large vocabularies are one of the characteristics of good readers and good students.

After our closing song I have an activity planned. I hope that you can join us. If you can't stay, you can take the materials with you.

CLOSING CHANT

It's Time to Go

One, two, look up here. (*Point to eyes.*)
Three four, lend an ear. (*Cup your ear.*)
Five, six, it's time to go
Seven, eight, it's getting late!
Nine, ten, I'll see you again.

END OF STORYTIME ACTIVITY

Make a get-well card—use images from the website www.llamallamabook.com. If you use screens in your storytime, this website has a site where you can make cards. Or if you prefer, make a QR code and give it to parents for use later. You could also give them paper, markers, and so on, to design their own. Remind everyone to sign their names.

Early Literacy Aside for writing activity

Writing and reading develop concurrently. It is fun to watch how children's writing abilities progress over time. Writing helps children make the connection between what they say and the written word, even if you can't read their writing yet. This is an important part of understanding how reading works, called print awareness. It will help them figure out, or decode, words once they are reading.

ALTERNATE MATH ACTIVITY

Sequencing: Have images of this available for the children to put in order.

First you have a germ.
Then you get sick.
Then you rest.
Then you get better.

Early Literacy Aside for Math Activity

Playing with putting events in order helps children become familiar with the concept that numbers have an order, too.

ALTERNATE SCIENCE ACTIVITY

Using tools: Put out a selection of books with good images of cells, bacteria, and other microscopic things. Use a magnifying glass or a small hand lens to show children how miniscule things can look bigger, like in the book.

Early Literacy Aside for Science Activity

Using tools is a part of science exploration. It is interesting for children to look at things in this way, and it helps prepare them for other opportunities for this kind of exploration.

ALTERNATE BOOK

Bear Feels Sick, by Karma Wilson (Margaret K. McElderry Books, 2007)

5. Hooray for Trucks!

STORYTIME INTRODUCTION

Welcome, everyone, to storytime. My name is (*your name*). It is always good to see you all here. We encourage everyone to participate! Thank you for bringing your children to the library.

OPENING CHANT

Welcome to Storytime

One, two, look up here.
Three, four, lend an ear.
Five, six, did you hear?
Seven, eight, don't be late.
Nine, ten, I can't wait!
We'll have some fun.
We've just begun!
Welcome to storytime.

EARLY LITERACY ASIDE: EXPLAIN

Today's early literacy component is print awareness, which is knowing how books work, and that print is everywhere and has meaning. During storytime I will point out how you can do this with your children when you talk, read, write, sing, and play together.

THEME TALK

Our first book is about a garbage truck. What does a garbage truck do? That's right—it picks up our trash. What else do you know about them?

BOOK

I Stink! by Kate and Jim McMullan (HarperCollins, 2007)

Our first book is called *I Stink!* It is by Kate and Jim McMullan.

This is a great opportunity to use a really big, deep voice when reading.

SONG

I've Been Working

(To the tune of "I've Been Working on the Railroad,"
available at http://kids.niehs.nih.gov/games/songs/childrens/railroadmid.htm)

I've been working on the dump truck
All the live long day.
I've been working on the dump truck
Since the break of day.
Can't you hear the horn? It's honking—
Rise up so early in the morn.
Don't you hear the foreman shouting—
Hey there, honk your horn.
Hey there, won't you honk?
Hey there, won't you honk?
Hey there, won't you honk your horn?
Hey there, won't you honk?
Hey there, won't you honk?
Hey there, won't you honk your horn?

BOOK

Truck, by Donald Crews (Greenwillow, 1991)

Our next book is called *Truck*, by Donald Crews.

Read the book through once. Go back and looking at the pictures, point out the different signs that are along the road and on the truck.

ACTIVITY

Prepare ahead of time signs of different shapes and sizes. For example a stop sign is an octagon, and a yield sign is a triangle. Have enough signs for each child to have one. Glue one of each onto a chart for sorting.

Now you all have a sign that has a shape. Each shape means something different. (*Explain what the shapes mean.*) Let's see how many we have of each one.

Have each child bring one up and match the shape, putting it in the appropriate column. Talk about which column has more.

EARLY LITERACY ASIDE: EXAMPLE

When we point out signs along the road and in stores we are helping our children see that print has meaning. We can also help them see this when we point out words as we read books.

INFORMATIONAL BOOK

Building a Road, **by JoAnn Early Macken (Capstone Press, 2008) (or any other informational book about trucks)**
Now we are going to read a book about how trucks help to build a road. It is called *Building a Road*, by JoAnn Early Macken.

Make a point of talking about all of the images in this book. Don't just read the words! Ask the children questions about what they are seeing. Expand on and repeat what they say. Remember to affirm their comments, too.

EARLY LITERACY ASIDE: EMPOWER

Words are everywhere. Remember that pointing out words to your children as you go about your daily life helps develop their print awareness, which will help them learn how to read. Please stay for a while longer so we can do an activity together. If you can't stay, you can take the materials with you.

CLOSING CHANT

Storytime Is Over

One, two, look up here.
Three, four, lend an ear.
Five, six, I'm sorry to say.
Seven, eight, that's it for today.
Nine, ten, I'm glad you came.
Now storytime is over!

END OF STORYTIME ACTIVITY

For either of the first two activities below, tell adults about asking children questions and offering information in order to build their children's vocabulary and background knowledge (e.g., Where is the truck going? What kind of truck is it? What does it do? How big is it?).

- *Make a steering wheel. Have premade steering wheel, or ask adults to help. Attach a paper plate to a large piece of paper using a brad. Have steering wheels ready for the children to take with them. Include a small sheet of paper with questions about the truck on it.*
- *Take small, dessert-size paper plates. Put a brad in the center of each one. Tell the children that these are the wheels of their trucks. Give them a piece of construction paper and ask them where they would like to put their wheels. Encourage them to draw a truck around the wheels.*

- *Play the game Red Light, Green Light. Have shapes and colors made for different signs. Encourage the children to take them home. Remind the adults and care providers that they might want to play Red Light, Green Light at home or in child care.*

ALTERNATE SCIENCE ACTIVITY

In storytime today we read a book called *I Stink!* about things that stink or smell bad. Let's smell some things that don't smell bad, but smell good!

Put little dabs of spices and foods (e.g., cinnamon, vanilla, cloves, garlic, onion, lemon) on small pieces of paper. Have the children smell them and tell you what they smell like, and encourage everybody to talk about the smells. Remind adults to use interesting vocabulary words.

MATH CONCEPTS DURING STORYTIME

You can add math to the science activity above by making a chart listing the smells and the preferences of the children. Come together as a group to make a chart of which smells everyone likes best. Have children write their name on a sticky note, and then put that note under the word or symbol that represents their favorite smell. Talk about which smell has the most votes. Charts and graphs are one of the places where math and science intersect.

Words That Describe Smells

Acrid	Delicious	Medicinal	Rancid	Sour	Stinky
Bitter	Fragrant	Minty	Rotten	Spicy	Strong
Burning	Fresh	Pungent	Salty	Stale	Sweet
Clean	Fruity	Putrid	Smoky	Stench	

ALTERNATE BOOKS

Get to Work, Trucks! by Don Carter (Roaring Brook Press, 2002)
Good Night, Good Night, Construction Site, by Sherry Duskey Rinker (Chronicle Books, 2011)
Red Truck, by Kersten Hamilton (Viking Juvenile, 2008)

Part III

Making It Your Own

chapter 10

Building Your Early Literacy Enhanced Storytime

THE PURPOSE OF THIS PART OF THE BOOK IS TO GIVE YOU THE TOOLS AND SHOW YOU the process for turning your own storytime into an early literacy enhanced storytime—a storytime in which we intentionally explain to adults how they can help their children develop the foundation for later reading. Our storytimes are full of early literacy, and we model ways to share books and activities that support early literacy. The early literacy enhanced storytime adds intentionality and articulation to the traditional storytime.

Early literacy enhanced storytimes follow the same criteria that govern the choosing of books and materials for your traditional storytimes. You will still choose books, songs, and activities that you enjoy, that you think children will enjoy, that are appropriate for the age or developmental stage of the group you are targeting, and that work in a group setting. Only after all these conditions have been met do you then look at a storytime theme—if you choose to use a theme. Next you figure out which one of the early literacy components you are highlighting for that storytime. You do not plan your storytime around an early literacy component; you highlight one of the components during the course of your storytime. Even though all early literacy components are usually part of each storytime, choose only one to highlight; otherwise, adults are overloaded with information and leave with nothing substantial.

Books are so wonderfully rich and flexible. It is how we *use* a book that makes it pertinent to a particular component. Whether or not a book rhymes, you can still take any word from the book and rhyme it, and you have phonological aware-ness! Even if the children know the meaning of every word in a book, you can always give them a less familiar word for one with which they are familiar, and you have vocabulary!

Because of this flexibility with books and other storytime elements, like flan-nelboards, puppets, and so on, depending on what we do, any one storytime can support any of the early literacy components. It would indeed be possible for us to talk about several of the early literacy components in one storytime, but we do not want to overwhelm adults with information. By giving three brief tidbits of information about one component, we make succinct points and allow adults to come away with some ideas about the hows and whys of early literacy.

Even though you highlight only one early literacy component per storytime, you don't want to leave adults with the impression that all they have to do is work on that one component and their children will be ready to read. Mention to parents and caregivers that this component is one of five that children need in order to learn to read; having a poster or visual of the components in the storytime area is helpful (see figure 10.1; to download an English poster, see www.lva.virginia.gov/lib-edu/ldnd/early-literacy/everchildr2r.pdf; to download a Spanish poster, see www.lva.virginia.gov/lib-edu/ldnd/early-literacy/everchildr2r-spanish.pdf). Also, highlight each of the five early lit-eracy components over the course of five storytimes, rather than high-lighting the same component for several storytimes in a row. Remind adults that laying a foundation for later reading is a process that takes years. Some components go on for a lifetime, since we always con-tinue to acquire new vocabulary and knowledge!

You will notice in the planning steps presented here that you first choose your example early literacy aside. Look for an item in your sto-rytime that lends itself comfortably to one of the early literacy compo-nents. You have already planned what you think will be a successful storytime, so choose a good match between what you are doing and an early literacy component. Don't

Figure 10.1

think, "What early literacy tip am I going to say; let me find something I can do that with." Instead, look over your storytime and see which book or item lends itself to a particular early literacy component that you would like to highlight. Our storytimes are full of early literacy, but you need only one example of the early literacy component, the example early literacy aside, for the actual storytime. This is because the explain aside is general, and the empower aside offers ideas on ways that adults can continue supporting the early literacy component at home.

Because we recommend that you cover the five components over the course of five storytimes, you may find that, at times, you have to think first of the component. So, let's say the component you have not yet covered over the course of several storytimes is letter knowledge. You may be looking at a storytime and thinking, "What can I do for letter knowledge in this storytime?" Again, it is always possible to find something in your storytime to support a particular early literacy component because books are so versatile. Just remember that you can use any part of storytime—books, activities, songs—as the basis for your early literacy asides.

Where to Begin: Creating an Early Literacy Enhanced Storytime

1. **Start with your own storytime:** Choose books and other items you like, that the children will like, that are appropriate for the targeted age group, and that work well in a group setting.
2. **Look over your storytime:** Look over your storytime and see which item particularly lends itself to an early literacy component. Make sure it's something you would have fun with and find interesting.
3. **Think about how to highlight early literacy:** Think about the item you have decided on and what you might need to do to highlight the early literacy component. For example, if you highlight print awareness with a book, you might start with the book upside down and see if the children know it needs to be turned right side up, or you might run your finger under the title and author of the book or under a repeated phrase as you read the book, or you might take words from a rhyming book and emphasize them in a song to focus on phonological awareness.
4. **Early literacy aside—Example:** Think about and write down the example early literacy aside that you will share with adults. You can refer to the list of asides in chapter 12, which are arranged by early literacy component, but don't feel restricted to this list.
5. **Early literacy aside—Explain:** Once you have determined your example aside, you know what you want to explain in your explain early literacy

aside. This is an introductory aside in which you let adults know what you will highlight in storytime. You can refer to the listings of asides in chapter 12 for some possibilities.

6. **Early literacy aside—Empower:** Think about and write down your empower aside. What do you want adults to continue doing after they have left storytime? This is a good time to think about some of the practices that are harder to include in storytime, like writing and playing. Use the list of asides in chapter 12 for some ideas. For those who do craft or other activities at the end of storytime or after storytime, you might include the empower aside during this time, because these are activities that can also be continued and built on at home or in child care.

7. **Review your asides:** Are they effective? Effective asides give a research-based reason for why or how an activity (e.g., playing rhyming games, saying a repeated phrase) or practice (e.g., singing, talking, reading, writing, playing) supports an early literacy component (e.g., phonological awareness, vocabulary, print awareness, background knowledge, letter knowledge) or reading skill (e.g., decoding, or recognizing words and relating letters and sounds to formulate words; comprehension, or understanding what is being read).

8. **Review your storytime plan:** Although your storytime will remain basically the same, you might make some changes in addition to the three asides. For example, if you extend a storytime element by adding on an activity or returning to a page in a book to talk about it, you may find you need to cut out or shorten another storytime element to accommodate these activities. Make any needed adjustments.

9. **There you have it!**

Use the form shown in figure 10.2 if you find it helpful (the full-size form is available as web extra 10.1 at www.alaeditions.org/webextras).

Keep the goal of encouraging intentional interactions between adults and children when you plan activities for after storytime. As you present and interact around the craft activities, keep in mind that there are two elements to learning: the context of learning, or the learning environment, and the content of learning, which should support early literacy development.

Figure 10.2

Planning Form

ASIDE	YOUR EARLY LITERACY ASIDES
Early literacy aside: **EXPLAIN**	
Early literacy aside: **EXAMPLE**	**WHAT YOU WILL DO:**
	YOUR ASIDE:
Early literacy aside: **EMPOWER**	

Completed Planning Form

ASIDE	YOUR EARLY LITERACY ASIDES
Early literacy aside: **EXPLAIN**	Today our early literacy tip is on vocabulary, or knowing the meanings of words. Reading aloud to your child is a powerful way of talking with your child. It provides many different words than they hear in regular conversation. The more words children know, the easier it will be to understand what they read when they start reading.
Early literacy aside: **EXAMPLE**	**WHAT YOU WILL DO:** **Cat and Mouse, by Ian Schoenherr (Greenwillow Books, 2008)** I will read the book *Cat and Mouse*. When I get to the page that says, "I'll never vex her, nor make her displeased," I'll read those words and then say, "I'll never *vex* her means I won't make her angry."
	YOUR ASIDE: After I finish reading the whole book, I'll say, "Parents, did you notice that I explained the word *vex*, and I didn't just substitute the word *angry*? Use those harder words and explain them with simpler ones. That's how children learn new words!"
Early literacy aside: **EMPOWER**	Today I pointed out the rich vocabulary in books—like the word *vex*, which we don't use in daily conversation. As you sing, talk, read, write, and play with your children throughout the day, you can build their vocabulary by using less familiar words and explaining them from time to time.

CONTEXT: CREATING A SAFE ENVIRONMENT

Children learn best in an environment that is safe, not just physically but also socially and emotionally. Learning takes place more easily when children enjoy what they are doing, feel safe enough to experiment and to say what they are thinking, and know they will find acceptance. There are four ways we can build this emotionally safe environment:

1. Through personal demeanor and engagement—including active listening and smiling
2. By involving all participants, children and adults, in activities
3. By emphasizing process over product
4. By following the child's lead and asking open-ended questions

First, the storytime presenter's own demeanor with both children and adults sets the stage for engagement in and with the craft or activity, as well as with the whole storytime experience. Just as participants readily pick up on how we feel about the books we present, they also take their cues from the approach you take with the activities. Being open and relaxed will help make the total experience an engaging one.

Second, the presenter needs to allow for each individual's personal and creative expression by having enough materials for both children and adults. This helps adults focus on their own projects and makes it less likely that they will try to make their child's craft perfect. Adults like to express themselves, too, but the way they express themselves is different from how children do. We all need outlets for expression, and storytime crafts and activities can provide such outlets. Some adults have not had the opportunity in their own lives to play around with arts and craft activities, so they experiment in their own ways. Even though we have materials for each individual, once everyone has worked on their own projects, it is good to encourage communication among them to allow them to talk about what they made and what they are thinking about it.

Third, it's important to emphasize process over product. The participants' crafts should not be expected to look a specific way. Young children especially learn through exploration of materials and ideas. There is no one way, no perfect or correct finished product. If a child draws a scribble and says that it depicts a dog, that scribble should be respected because it represents a dog to the child. The child can use the drawing to help retell a story or to talk about a dog. If you choose to show a sample of a finished product, it should resemble the work of a child.

A key part of the craft process occurs when adults describe what they are doing to children and children describe what they are doing to adults. To ensure that activities give priority to process over product, think in terms of "process forms product" or "let process lead to product."

Fourth, asking open-ended questions empowers children to take the lead and helps promote an emotionally safe learning environment. Open-ended questions are ones that cannot be answered with yes or no. They include questions such as the following:

- What did you draw or make?
- How did you make that?
- What did you use to make it?
- Can you show me what it does?
- What does it say?
- What are you going to do next?
- What do you like about this?
- What words would you like me to write on your paper?
- What's happening here?

Ask a few such questions judiciously, and gauge each child's willingness to respond. Be careful not to put children on the spot by asking too many questions. Instead, use well-placed questions to encourage children's thinking, imagination, and language while acknowledging their work. Sometimes you can encourage children's talk by simply repeating what they say and then giving them time to think and respond. Modeling these behaviors is one way to encourage them. Offering a tip or two about some specific ways to encourage children's language can be helpful to adults, whether you are acknowledging what they are doing that supports language development or whether you are making a suggestion on ways to support language development.

CONTENT: SUPPORTING EARLY LITERACY DEVELOPMENT

The storytime presenter makes a difference. The way you talk with children, the way you describe a craft or activity, and your interaction with the participants as they work on and finish an activity all influence their responses to you, to the activities they are doing, and to the way they feel about the storytime experience. Use a rich vocabulary to describe the craft-making process, and repeat nouns, adjectives, and adverbs instead of using pronouns. Encourage participants to use the object they made to talk or to retell a story. Follow children's leads as they talk about what they are doing.

Here is an example of the implementation of early literacy storytimes given throughout the Arapahoe (CO) Library District. Several helpful documents developed at the library are posted at www.alaeditions.org/webextras.

GROWING STORYTIME COMPETENCY: PROCESSES AND TOOLS FROM THE ARAPAHOE (CO) LIBRARY DISTRICT

Lori Romero, coordinator and supervisor
for the Child and Family Library Services Department

Melissa Depper, child and family library services librarian,
storytime presenter and trainer

The Arapahoe Library District in the South Denver metro area boasts popular storytimes as a core service—one that brings significant numbers of families into the library each day. More than fifty storytimes for babies, toddlers, preschoolers, and families are provided in English, Spanish, and Russian each week. The storytimes are sprinkled throughout our eight libraries, at preschools and area childcare homes. We see an increasingly diverse population and touch a wide variety of socioeconomic levels within the boundaries of our library system.

Thanks to Every Child Ready to Read research and our visionary district leadership, we have been able to take the time to forge ahead with a thorough plan for continuous improvement, seeking to understand, evaluate, and make the most of early literacy storytime experiences for our children and families. We began by asking questions and analyzing answers. "What, exactly, makes a storytime outstanding?" "Are we doing those things consistently?" "How can we really make a difference?"

According to attendance data and patron survey comments, we have been successful in providing storytime experiences that are consistently perceived as both enlightening and fun. As we began learning more and more about brain development and the critical importance of building the foundation for literacy from infancy, we knew we were uniquely positioned and had the potential to reach our eager families in even more significant and intentional ways during storytime.

Looking back at patron feedback, we noted several general comments related to fun, enjoyment, convenience of storytime schedules, great books, and so on. What patrons mentioned most often as making a difference in storytime quality, however, was our staff: their preparedness, skill level, enthusiasm, and engagement with children.

Armed with a clear focus on our most valuable assets and change agents—our storytime providers, our background knowledge of early literacy development, and our leveraging of a strong foundation and support from our district leadership—we got to work.

The Arapahoe Library District's mission statement includes providing outstanding and personalized service, along with a core objective of increasing literacy empowerment by preparing the youngest children to learn to read. The value of early childhood literacy and the role of the library are at the heart of all levels of our strategic planning. In addition, the goals of our Child and Family Library Services Youth Services Team center on empowering parents as first teachers.

This core foundation guides our work. Linking our quality storytime initiative's activities with library district goals and objectives was critical to building traction and getting buy-in from all staff.

Our first step was to identify the individual components that make an outstanding literacy-based storytime. We decided to develop storytime competencies that weave research, patron feedback, and our district goals into a product that would clarify best practices and make sense to our storytime providers. Although careful to keep entertainment, creativity, and fun in the competencies, it was important for us to help staff really notice what they were doing and to understand why they were doing the things they do in storytimes. Instead of focusing on theme, activities, or number of songs and books, our competencies broke the storytime experience down into bite-size pieces, thus magnifying what we believe storytime staff needs to carefully consider before, during, and after each storytime session to meet standards of high quality. We asked, "What do storytime providers really need to know and be able to do?"

Digging in deep to answer this question was time consuming, but in the end, it was well worth the effort. The analysis evolved into a storytime competencies document that is well used. The document serves as a districtwide training tool and is a guide both for crafting and evaluating quality, literacy-based storytime experiences. The competencies direct staff to focus on three broad categories: preparation, delivery, and engagement in storytime. Key storytime elements embedded in these larger categories include setting the stage, content, presentation, literacy message, interaction, management, and professional development. The detailed competencies help guide storytime providers with planning (see web extra 10.2 at www.alaeditions.org/webextras).

The competencies also enable a more focused and consistent evaluation of staff performance. Although several of our veteran children's librarians had observed storytimes and provided practical feedback for storytime colleagues in the past, when our Child and Family Library Services Department was formed, we knew the conditions were ripe to lay the groundwork for more purposeful and results-oriented storytime evaluation and robust staff training to go alongside.

Our directors, managers, and supervisors agreed to learn more about early literacy, the competencies, and evaluation of storytimes. The Child and Family Literacy Team designed training opportunities, including both live and videotaped samples of powerful storytimes featuring our storytime staff in action. This time spent training, along with a new competency-based storytime observation guide for supervisors (see web extras 10.3 and 10.4 at www.alaeditions.org/webextras), served to launch the initial phase of the evaluation process. The short and simple observation guides target specific, observable behaviors that lead to rich and articulate conversations, common language, and ongoing collaboration in every library. Library supervisors committed to observing, supporting, and evaluating storytime staff two times throughout the year as a part of performance plans. We believe that embedding this process into our plan is making a big difference. The supervisor observation forms are used side by side with the storytime competencies document, and the design of the tools allows for creative variations in personal style of storytimes while also matching up important objectives. We are grateful for this concrete way to help both supervisors and staff, and we are gathering positive feedback about the process and tools. Staff are always encouraged to come back to the Child and Family Library Services Team to get further support; and we are responding with more ongoing and varied training opportunities based on the storytime competencies.

The storytime evaluation plan at the Arapahoe Library District is evolving. We will continue to build our collection of program data, use current research, and develop strategies to address the day-to-day improvement of our storytimes. We are confident that we are off to a great start in the process. We believe that it was wise to focus first on district goals and our best resource, the storytime staff, and we feel that we have laid solid groundwork for the next steps in the process. We are proud of our thoughtful sequence of competencies, training, and evaluation tools, and we will continue to grow our early childhood literacy storytime initiative at the library so that every child is ready to read when they enter school.

chapter 11

Storytime Extras

THIS CHAPTER CONSISTS OF NURSERY RHYMES, SONGS, MOVEMENT ACTIVITIES, AND crafts that you can adapt to fit your storytimes.

Sometimes we print the words to songs and rhymes and hand them out for the adults to take home. This practice is beneficial, especially if you include an early literacy tip on the handout. However, during storytime, it is hard for adults to hold the handout, read it, and also do motions to the rhymes or songs with their children. Having everyone follow along and waiting to give out the handout at the end of storytime frees adults to participate with their children. Waiting also has the added benefit of promoting a "group sense"; for example, everyone saying rhymes or singing songs together. Some presenters project the words using a PowerPoint presentation, which is handy if the library has the setup to do so and the room does not have to be too dark. Words to the rhymes and songs can also be printed out on flip charts or posters. You can enlarge the rhyme on a copier or use a banner program, such as the one at www.earlylit.net/storytimes/flipcharts.shtml.

For each item below, the way the early literacy component is being highlighted is described. Be sure to include an early literacy aside from the sample early literacy asides in chapter 12 or ones you develop yourself.

Nursery Rhymes

The reasons for making nursery rhymes part of storytime range from the philosophical to the practical. From a cultural perspective, nursery rhymes are a childhood tradition. They have been passed down for generations, are referred to in books and speeches, and have become an accepted part of general knowledge (or a child's background knowledge). They also help children develop early literacy skills, especially phonological awareness. One study tells us that young children who learn nursery rhymes have stronger phonological skills than those who don't.[1] From the practical point of view, nursery rhymes are readily available and in the public domain. We may use them, play with them, and reproduce them easily and legally. And of course, the rhythm and rhyme of the words bring delight and enjoyment to children and adults alike.

Use these rhymes and activities in any way that fits your needs. We have included suggestions for using nursery rhymes with several different literacy components, and you can add your favorites to the ones in this section. When you reproduce the rhymes, be sure to include images to refer to.

LITTLE BOY BLUE

Little Boy Blue, come blow your horn.
The sheep's in the meadow, the cow's in the corn.
Where is the boy who looks after the sheep?
He's under the haystack, fast asleep.
Will you wake him? No, not I;
For if I do, he's sure to cry.

Early Literacy Component: Phonological Awareness
What you do: Read the rhyme and then say it together.
What you say: "There are words in this poem that rhyme, or share a sound—
   horn and *corn*, *sheep* and *asleep*, *I* and *cry*. We are going to read the rhyme
   aloud once more. This time through, you tell me what the word is that
   is missing." (*Read the rhyme, leaving out the second rhyming word of
   each pair.*)

Early Literacy Component: Background Knowledge

What you do: Read the rhyme several times and have parents and children say it together. Then ask questions to help children learn about living on a farm.

What you say: "Why did Little Boy Blue need to get up? Where was he sleeping? Where do you sleep? What do you think the sheep is doing in that corn-field? What would you do to get the sheep out of the corn?"

Early Literacy Component: Print Conventions and Awareness

What you do: Read the rhyme. As you reread it, point to the words as you say them. When you read the word *haystack*, you can also point to the picture of the haystack.

What you say: Point only—you don't need to say anything special to the children.

Early Literacy Component: Vocabulary

What you do: Talk about the images. Point out and define the horn and the hay-stack.

What you say: "How do you feel when you wake up? Why would Little Boy Blue cry? What other words can you use to talk about how you feel when you don't get enough sleep (*grouchy, grumpy, tired, weary*)?"

Early Literacy Component: Letter Knowledge

What you do: Go through the rhyme together and look for all of the *B*s.

What you say: "Let's count the letter *B* together. We need to look for capital let-ters and lowercase letters. (*Think out loud that the letter* d *looks like a* b *but is different*) Look how much a *b* looks like a *d*. We need to be careful when we look for these letters!"

JELLY ON A PLATE

Jelly on a plate,
  (*Cup your hands as if holding a plate.*
  Shake the plate side to side.)
Jelly on a plate,
Wibble, wobble, wibble, wobble,
Jelly on a plate.

Sausage in a pan,
  (*Pretend to cook sausage in a pan.*)
Sausage in a pan,
Frizzle, frazzle, frizzle, frazzle,
Sausage in a pan.

Baby on the floor,
  (*Put the baby on the floor, or mime doing so for bigger kids.*)
Baby on the floor,
Pick him up, pick him up, (*Pick the baby up.*)
Baby on the floor. (*Put the baby back down.*)

Early Literacy Component: Phonological Awareness

What you do: Recite the rhyme with action; say it together.

What you say: (*For older children*) "There are some funny words in this rhyme—*wibble, wobble, frizzle, frazzle!* Let's make some more up. How about *dribble, drabble? Slibble, slabble?* Let's try saying those words in the rhyme."

Early Literacy Component: Vocabulary; Background Knowledge

What you do: Recite the rhyme several times with actions; say it together.

What you say: "What else wibble wobbles? How might you look if you wibble wobbled? Let's see how you look when you shake, tremble, or quake." (*You could also talk about different foods that wibble wobble or are fried in a pan.*)

Early Literacy Component: Print Conventions and Awareness

What you do: Show the children the picture of the jelly or the sausage. Show them the real things or pictures of them as well, pointing out the words of the items on the packaging.

What you say: "Looking at the pictures and the words on the labels helps us guess what is inside the package."

Early Literacy Component: Letter Knowledge

What you say: Talk about the different shapes—of the pan, the sausage, and so on. Or, for preschoolers, use this rhyme with a letter that you are playing with, changing the "wibble, wobble" to start with the focus letter—"bibble, bobble" for the letter *b*, for example.

JACK BE NIMBLE

Jack be nimble,
Jack be quick,
Jack jump over the candlestick.

Early Literacy Component: Phonological Awareness

What you do: Read the rhyme several times, and then say it together. Find a word
or a pair of words with one syllable whose rhyme you'd like to play with.
See example with lick and tick below.

What you say: (*For young children*) "Adults, you are going to bounce your child
on your knee to the rhythm of the rhyme. When it comes to 'jump over
the candlestick,' pick up your child, and move him or her from one side of
your knee to the other in an arch."

(*For preschoolers*) "We are going to find words that rhyme, or sound alike at
the end, the way that *tick* and *lick* do. The sound they share is /ik/. That is the
part that rhymes. You can change the first sound and the words will still rhyme.
For example, *tick*. I can take out the *t*, which leaves me with /ik/. I can use the *l*,
which gives me *lick*."

"We can sing a rhyming song, using words that share ending sounds." (*Sing to
the tune of "Skip to My Lou," available at http://kids.niehs.nih.gov/games/songs/
childrens/skiptomp3.htm.*)

> *Lick*, *tick*, share ending sounds,
> *Lick*, *tick*, share ending sounds,
> *Lick*, *tick*, share ending sounds.
> This makes them rhyming words.

(*Alternately, sing to the tune of "Frère Jacques," available at www.kidsongs.com/
lyrics/frere-jacques.html.*)

> *Lick* and *tick*
> *Lick* and *tick*
> Hear the rhyme?
> Hear the rhyme?
> They share ending sounds.
> They share ending sounds.
> Hear them rhyme.
> Hear them rhyme.

(*Or, sing to the tune of "London Bridge Is Falling Down," available at www
.kididdles.com/lyrics/l037.html.*)

> *Tick* and *lick* are rhyming words, rhyming words, rhyming words,
> *Tick* and *lick* are rhyming words,
> They share ending sounds.

Early Literacy Component: Background Knowledge

What you need: candlestick, candle, or pictures of them

What you do: (*For preschoolers*) Read the rhyme together, pointing to each word as you read it. Bring in a candlestick to show the children what it looks like. Use an unlit candle in a candlestick or your fist with your thumb sticking up as a candle.

What you say: "Have your child jump over the candlestick as you say the rhyme. If they can't jump over it, they can jump near it."

Early Literacy Component: Print Conventions and Awareness

What you need: Children's names written on paper and place in a bowl or on a flannelboard

What you do: (*For older children*) Have all of the children's names in a bowl or on a flannelboard. Pull a name out of the bowl. Point to it and say it. You are going to substitute the child's name for *Jack*. If there are a lot of children, split them up into smaller groups. Read or have children read the name on their own name tag or another person's name tag.

What you say: "We are going to take turns being Jack. When I take your name out of the bowl, we are going to read it aloud and then you get a turn to jump over the candlestick."

Early Literacy Component: Vocabulary

What you do: (*For babies*) Lift the baby up and over as they hear the word for the motion. (*For older children*) Read and say the rhyme together.

What you say: (*For babies*) "Babies love it when we match movements to the words!" (*For older children*) "*Nimble* isn't a word we hear often. *Nimble* is another word for *agile*, or not clumsy. What other words can you think of that mean the same thing? *Lively*, *swift*, or *sprightly*. These words are the opposite of *slow*, *clumsy*, and *awkward*."

Early Literacy Component: Phonological Awareness

What you do: Say a rhyme. Change the rhyme so that the verb matches the name that starts with the letter that you are playing with. For example:

Kyle be nimble . . . Kyle kicked over . . .
Penny be nimble . . . Penny pushed over . . .
Sam be nimble . . . Sam skipped over . . .
Ben be nimble . . . Ben bumped into . . .

EARLY IN THE MORNING

Early in the morning at eight o'clock
   (*Look at wrist, as if you have a watch on.*)
You can hear the postman's knock.
   (*Cup ear, and mime knocking twice to match the beat.*)
Up jumps Ella to answer the door. (*All jump up.*)
One letter, two letter, three letters, four! (*Act out picking up letters.*)

Early Literacy Component: Phonological Awareness

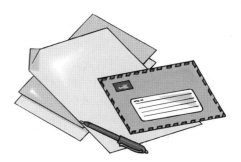

What you do: Say the rhyme using actions noted. Repeat a couple of times, emphasizing the rhyming words.

What you say: "Did you hear that? *Door* rhymes with *four*! *Clock* and *knock* rhyme, too!"

Early Literacy Component: Background Knowledge

What you do: (*For preschoolers*) Read or say the rhyme together several times. Ask some open-ended questions, questions that cannot be answered with just one word.

What you say: "What is Ella doing in the morning? Who comes to the door? When does the mail come to your house? Who gets mail? What comes in the mail?"

Early Literacy Component: Print Conventions and Awareness

What you need: Paper, crayons or pencils

What you do: After storytime, the children are going to write a letter. Another option is to have adults and children write a note to library staff. Have a cardboard box with a slot in it so they can "mail" the note they have written. Adults can write what the child is saying. At the next storytime, you can display the notes with your responses.

What you say: "Have your child write a note for someone. Make sure your child writes his or her name! What your child writes may look like scribbles. That's fine. If your child doesn't mind, you can write at the bottom what your child tells you it says. Put it in an envelope and mail it, if possible. Otherwise, you can fold it up and write the receiver's name on it for hand delivery."

Early Literacy Component: Vocabulary

What you say: (*For older children*) "Another word for *postman* is *mailman* or *mail carrier*. Why do you think he is called a postman? Because he gets mail from the post office, that's right. Where can you put mail? Into a mailbox. How else does the mail carrier get your letters?"

Early Literacy Component: Letter Knowledge

What you need: Prepare ahead of time envelopes with letters corresponding to the first letter of each child's name.

What you do: Play mailman by delivering the envelopes to the appropriate person. You can hold up the envelope and guess what letter it is together by sounding it. For example, you could say for the letter *D* that is makes the /d/ sound, like in *dog*. If the group is big, split up, or save this for an activity after storytime.

What you say: "Children's names are important to them! We can use their names as a first step in teaching them the alphabet."

PANCAKE DAY

Great *A*, little *a*,
This is pancake day.
Toss the ball high,
   (*Suit actions to words.*)
Throw the ball low,
Those that come after
May sing hi-ho!

Early Literacy Component: Phonological Awareness

What you do: Say the rhyme with actions noted.

What you say: (*For preschoolers*) "What else could we sing instead of hi-ho? How about flay-flo? What other sound switches could we make? Changing the first sound in a word helps children hear the smaller sounds in words while playing a fun word game."

Early Literacy Component: Vocabulary

What you need: A ball for each adult-child pair

What you do: Hold the ball up high and then down low. You can also roll it back and forth to the child, while you talk about where the ball is going—close to the child, next to, behind, above, below, and so on. This could also be an activity for after storytime.

Early Literacy Component: Background Knowledge

What you need: A cookbook

What you do: Show everyone the cookbook.

What you say: "This is a cookbook. It gives instructions on how to prepare different kinds of foods. Let's see what it says about pancakes."

Early Literacy Component: Print Conventions and Awareness

What you need: (*For older children*) Bring in some containers of the ingredients used in making pancakes, or bring in frozen pancakes.

What you do: Point out words on the containers.

What you say: "What do you think this container has in it? What makes you think that? What clues do you see on the label?"

Early Literacy Component: Letter Knowledge

What you need: (*For infants and toddlers*) Ball and blocks

What you do: (*For infants and toddlers*) As the child is feeling a ball or blocks, talk about the shapes.

(*For preschoolers*) Say the rhyme together. You can substitute whatever letter you are playing with for the letter *A*. You might use the first letter of each child's name. Draw the letter in the air as you say it. Show them the difference between a "great" letter and a "little" letter.

What you say: (*For infants and toddlers*) "A ball is round; this block is a triangle." (*Also describe objects, talk about the textures and colors, and how two items are alike and different.*)

(*For preschoolers*) You can see the difference between the uppercase or big letter and the lowercase or little one when you draw them in the air.

HICKORY DICKORY DOCK

> Hickory dickory dock
> (*Everyone stands up; swing hands clasped together as a pendulum.*)
> The mouse ran up the clock
> (*Squat down to be the little mouse and then make climbing motion.*)
> The clock struck one (*Do a jumping jack, clapping hands above head.*)
> The mouse ran down
> (*Stand tall with hands in front of mouth like a mouse, then squat down.*)
> Hickory dickory dock (*Swing hands clasped together as a pendulum.*)

Early Literacy Component: Phonological Awareness

What you do: Act out the nursery rhyme. Any rhyme with two characters lends itself to being acted out. Repeat, having children pay attention to the syllables and do motions in the rhythm of the syllables.

What you say: "Good job on acting out the rhyme. Now let's try it again and do the actions to the rhythm of the words." (*Demonstrate.*)

Early Literacy Component: Vocabulary

What you need: (*For older children*) Bring in a picture of an old-fashioned clock that has a pendulum, along with pictures of a digital clock and a clock with hands, watches, and so on (or the real things, if you have them).

What you say: "There are many different kinds of clocks. What do we use clocks for? That's right, to tell time. (*Make sure to use the names of different kinds of clocks.*) Children learn new vocabulary words more easily when they have an object to associate with the meaning of the word."

Early Literacy Component: Letter Knowledge

What you need: (*For older children*) Bring in a picture of an old-fashioned clock that has a pendulum, along with pictures of a digital clock and a clock with hands, watches, and so on (or the real things, if you have them).

What you say: "How are these clocks alike? How are they different? It is interesting that things that look quite different from each other do the same thing, like tell time."

Early Literacy Component: Background Knowledge

What you do: The adult is one character, and the child another. This is adaptable to any nursery rhyme that has two characters.

(*For toddlers and two-year-olds*): Do this as a fingerplay, first using bent arm as clock and fingers of opposite hand as mouse.

(*For preschoolers*) Do the standing version above. Now have the adults be the clock and children be mice.

What you say: "The grown-up is the clock and the children are the mice. Be careful that the pendulum doesn't strike the mouse!"

Songs, Games, and Movement Activities

Songs and movement activities can be used in a variety of ways:

- as stretches between books
- as transitions between storytime components
- as connections to early literacy components
- as an activity to do after storytime

Songs and movement activities (including fingerplays and stretches) provide a break from sitting still for stories and books, they keep or regain children's attention in a playful way, and they facilitate learning. Songs and movement activities offer opportunities to highlight early literacy components and make learning fun.

When storytime presenters demonstrate song and movement activities and encourage both children and adults to participate, they make it easier for adults to support their children's early literacy development every day. Adults who participate are then able to sing and play with what they learned in storytime.

ANIMAL SOUNDS:
SONG ADAPTATION OF "DID YOU EVER SEE A LASSIE?"

(You can find the tune at www.kidsongs.com/lyrics/did-you-ever-see-a-lassie.html.)

Early Literacy Component:
Phonological Awareness (Environmental Sounds); Vocabulary

Use with: Any book with animals or animal sounds
What you do: Read the book.
What you say: "We are going to sing a song with the different sounds that animals make."

> Did you ever hear a chick, a chick, a chick?
> Did you ever hear a chick peep this way and that?
> Peep this way and that way,
> Peep this way and that way.
> Did you ever hear a chick peep this way and that?

Repeat with other verses, substitution *cat* and *meow*, *dog* and *bark*, *horse* and *neigh*, and *sheep* and *bleat*.

Early Literacy Component: Vocabulary; Background Knowledge

What you do: Decide which verbs you want to use with each animal and how to physically show the movements.
What you say: "There are different ways of describing how animals and people move. We are going to sing a song that uses some of these words."

> Did you ever see a horse, a horse, a horse?
> Did you ever see a horse trot this way and that?
> Trot this way and that way,
> Trot this way and that way.
> Did you ever see a horse trot this way and that?

Did you ever see a snake, a snake, a snake?
Did you ever see a snake slither this way and that?
Slither this way and that way,
Slither this way and that way.
Did you ever see a snake slither this way and that?

Repeat with other verses, substituting *tiger* and *pounce*, *cat* and *prance*, *baby* and *crawl*, and *rabbit* and *hop*.

RHYMING WORDS: SONG ADAPTATION OF "MARY HAD A LITTLE LAMB"

(You can find the tune at http://kids.niehs.nih.gov/games/songs/childrens/maryhadmp3.htm.)

Early Literacy Component: Phonological Awareness (Rhyming)

Use with: Any book

What you do: Read the book. Come back to a page where two words rhyme.
Sing a song to emphasize rhyming words. Or, you can select a word from
the book, one that has a lot of possible rhyming words. Pick a word and
some words that rhyme with it. Sing the song.

What you say: After singing a verse, ask the children to come up with more
words from the same rhyme family. Nonsense words are fine, too.
Or say, "I am going to pick a word from the book. We are going to think of some
words that rhyme with it. We are going to put those words into the rhyming song."

King and *ring* share ending sounds,
Ending sounds,
Ending sounds.
King and *ring* share ending sounds.
Rhymes are all around.

CLAPPING SYLLABLES

Early Literacy Component: Phonological Awareness (Segmentation—breaking words into parts)

Use with: Children's names; book that has multisyllabic words

What you do: Read the book. Go back through it, pointing out the words that you
will play with.

What you say: "We are going to see how many parts (*choose a word from the
book*) can be broken into. For each sound chunk, we are going to clap
(*or jump, or snap fingers*)." Give some examples:

Tur-nip (two claps)

Rose (one clap)

Di-no-saur (three claps)

HIGHLIGHT BEGINNING SOUND: SONG—"HERE WE GO LOOBY LOO"

(You can find the tune at http://kids.niehs.nih.gov/games/songs/childrens/lobbyloomp3.htm.)

Early Literacy Component: Phonological Awareness (Beginning Sounds)

What you do: Decide which beginning sounds you will be playing with. Showing parents that nonsense words can be used in word play can make it more fun.

What you say: "We are going to sing a song. The first time through we will sing using the /l/ sound. Each time after that, we will change some of the words. It will be like this." (*Sing it through.*)

Here we go *looby loo*,

Here we go *looby light*.

Here we go *looby loo*,

All on a Sunday night.

You put your right hand in,

You take your right hand out,

You give your right had a shake, shake, shake,

And you turn yourself around.

Assume, for example, that you are focusing on the /s/ sound:

Here we go sooby soo,

Here we go sooby sight.

Here we go sooby soo,

All on a Saturday night . . .

Continue with other body parts.

NAMES OF BABY ANIMALS:
SONG ADAPTATION OF "FIVE LITTLE DUCKS WENT OUT ONE DAY"

(You can find the tune at www.kididdles.com/lyrics/f005.html.)

Early Literacy Component: Vocabulary; Background Knowledge

Use with: Books with animals or animals and their offspring

What you do: Read the book.

What you say: "Animal babies often have names that are different than their parents' names. For example, a baby dog is a puppy. This book has lots of different animal names in it. After we read it, we are going to sing a song that has different parent and baby names in it."

Five little ducklings went out to play
Over the hill and far away.
Mother Duck said, "Quack, quack, quack."
Four little ducklings came running back.

Five little colts . . .
Mother Mare said, "Neigh, neigh, neigh."
Four little colts came home that day.

Five little foals . . .
Father Stallion said, "Neigh, neigh, neigh."
Four little foals came home that day.

Five little kittens . . .
Mother Cat said, "Meow, meow, meow."
Four little kittens came back somehow.

Five little calves . . .
Mother Cow said, "Moo, moo, moo."
Four little calves came home, too.

NAME THAT BODY PART: ACTION SONG—"THE HOKEY POKEY"

(You can find the tune at http://kids.niehs.nih.gov/games/songs/childrens/hokeymp3.htm.)

Early Literacy Component: Vocabulary

Use with: Books about human or animal bodies, or about clothing

What you do: Decide which body parts or clothes you want to talk about.

What you say: "We are going to do the hokey pokey using different parts of our bodies." Tell and show everyone what the parts are before you start the song. You may need to let them practice before they do the actions as part of the song:

Put your knuckle in, put your knuckle out
Put your knuckle in, and shake it all about.
You do the hokey pokey and you turn yourself around.
That's what it's all about.

Put your ankle in . . .
Put your thigh in . . .
Put your spine in . . .

For clothing, use *collar*, *cuff*, *shoelace*, *belt loop*, and so on. If using animals, say, "Horses, for example, have manes and hooves. Sharks have dorsal fins, snouts, and gills." You can change the name of the animal within the song.

PLAYING WITH PREPOSITIONS GAME

Early Literacy Component: Vocabulary; Background Knowledge (Conceptual Thinking)

Use with: Item from any theme

What you do: Choose a photo or drawing of an object related to the storytime theme. Make enough copies of it to provide one per participant (adults and children). Hand out the pictures. Demonstrate. For example, "I am putting my picture of the apple between my legs." Then have children take turns describing where they are putting their picture and have others copy what that child does. Group members follow each other's directions. For example, if a child says, "Put the leaf on your cheek," every participant puts her leaf on her cheek.

What you say: "Some prepositions, such as *next to*, *in front of*, and *in between*, may be complicated for children and require extra practice."

Additional activity: To encourage greater physical involvement, use a rope or string and have participants stand on it, go around it, and so forth.

RETELLING STORIES:
SONG ADAPTATION OF "THE FARMER IN THE DELL"

(You can find the tune at http://kids.niehs.nih.gov/games/songs/childrens/farmermp3.htm.)

Early Literacy Component: Background Knowledge (Narrative Skills and Book and Story Knowledge)

Use with: Book with a strong narrative line, cumulative tale

What you do: Read the book and tell the story.

What you say: "We are going to retell the story, using this song. It goes like this." From the example below, based on "The Gingerbread Boy," you can get the idea of how this might work. Sing the song as you go back through the book and look at the pictures, or use picture cards or a flannelboard:

The woman baked the cookie.
The woman baked the cookie.
Hi-ho the derry oh!
The woman baked the cookie.

The boy jumped out of the oven.
The boy jumped out of the oven.
Hi-ho the derry oh!
The boy jumped out of the oven.

The cow chased the boy.
The cow chased the boy.
Hi-ho the derry oh!
The cow chased the boy.

LOVE OF READING:
SONG ADAPTATION OF "IF YOU'RE HAPPY AND YOU KNOW IT"

(You can find the tune at www.kididdles.com/lyrics/i007.html.)

Early Literacy Component: Background Knowledge (Print Motivation)

Use with: As opening or closing song, to introduce books, or as an anytime song!

What you do: Introduce the song.

What you say: "Let's sing a song about how much we enjoy books."

If you love to read books,
Clap your hands. (*Clap, clap.*)
If you love to read books,
Clap your hands. (*Clap, clap.*)
If you love to read books,
Then your brain will surely know it. (*Tap your head.*)
If you love to read books,
Clap your hands. (*Clap, clap.*)

If you love to read books,
Shout hooray. (*"Hooray!"*)
If you love to read books,
Shout hooray. (*"Hooray!"*)
If you love to read books,
Then your brain will surely know it. (*Tap your head.*)
If you love to read books,
Shout hooray. (*"Hooray!"*)

FONTS IN BOOKS

Early Literacy Component: Print Conventions and Awareness

Use with: Books in which the fonts convey meaning

What you do: Read a book in which any of the following occur:

- Print matches the word it describes, such as shaky print that spells the word *spooky*.
- Print moves across the page in irregular ways.
- Text is set in a variety of typefaces—modern, old-fashioned, simple, elaborate, jagged, flowing.
- The book uses words that contain letters of different sizes.

What you say: Before, during, or after reading the book, talk about the different kinds of print while pointing out the typeface.

PLAYING WITH PACKAGING FOR FOOD THEMES

Early Literacy Component: Print Conventions and Awareness

Use with: Themes related to food, including shopping, restaurant, cooking, different kinds of food (e.g., cookies, pizza)

What you do: Bring in containers, sale papers from the grocery store, pencils or crayons, and scrap paper.

What you say: As children and adults play after storytime: "You can read what is inside of a package by looking at the pictures of what is inside and by reading the words. Adults, see what your children can tell you by looking at the containers." You can add writing to play by having pencils or crayons and paper to make lists and signs.

NAME TAGS AND NAME WRITING

Early Literacy Component: Print Conventions and Awareness

Use with: Any storytime

What you do: Have materials available so adults and children can make name tags. If you do not have materials for each person to have a name tag or if the group is too large, consider having several sign-in sheets where participants can write or scribble their names. You can put up mural paper for people to write their names for the whole week—everyone who has come to storytime! Remember, writing can be a drawing, scribble, letter look-alikes, or letters.

What you say: "Please write your names on the name tags. Encourage your child to write his or her own name."

TRANSITIONING:
SONG ADAPTATION OF "LONDON BRIDGE IS FALLING DOWN"

(You can find the tune at www.kididdles.com/lyrics/l037.html.)

Early Literacy Component: Background Knowledge (Print Motivation)

What you do: Use this as a transition song for reading-together time. During or at the end of storytime, the children choose a book from a basket or a display and take it over to their adult for book-sharing time.

What you say: "It's our reading-together time now. Take a few minutes to share a book with your children. You may not finish the whole thing. Today, take time to ask your child an open-ended question, a question that cannot be answered with one word, about one of the pictures."

> Please, won't you read a book with me,
> Book with me, book with me.
> Please, won't you read a book with me.
> Someday, I'll read to you!

As you gather books back:

> Please won't you give the book to me,
> Book to me, book to me
> Please won't you give the book to me
> Now your story's done.

DRAWING SHAPES:
SONG ADAPTATION OF "THERE'S A SPIDER ON THE FLOOR"

(You can find the tune at www.boyscouttrail.com/content/song/song-1325.asp.)

Early Literacy Component: Letter Knowledge (Shapes)

Use with: Book or rhyme with shapes, or just a stretch between books

What you do: Substitute any shape or letter for the word in italics.

What you say: "We are going to draw shapes (or letters) in the air. Here is a *square*. It has four lines for straight sides and all the lines are equal in length."

> Draw a *square* in the air, in the air.
> (*Use your finger to draw a square in the air.*)

Draw a *square* in the air, in the air. (*Draw a square in the air.*)
Draw a *square* in the air. (*Draw a square in the air.*)
Now draw it everywhere. (*Draw squares in several directions.*)
Draw a *square* in the air, in the air. (*Draw a square in the air.*)

DRAWING SHAPES: SONG ADAPTATION OF "THIS OLD MAN"
(You can find the tune at www.kididdles.com/lyrics/t032.html.)

Early Literacy Component: Letter Knowledge (Shapes)
Use with: Book or rhyme with shapes, or just a stretch between books
What you do: Substitute any shape or letter for the word in italics.
What you say: "We are going to draw shapes (or letters) in the air. Here is a *circle*. It is completely round."

Circle is here. (*Draw a circle in the air.*)
Circle is there. (*Draw a circle in the air.*)
Circle is here and it is there. (*Point to where the circles were.*)
With a clap, clap, jump up, and turn yourself around.
Circle is here and everywhere. (*Point to where the circles were.*)

PLAYING WITH LETTERS

Early Literacy Component: Letter Knowledge
Use with: Any book
What you do: Take a letter from the title or a shape you see in a picture of the book. Shapes and letters lend themselves to movement. Take a few minutes to draw the shape or letter you want to focus on, and refer to your drawing as you do the activities. For younger children, you may decide to use shapes only:

- Show participants how to make the shape or letter with their fingers.
- Model how participants can make their entire bodies into the shape or letter. Try it in pairs.
- Draw the shape or letter on your arms or legs and tell participants to do the same.
- Tell children to trace the shape or letter on the back of an adult.
- Tape a large version the shape or letter to the floor, and have the children walk along its outline.

What you say: Explain what you are doing as described above.

SONG: "B-I-N-G-O"

(You can find the tune at http://kids.niehs.nih.gov/games/songs/childrens/bingomp3.htm.)

Early Literacy Component: Letter Knowledge

What you do: Decide which five-letter word you want to substitute for *bingo*.

What you say: "We are going to sing a song, dropping letters as we go along." You may or may not have cards with the letters spelling out the word. If you use cards, children can take turns holding them up or taking them down at the appropriate time. You can use this song to spell and clap out words of varying lengths. You will need to experiment to see how the letters fit the rhythm of the song. For preschoolers you might try the song this way, reversing the letters and claps:

B-*clap-clap-clap-clap*
B-I-*clap-clap-clap*
B-I-N-*clap-clap*
B-I-N-G-*clap*
B-I-N-G-O

This way they get more practice saying the letters as you point to them. It may be challenging at first to those who are used to the traditional way.

There was a farmer had a dog,
And Bingo was his name-O.
B-I-N-G-O!
B-I-N-G-O!
B-I-N-G-O!
And Bingo was his name-O!

Try substitutions like the following:

There is a food I love to eat,
And pizza is its name-O!
And fruit . . .
And apple . . .
And grape . . .

There is a drink I love so much,
And juice is what it's called-O!

There's an animal I love so much,
And puppy's what it's called-O!
And horse is . . .
And kitty's . . .

Craft Activities

Let's look now at the craft activities. Many books and websites offer ideas for crafts for young children. We have chosen to focus on crafts and activities using materials that are readily available and do not cost much. In addition, we have provided variations that make the crafts more open ended. You will notice that some of the ideas are more activity than craft. Participants may not necessarily take home a product but may instead take away an idea for a game to play or something to make at home. This approach supports an open-ended, child-directed orientation to supporting children's language development. Just as any book can support the early literacy components, the same can be said of craft activities. The key to early literacy development is the role that adults play in enriching children's language environment and interactions.

We encourage adults to participate in storytimes for preschoolers. However, for a variety of reasons, some parents or caregivers may not attend. Inviting adults to join the group for the last five to ten minutes of storytime is one way to encourage them to interact with their children around the storytime experience. During this time, you can also suggest specific, simple ways that they can support their children's early literacy development at home with enjoyable activities.

These craft activity ideas can be used during or following storytimes for two- to five-year-olds. The crafts can be adapted for preschoolers of all ages and abilities. The drawings produced by a two-year-old will be more scribbled than those made by a five-year-old, but everyone can enjoy the craft. Adults can be encouraged to help their children in supportive, nonintrusive ways.

Many people search for activities by theme first. Our approach is to start with simple, easily available materials and to brainstorm how they might be used to support early literacy. Because the activities are open ended, they are easy to adapt to a desired theme or book. Typical activities include the following:

- Make a character or an object to talk about or to tell or retell a story.
- Have fun acting out a scene from a book.
- Make a book.
- Make something with shapes.
- Make letters.
- Match shapes, letters, or patterns.
- Make animal sounds.

For each craft or activity we have included the following:

What you need: the materials needed

What you do: instructions on how to make the craft or do the activity

What you say: what the storytime presenter says to the adults and
children and, by extension, what the adults say as they interact
with children

In addition to doing the crafts and activities here, think about the ones you already
do and feel comfortable with. Consider how you might adapt them to focus more
on process over product, adapt them to be more open ended, use them to enrich
children's language experience, or use them to convey early literacy information
to parents and caregivers.

FOLD A CARD

Early Literacy Component: Background Knowledge (Narrative Skills); Print Conventions and Awareness

What you need:

One 3-by-5-inch card per person for each character or item in a book

Crayons or washable markers

What you do: Demonstrate that when you fold the card or paper in half, it stands
up all by itself, like a tent! That piece of paper can then become anything—a person, a truck, a frog, a hat, a sign, a house. Have the participants
fold and draw on their cards to build on a story you have shared with
them. Some children, especially older preschoolers, may enjoy using the
cards to make up their own stories.

What you say: "Fold your cards in half and draw people and things that you
heard about in a storytime story." Comment on the child's drawing, such
as: "Which character are you making there?" or "You are using lots of different colors." Encourage the child to retell the story. "Now you are done
with drawing the characters. Tell me what happened first in the story and
hold up the card. If you like you can put on a little show."

FEELINGS ON A PLATE

Early Literacy Component: Vocabulary

What you need:

Paper plates for each participant

Crayons or washable markers

What you do: Have participants draw a face with a different feeling on each paper plate.

What you say: Have the children talk about the feelings they have drawn. Among the possible questions and comments are "What is this person feeling?" "Oh yes, she looks . . ." "I felt _____ when _____. When have you felt _____?" "Who felt _____ in the story?" Children may converse with the adult who brought them, with other children, and with you. (See the list of words that describe feelings in chapter 9.)

MAKE A BOOK

Early Literacy Component: Background Knowledge (Narrative Skills); Print Conventions and Awareness

Use with: Book or story with strong narrative line, a retellable story

What you need:

Four 3-by-5-inch cards or paper of your choice of size per person

Crayons or washable markers

Stapler (for your use ahead of time)

What you do: Before storytime begins, create booklets by stapling four 3-by-5-inch cards together. During activity time, pass out a stapled booklet to each person.

What you say: "You are going to be creating a book by drawing a picture on each card." Specify a subject, such as the storytime theme or a particular book. Model how to talk about a book by asking children questions about one of the pictures. Ask them to tell you about what they have drawn. Model leaving the child enough time to respond. Then have adults talk about what they have drawn in their books and have them ask their children questions about the drawings in their booklets. Encourage parents to save both their children's booklets and their own for further discussion at home.

CONCENTRATION GAME

Early Literacy Component: Phonological Awareness (Rhyming or Beginning Sounds)

What you need:

Three cards or pieces of paper for each person (or more, depending on the children's ages and the desired level of difficulty)

Pictures cut from magazines or clip art

Glue

What you do: Have the group play a game of concentration using picture cards of words that rhyme. Depending on the group and the time available, children and their adults may work together to create their cards, or you may make all cards in advance. If participants make their own playing materials, give each person three cards and give each child-adult pair some glue and a batch of pictures, making sure that each batch contains at least three pairs of pictures depicting words that rhyme. If you have already made the cards, give three pairs of rhyming pictures to each child-adult pair.

What you say: If participants make their own cards, ask the child-adult pairs to look through their pictures and pick two that contain words that rhyme. Tell the adult to glue one of the pictures to a card and to help the child glue the other picture to one of his or her cards. They should repeat the process with different rhyming words until they have made three sets of cards.

To play concentration, the pairs place all their cards face down. One player turns over a card and says what the picture is. The same person turns over another card and says what the picture is. If the items in the pictures rhyme, the person keeps the cards. If not, the player turns the cards face down again, and the other player takes a turn. Play continues until all the cards have been matched.

Point out that as children turn the cards over and name the objects, adults can repeat the words clearly and slowly to help children determine whether or not they rhyme. If the child says that two words rhyme when they don't, the adult can say, "No, *bug* and *bee* do not rhyme; they don't sound alike at the end. Let's think of a word that does rhyme with *bug: rug, plug, tug.*"

You can do this same activity matching beginning sounds.

BINOCULARS

Early Literacy Component: Phonological Awareness; Vocabulary; Background Knowledge

What you need:

Two toilet-paper rolls per person
Tape or rubber bands for adults to
   band rolls together

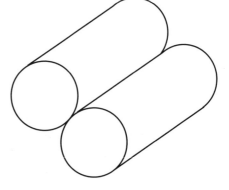

What you do: Bring in a pair of binoculars, if possible. Have the group use toilet-paper rolls and tape or rubber bands to make binoculars. Pass out two toilet-paper rolls per person.

What you say: Explain what binoculars do. Tell participants they will make something that looks like binoculars using toilet-paper rolls. Tell adults that children can hold their two toilet-paper rolls together, side by side, so that they can wrap tape or rubber bands around them to hold them together. Then encourage participants to look through their binoculars at the world around them. Note that real binoculars magnify things and make them look closer. However, even though handmade binoculars don't do that, it's still possible to focus on lots of things. Demonstrate several activities that adults can then do with the children.

As the children look through their binoculars, ask, "What do you see?" Then say, "Tell me about it." Have the children continue looking at and describing objects and people in the room. Add some information to what the children say.

Look around for words that rhyme with a given word: "I spy something yellow that rhymes with *bug—rug*!"

Optional: Cover one end of the binoculars with colored cellophane. As the children look through their binoculars, have them talk about what they see through the colors.

WRITE A MESSAGE

Early Literacy Component: Print Conventions and Awareness; Letter Knowledge

What you need:

> One piece of paper or half a piece of paper for each person
> Pencils, crayons, or washable markers

What you do: Write or draw on the piece of paper.

What you say: "Adults, you are going to write a message and see if your child can figure out what it says." The "message" can be in words, pictures, or both—for example, the words "I love you" and a heart. The child reads the message and then writes a message on his or her piece of paper. It may be squiggles; that's fine. The child reads his or her message to the adult.

DRAW PARTS OF THE BODY

Early Literacy Component: Vocabulary; Background Knowledge

Use with: Book or theme of body parts

What you need:

> One piece of paper per person (to trace the child's entire body, you
>   can buy butcher or art paper by the roll)
> Crayons or washable markers

What you do: Child places hand on paper. Adult (or child, if able) traces around the open hand. Label the different parts of the hand: thumb, index finger, middle finger, ring finger, and pinkie. Also use words like *palm*, *heel*,

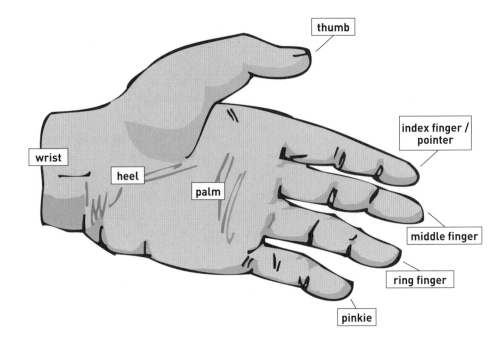

wrist, knuckle, nail, cuticle, and vein. With large pieces of paper, like mural paper, you can do the same thing tracing the whole body.

What you say: Point to one of the fingers and say, "What is this finger called? That's right, your thumb. Do you know what this is called? (*Point to a knuckle.*) Did you know that not only your foot has a heel, but your hand does, too, right above your wrist. You can press down on things very hard with the heel of your hand."

PLATEFUL OF FOOD

Early Literacy Component: Vocabulary; Phonological Awareness (Beginning Sounds)

Use with: Books or theme of food, shopping, eating

What you need:

Paper plates, one per person

Scissors

Newspaper advertisements of food

What you do: Give each person a plate and some pages of ads. Give scissors to each child-adult pair.

What you say: "Let's look for your favorite foods to cut out and put on your plate." You might ask why children like a particular food. Use synonyms to help them describe them: *delicious, scrumptious, delightful.*

Or alternatively, say that you are looking for foods that start with a particular sound. These are the foods that children will cut out and put on their plates.

MAKE YOUR OWN PUZZLE

Early Literacy Component: Letter Knowledge
Use with: Any book or theme
What you need:
>Paper plate or piece of thin cardboard, one per person
>Old book jackets, copies of book jackets, or other pictures
>Scissors
>Glue

What you do: In advance, cut out the picture and glue it to the middle of a paper plate or cardboard. Give each participant a plate or piece of cardboard with the picture on it. Ask adults to help children cut the plate into pieces to make a puzzle. Cut fewer or more puzzle pieces according to the child's abilities.

What you say: First, talk about the picture on the whole plate. Ask open-ended questions, like "What is this called?" And then affirm children's answers: "That's right, this is a . . ." Then describe the picture more, adding adjectives to your description. Then say, "Now let's take the puzzle apart and see if you can put it together again. Look! You made your own puzzle. You can make more at home."

MAKE YOUR OWN BLOCKS

Early Literacy Component: Vocabulary; Background Knowledge
Use with: Books or themes about building, size, position
What you need:
>Cereal, shoe, and oatmeal boxes
>Contact paper or clear book tape (to make the boxes sturdier),
>   optional
>Tape

What you do: Put the boxes out for the children to play with. Encourage stacking, building, and knocking over (with permission of the builder, of course).

What you say: It might be easiest to start out building towers. Make comments like, "Which box should we put on the bottom? Why? Let's see what happens if we put a little one on the bottom." Talk about the size and position of boxes—on top of, underneath, and so on.

BOXES AS INSTRUMENTS

Early Literacy Component: Phonological Awareness

What you need:

Empty cylindrical oatmeal containers

Paper to wrap them in, optional

What you do: Encourage everyone to bang the tops of the boxes, as if they were drums. Put on some music, if you want, and bang away to the rhythm of the music! Now stop and see how softly you can tap the boxes. "How does it sound if you tap with one finger, with all your fingers, with the flat palm of your hand? Can you follow my rhythm—start simple!"

What you say: You can vary the sound by putting lids on boxes and putting things in them. Also, different-sized boxes make different kinds of sounds!

COOKIE-CUTTER PUZZLE MATCH

Early Literacy Component: Letter Knowledge

What you need:

Cardboard in different colors

Cookie cutters

Washable markers

Scissors

What you do: In advance, trace the cookie-cutter shapes onto cardboard or paper, several copies of each. Cut them out. Each adult-child pair chooses three or four of these cutouts. Pass out a sheet of cardboard and have markers available. Adults trace the cookie-cutter shapes they chose with a wide marker onto the cardboard sheet. This is the tray, or bottom part, of a matching puzzle game. Children match the cutout shape to the outline on the cardboard sheet. You can also encourage adults to put the shapes into a pattern that children can match and then make on their own.

What you say: Talk about the different shapes of the pieces. Talk about the similarities and differences in the pieces. You can match them by color, shape, or category (e.g., animals, people, toys).

MAKE YOUR OWN LOTTO GAME

Early Literacy Component: Vocabulary; Phonological Awareness (Rhyming and Beginning Sounds)

What you need:

> Use the website www.dltk-cards.com/bingo/ to make lotto cards, choosing the theme or printing blanks
>
> Cardboard approximately 6 inches by 8½ inches, or to fit your printout

What you do: Play lotto (or bingo) by passing out one card to each person. Pass out "markers," which can be large buttons or circles, to each person, enough for one per square, depending on how many squares in the cards you made (e.g., three by three, four by four). The fewer the squares, the easier and shorter the game is.

For vocabulary, using your pieces of all the pictures, hold up and then name and talk about the pictures, using synonyms and some adjectives to describe the picture. Now place all your pieces face down. Turn over one piece. Have a child say what it is and have everyone look for it on their card. If they have it, they cover it with one of their markers.

For phonological awareness (rhyming), using your pieces of all the pictures, hold up each one and say the name of the picture. Have the children think of words that rhyme with that word. They can be silly words, too! Place all your pieces face down. Turn over one piece, but do not show it to participants. Think of a word that rhymes with the picture you picked up and say it to the group. If they have a picture that rhymes with your word, they cover it with one of their markers.

For phonological awareness (beginning sounds), using your pieces of all the pictures, hold up each one and say the name of the picture. Say the beginning sound. Have children think of words that start with the same sound. Place all your pieces face down. Turn over one piece, but do not show it to the participants. Think of a word that starts with the same sound as the picture you picked up and say it to the group. If they have a picture of a word that starts with that sound, they cover it with one of their markers.

Players complete lotto when they have covered all the space in a row (horizontally or vertically or diagonally) or when they have covered the whole card. Everyone claps for the winner!

You can make sets of cards and put them in plastic bags and have adults and children play in pairs or small groups.

What you say: "Playing games with your preschool children helps them think in many different ways. Play a game just long enough for them to enjoy it."

COLLAGE OF SHAPES

Early Literacy Component: Letter Knowledge (Shapes); Background Knowledge (Conceptual Thinking)

Use with: Any book or theme

What you need:

> Construction paper of different colors, cut into shapes
>
> Paper, one sheet per participant
>
> Glue

What you do: After reading a book, talk about the shapes in one or two of the pictures. Hand out a sheet of paper to each person. Lay out the paper shapes and have participants make a picture using the shapes. The pictures could be related to the theme. For example, they could make animals out of shapes, boats, trees, houses, and so on.

What you say: "Adults, your children may make a picture of something or a design. Have your child describe his or her picture. Talk about what you see. Then talk about your own picture and what you made."

You will have many more ideas of ways to enhance your storytimes using rhymes, flannelboards, songs, movement, and craft activities. Pointing out the connection between these activities and later reading helps parents and caregivers see how play and playful interactions with their children go a long way to supporting later reading.

NOTE

1. L. J. Harper, "Nursery Rhyme Knowledge and Phonological Awareness in Preschool Children," *Journal of Language and Literacy Education* 7, no. 1 (2011): 65–78, http://jolle.coe.uga.edu/archive/2011_1/harper.pdf.

chapter 12

Early Literacy
Asides

THIS CHAPTER PROVIDES SOME EXAMPLES OF EARLY LITERACY ASIDES THAT YOU CAN use in your storytimes. It is important that asides are effective in communicating to adults the role that they play in helping their children get ready to read.

An effective aside gives a research-based reason for why or how an activity (e.g., playing rhyming games, saying a repeated phrase) or practice (e.g., singing, talking, reading, writing, playing) supports an early literacy component or reading skill (e.g., decoding, or recognizing words and relating letters and sounds to formulate words; comprehension, or understanding what is being read). An ineffective aside is "Singing will help your children learn to read." This type of aside is too general; it does not give a reason for why the practice is important. An effective aside is "Singing slows down language so children hear the smaller sounds in words. This will help them later to sound out words when they learn to read." Another effective aside is "Singing with children helps them to hear the smaller sounds in words because there is often a different note for each syllable. This skill (is called phonological awareness, and it) will help them when they try to sound out words as they learn to read."

For the purpose of conveying the research, we have used the term *early literacy components*, particularly because background knowledge is not a skill, but the result of several skills. When speaking with adults, it may be easier to use the term *skill* instead of *component* in the asides. Whichever approach you decide on, leading with the component or the practice, the aside must be an effective one.

Until we become comfortable with new information, it helps to have a kind of script of what we want to tell others. Perhaps some of the following suggestions will be helpful. *Feel free to reword them to suit your own style.* These suggestions are not meant to be limiting. We have written the asides in a variety of styles to show that there is more than one way to state research, so there is some repetition. You can share your own early literacy asides based on information you have gathered by reading books or articles.

Because the practices are directly tied back to the components via effective asides, they are not dealt with separately in this list. The words for the five practices (sing, talk, read, write, play) are in boldface when information is given on how that practice supports early literacy or later reading. The word for the practice does not appear in bold if it is only mentioned. In this chapter, parentheses indicate optional wording. We also suggest the age of the child for whom the aside works best.

The designations represent stages: early talker (ET) for newborn to two-year-olds, talker (T) for two- and three-year-olds, and prereaders (PR) for four- and five-year-olds.

Asides That Support Phonological Awareness

1. Researchers have found that one of the early literacy skills children need to be able to learn to read is (phonological awareness,) the ability to hear and play with the smaller sounds in words. There are many ways to help your children hear sounds as you sing, talk, read, write, and play with them throughout the day. Today in storytime I'll point out some ways to help children with [choose one] rhyming words, (or) breaking words into syllables, (or) hearing the beginning sounds in words. (ET, T, PR)

2. Hearing the rhythm of language when you read or say rhymes with your children contributes to phonological awareness, or the ability to hear the smaller sounds in words. It is one of the skills that researchers have found helps children sound out words when they learn to read. (ET, T, PR)

3. Saying the sounds that animals make and encouraging your children to make those sounds is the beginning of (phonological awareness, or) hearing the smaller sounds in words. This will help them as they decode or sound out words once they are learning how to read. (ET, T, PR)

4. **Singing** nursery rhymes helps children get ready to read. Listening to rhymes helps them hear the smaller sounds in words (develop phonolog-

---

ET = early talker (newborn to two years old), **T** = talker (two to three years old), **PR** = prereader (four to five years old); **[ ]** = directions to presenter, **( )** = optional

ical awareness. Phonological awareness is the term used for the ability to hear and play with sounds in words), an important skill for learning to read. (ET, T)

5. **Talking** with your babies is so important—they need to hear the sounds of your language! Until about six months of age your babies are "universal linguists." They can tell the difference among each of the 150 sounds of human speech. By twelve months, they recognize the speech sounds of only the languages they hear being spoken by the people who talk and play with them. Hearing the smaller sounds of words is called phonological awareness. It's key to learning how to read. (ET)

6. Saying nursery rhymes is one good way for your children to hear the sounds of language, which will help them break words into parts when they are learning how to read. If you are comfortable talking with your children in a language other than English, **talk** with them in that language, so they hear its sounds. (ET, T, PR)

7. [When using a big book with infants] You know that high-pitched voice we use with babies and puppies? It's called "parentese." **Talking** with babies this way helps them get ready to read. Don't worry about whether or not your children can see this big book. We'll read it together. Your children love the sound of your voice. Children need to hear the difference between sounds to be able to decode or sound out words when they are reading. (ET)

8. Researchers find that speaking in "parentese," that high-pitched, slow voice we use with babies and puppies, keeps your babies' attention longer than using your regular voice until they are about nine months old. The rhythm of words is part of (phonological awareness, or) the ability to hear and play with the smaller sounds in words. Children need to be taught this skill to learn to read. Watch your children as we read the book together. (ET)

9. [Rhyming book] **Reading** and **talking** about what you read help your children get ready to read. After you've read a rhyming book with your children, come back to a page with rhyming words and talk about two words that rhyme. Children sometimes like to fill in the rhyming word, especially if they have heard the book before. If your children are able, then stop just before you say the second word of the rhyming pair and let your children fill in the word. Recognizing and making rhymes will help them sound out words, which is part of getting ready to read. (T, PR)

10. **Talking** about words that rhyme helps children become more aware of the smaller sounds in words, (which is the early literacy skill of phonolog-

---

ET = early talker (newborn to two years old), **T** = talker (two to three years old),
PR = prereader (four to five years old); **[ ]** = directions to presenter, **( )** = optional

ical awareness,) which will help them decode, or figure out, a word when they are reading. Pick a word (*tree*) and see if your children can think of a rhyming word. If that is too hard, then see if your children can recognize a rhyming word, which is easier—does *tree* rhyme with *cat*? Does *tree* rhyme with *me*? (T, PR)

11. Even though young children do not understand the meanings of the rhymes, it is important for them to hear them. By six months babies are already able to recognize the sounds of the languages that you use when you **talk** with them. Talking with your babies makes their brains more efficient in processing and learning the languages they hear. You are helping them get ready to read. (ET)

12. Rhyming is one way children learn to hear that words are made up of smaller parts. By saying rhymes and **singing** songs with your children, you are supporting phonological awareness. This will help them when they later try to sound out words to read. (ET, T, PR)

13. One way that you support phonological awareness, or hearing the smaller sounds in words, starts with just hearing sounds. When you are **playing** or **reading** together, you can say animal sounds, the sounds of cars, a door-bell, any sound, and have your children try to repeat what you say. Did you know that different languages have different words for the sounds animals make? These activities are helping your child hear words in a way that will help him or her decode words while learning how to read. (ET, T)

14. **Playing** rhyming games in the car, while waiting for an appointment, or anywhere, can be a fun way to help your children hear the smaller sounds in words. Remember, children can recognize a rhyme before they can make the rhyme. So, if it's too hard to make rhymes, let them start by hearing rhymes and recognizing them. For example, the question "Does *cat* rhyme with *bat*?" is easier for young children to answer than the question, "What rhymes with *cat*?" Children not only enjoy playing with words and their sounds, but these activities will help them when they have to decode or sound out words as readers. (T, PR)

15. You may not know it, but **singing** songs with your baby or toddler helps him or her hear words being broken up into smaller sounds, because often each syllable has its own note. (This skill is part of phonological awareness.) You are helping your children get ready to read! (ET, T)

16. Preschoolers love being silly, and this includes being silly with words. You can play with words—making up nonsense words as you make up as many rhymes to one word as you can. Hearing those smaller sounds in

---

ET = early talker (newborn to two years old), **T** = talker (two to three years old),
PR = prereader (four to five years old); **[ ]** = directions to presenter, **( )** = optional

words is an important part of being able to sound out words when they learn to read. (PR)

17. [When using *The Eeensy Weensy Spider*, by Maryann Hoberman (Little, Brown, 2004), or piggyback songbook of your choice] **Singing** helps children hear the smaller sounds in words (which is part of the early literacy skill of phonological awareness). One way to sing songs is to share songbooks together. Preschoolers and older children often like to make up their own verses. By choosing sentences that fit the rhythm of the song and that use rhyming words, they have fun while developing phonological awareness. This will help them decode or sound out words once they are learning to read. (T, PR)

18. **Sing** to your children, even if you don't have perfect pitch. In songs, each syllable often has a different note. Without really thinking about it, children are hearing words being broken down into parts. This helps them when they have to sound out words when they are learning how to read. (ET, T, PR)

19. **Singing** slows down language. Let's say the words to this song [example: "London Bridge Is Falling Down"]. Now let's sing the song. Hear the difference in the ways we say and sing the words? Because children can hear the sounds of the words more easily when you are singing, you are helping them develop [phonological awareness,] the ability to hear and play with the smaller sounds in words, which will help them when they are decoding, or sounding out words. (ET, T)

20. Today we are going to play with the sounds in the song "Row, Row, Row Your Boat." We are going to be changing the first sounds in words and breaking words into their smaller parts. These skills are part of (phonological awareness, or) the ability to hear and play with the smaller sounds in words. These are skills that will help the children once they have to try to sound out words later when they learn to read. Let's sing together and you'll see what I mean! (PR)

21. Changing the beginning sound in a word helps children understand that words are made up of sounds. This will help them when they need to sound out words when they are reading. Four- and five-year-olds enjoy silliness, including nonsense words. We can mix in wordplay when we talk with our children. (PR)

22. At home, have your children think of other words that start with the same sound as the first sound in your children's names. Remember to focus on sounds, not letters! Good phonological skills, or the ability to hear and

ET = early talker (newborn to two years old), **T** = talker (two to three years old), **PR** = prereader (four to five years old); **[ ]** = directions to presenter, **( )** = optional

play with the smaller sounds in words, is a hallmark of good readers and helps them decode words when reading. Children learn best by doing activities that have meaning to them. (PR)

23. (When we separate a word into its sounds it is called segmentation, which is part of phonological awareness, one of the skills that researchers say that children need to get ready to read.) Doing things like clapping out the parts of words will help your children later when they have to break words into syllables as a way of sounding out (or decoding) words. (PR)

24. Take advantage of every opportunity to play with rhyme and the sounds of words. Hearing the smaller sounds in words is helping your children get ready to read. It will also help them to decode words once they are reading. Plus it's fun! Enjoy your time this week as you rhyme around town with your children! (T, PR)

25. Take advantage of every opportunity to play with words. Make up rhyming riddles or play the game I Spy with beginning sounds or rhymes as you wait in the doctor's office or anywhere else. Not only will your children learn to hear sounds in words, which helps them get ready to read, but also it will lessen the boredom and tension of waiting! When you **play** with your children like this you are helping them get ready to decode, or figure out what words are, when they learn to read. (T, PR)

26. We are going to clap out the syllables in everybody's names as part of the introduction. Clapping names helps children hear words divided into parts. This fun activity helps develop (their phonological awareness, or) breaking words into parts. This is one of the skills that researchers say is important for children to be able to learn to read. There are lots of ways for us to play with words with our children. (PR)

27. Here's a sheet with the words to the songs and rhymes we did today. We will repeat many of them next week as well as do some new ones. Keep **singing** and saying your favorites with your children. This is one way to strengthen (their phonological awareness, or) hearing smaller sounds in words. This is an important skill that will help your children sound out words when they learn to read. (ET)

28. During the day, stop for a moment and listen to the sounds around you. Ask your children what they hear and talk about it. Try to imitate the sounds you are hearing. Even little activities like this one help your children develop (phonological awareness,) the ability to hear and play with the smaller sounds in words, which will help your child sound out words when reading. (ET, T, PR)

ET = early talker (newborn to two years old), **T** = talker (two to three years old), **PR** = prereader (four to five years old); **[ ]** = directions to presenter, **( )** = optional

29. The roots of phonemic awareness, hearing each individual sound in a word, can be found in the nursery rhymes, movements, and word games that we play with our kids. Just by singing songs and playing with words we are helping them get ready to read because they will be better able to decode the written word. (ET, T)

30. Remember, with rhyming we concentrate only on the sounds, not on how things are spelled. In English, the spelling and the sound don't always match. Rhyming words don't have to make sense, so there's lots of room for silliness and wordplay all through the day while you're developing your children's (phonological awareness, or the) ability to hear and play with the smaller sounds in words, which will help them sound out words as a reader. In other words, you can use nonsense words, too! (T, PR)

Asides That Support Print Conventions and Print Awareness

1. Print awareness includes knowing how to handle a book and noticing print all around us. It is one of the skills researchers say is important to know before children learn to read. As you talk, sing, read, play, and write with your children throughout the day, you can find ways to help your children become aware of print. I'll point out some of the ways you can do this in storytime today. (ET, T, PR)

2. [When using a book with fonts that support word meaning or expression—large font for yelling, for example] We want children to understand print awareness, which is knowing that print has meaning. When we talk about the words on the page as we read them, children make the connection between the written word and the meaning of the word, which is helping them get ready to read. (T, PR)

3. [When reading a book by Mo Willems or other title that uses callouts or dialogue bubbles, read the book. Come back to a page with a callout bubble.] This callout bubble is showing us that this character is talking. Whenever you see that, that's what the bubble means. Adults, by pointing this out, you are showing your children a convention of print that will make it easier for them to understand how print works as they learn to read later on.

4. When children are young, they treat books as they would any other toy— they play with them! They might put them in their mouths and explore

---

ET = early talker (newborn to two years old), **T** = talker (two to three years old), **PR** = prereader (four to five years old); **[ ]** = directions to presenter, **( )** = optional

them by pushing and pulling and sometimes tearing them. When you let your young children explore and play with books, they are learning how to handle them. Keep some books in their toy box. You are helping your children develop print awareness because they are learning how books work. This is one of the skills that researchers have shown is an important part of a strong foundation for reading. (ET)

5. Today's early literacy skill is focusing on print awareness, or helping your children understand that print has meaning, one of the skills researchers say helps kids get ready to read. We see print all around us—on signs, T-shirts, banners, flyers—this is called environmental print. When your children notice a stop sign or the sign for your favorite restaurant, that's print awareness. They are "reading" the sign! (T)

6. [When demonstrating with a board book with one picture per page] Babies like books that have pictures of things that are familiar to them. Here is one with a picture of an apple. You can talk about the apple in the picture. Then get a real apple and show it to your children. Talk about how it tastes (sweet, tart), how it feels (round and smooth), how it feels when you bite it (crunchy). By showing children the real object, you are helping them realize that pictures represent real things. This will help them learn later that printed words represent real things. (ET)

7. When you are reading with your child, you can run your finger under the words of the title or a repeated phrase as you say it. This helps children understand that you are reading the text, not the pictures. (T, PR)

8. Did you all pick up (or write) a name tag? When we do things like make grocery lists or use name tags, the children see that print has a purpose. This helps them develop print awareness, one of the early literacy skills children need to have to be ready to read. (T, PR)

9. As you read books with your children, even babies, they will try turning the pages of the book. Even though they might not be too coordinated yet and even though it may take a little longer to share the book, taking the time to let them turn the pages develops their print awareness, or knowing how a book works. (ET)

10. I pointed to some of the words as we read them. I did that not just to help us read together but also because pointing to the words helps children understand that we are reading the text, not the pictures. (ET)

11. When we read picture books to children, researchers have found that 95 percent of their attention is on the pictures. By occasionally pointing to the words in the book, you are helping them realize that it is the text

ET = early talker (newborn to two years old), **T** = talker (two to three years old), **PR** = prereader (four to five years old); **[ ]** = directions to presenter, **( )** = optional

we are reading, not the pictures. Pictures are wonderful, of course! (PR)

12. [Example: *Bunny Cakes*, by Rosemary Wells (Puffin, 2000)] Here is a book where writing is important to the story. You can have your children draw pictures and "write" lists. They become aware that print is related to the spoken word—which is print awareness. (T, PR)

13. When you read with your children, from time to time hold the book upside down or backward. See if children notice that it is upside down. If not, point it out. Children need to know how to hold a book, which part is the cover, which part is the back of the book. This is one fun way to find out if they know this; it is a part of being ready to read. (T, PR)

14. Our early literacy tip today is on print awareness, one of the early literacy skills children need before they learn to read. **Reading** with children and helping them become comfortable with turning pages and seeing how books work is the beginning of print awareness. (ET, T, PR)

15. Have your children draw a picture. When they tell you about it, write down their words. This helps them understand that the written word represents the spoken word, one aspect of print awareness. (T, PR)

16. Children can learn the connection between the written and spoken word, print awareness, with this activity. Have your children tell you a story or something they have learned. Write down what they say as they tell it to you. You and your children can make your own books by stapling sheets of paper together. Then have your children read the book (tell the story) to you. (T, PR)

17. You can help your children see the relationship between the written and spoken word by using what is called environmental print, or words that are part of everyday life, like signs and labels that you can point out to your children as you read them. This is part of print awareness, a skill children need to be ready to read. (T, PR)

18. **Writing**, including scribbling, is one way to develop print awareness. Encourage your child to "read" to you what he or she has written. This helps to reinforce that writing and print have meaning, which is something children need to know to be ready to read.

19. **Writing** can be very motivating. When children write their own words, in whatever style they can, they start to see the connection between the spoken and the written word. Encourage your children to write. Begin by making a shopping list together the next time you go shopping. Doing things like this helps them see the relationship between letters and sounds too. All of this helps them get ready to learn how to read. (T, PR)

ET = early talker (newborn to two years old), **T** = talker (two to three years old), **PR** = prereader (four to five years old); **[ ]** = directions to presenter, **( )** = optional

20. Talk about writing when you make and send greeting cards. Have your child help and remember to ask her to sign his or her name along with yours! Don't worry if it is not legible. Your child is getting the idea that what he or she writes means something. Knowing that words have meaning is part of getting ready to read. (T, PR)

21. When children are playing, see how you might add print to their play. For example, if they are playing restaurant, you might ask them the name of the restaurant and then have them write it on a sign. You could add menus and a pad and pencil to have them take orders. There are lots of ways to add print to play.

22. Talk about the labels on containers. Even though children may not read letters, they can tell you what is in a container by looking at the logos and pictures on the box or can, which is supporting print awareness.

Asides That Support Letter Knowledge

1. Letter knowledge is knowing that letters are different from one another and that the same letter can be written in different ways. It also includes knowing that letters represent sounds. There are lots of fun things that you can do to help your children develop letter knowledge—by singing, talking, reading, writing, and playing with them. I'll mention a few of these as we go through out storytime today. (ET, T, PR)

2. One of the five early literacy components is letter knowledge. This means recognizing letters and the names of the letters and knowing that they represent a sound. **Reading** alphabet books is one way to help children become aware of letters and how they look. It is best not to quiz your children on the letters. Instead, start with the letters in your child's name. Knowing letters and their sounds will help them when they are learning how to decode and sound out words once they are reading. (PR)

3. You don't need an alphabet book to talk about letters. Take any book you are reading with your child and look for the first letter, or any letter, in his or her name. Knowing the letters of the alphabet and the sounds they make is an important first step in getting ready to read. (PR)

4. Many alphabet books do not really tell a story. When you and your child are reading that kind of book together, you don't need to read it from beginning to end. Instead, ask your child to choose a page that looks interesting to him or her. Talk about the letter and the picture(s) that go

ET = early talker (newborn to two years old), **T** = talker (two to three years old), **PR** = prereader (four to five years old); **[ ]** = directions to presenter, **( )** = optional

with it. Learning the alphabet should be a fun part of getting ready to read. (T, PR)

5. The letter your child is likely to be the most interested in is the first letter of his or her name. You can help your child learn that letter by pointing it out when you see it in a book or on a sign when you are doing errands or shopping. Learning how to read and write one's own name is an important step in learning the alphabet and in getting ready to read. (T, PR)

6. Letter knowledge starts with seeing and recognizing shapes. A baby playing with a ball feels its roundness. Later that will mean a circle and then the letter *O*. Lots of letters use the circle shape. Others use triangles or other shapes. Researchers have found that children identify letters by their shapes. Playing and exploring are a part of learning how to read! (ET)

7. To identify letters, children have to be able to distinguish things that are alike and different. For example a lowercase *n* and a lowercase *h* look almost the same—just the height of the line is different. So, noticing things that are alike and different and playing matching games helps later with letter knowledge, a prereading skill. (ET, T)

8. Young children learn through their senses. Touching, smelling, and tasting are as important as hearing and seeing. Give your children opportunities to feel different textures and shapes. When you talk with them, ask questions like, "What feels the same, what feels different?" These experiences help them later when they are trying to make out differences in the shapes of letters. (So, now as we play with these shakers, let them feel the shape and the texture. If their hands are too small to hold them, roll them on their bodies.) These activities are laying the foundation for knowing the difference between letters, a part of getting ready to read. (ET)

9. What is the beginning of letter knowledge for very young children? It is not doing letter flash cards with your baby. Babies learn through all their senses. Letting your children feel shapes will later help them make out shapes in letters. Talking to your children about what is alike and different in pictures or in the things you see around you helps your children distinguish similarities and differences, which will help later in distinguishing differences in letters. In order to be able to read, they need to understand this important concept. (ET, T)

10. You can name the letters and their sounds whenever you see them and wherever you go! Even using signs, like stop signs, when you are playing

ET = early talker (newborn to two years old), **T** = talker (two to three years old), **PR** = prereader (four to five years old); **[ ]** = directions to presenter, **( )** = optional

with your child or driving or walking around helps children learn letters, which is part of being ready to read. (T, PR)

11. Before children learn actual letters, they are aware of shapes. Before they have the coordination to hold a crayon and write, they can move their whole arms and bodies. Let's see you make a circle shape with your whole body! There are so many ways to help our children get ready to read! (T, PR)

12. Talk about subjects your children are interested in. Then show them the letters in those words—like *motorcycle* or *princess*. Children are more likely to remember letters when they have to do with things they are interested in than if you drill them with flash cards. Getting ready to read should be fun, not a chore! (PR)

13. Point out and talk about letters and their sounds wherever you go. The most interesting letters for most children are the ones in their names, so begin there and have fun! Children feel so proud when they can read their own names, when they are on the road to reading. (PR)

14. Children can learn letters in many ways that are fun and that will keep their attention. For example, they can make letters using their bodies and then their fingers. They can draw letters in the water when they take a bath, with chalk on the sidewalk, or with playdough. Keep it fun. Talk about the letters in your children's names or in the names of a topic they might be interested in (e.g., trucks, volcanoes, kittens). Learning letters helps them decode or read words once they are in school.

15. Research indicates that children benefit most from learning both the sound and the letter name at the same time. When you teach children letters, explain that the letter is called (name of letter) and represents the sound (name of sound). Start with letters that have meaning to your children (like those in their own name). You can write them on paper or in the air as you say them, too. Knowing letters and the sounds they represent will help them when they have to decode words they are reading. (PR)

16. Eventually, your children will be writing letters. Writing starts with scribbling, so encourage your child to draw. Learning how to read requires many different skills. This is one of them! (T)

17. Children learn best by doing. Remember that playing with letters should be meaningful to them. Show your kids letters that have to do with objects and words that they know and are interested in—what letters are in the word *motorcycle*? (PR)

18. Singing the alphabet song is one way that children learn the names of the letters. Lots of children know the song but have no idea what the letters

are. Saying the names of letters, even by rote, is a first step to learning letters. You can sing the alphabet to different tunes—try singing it to "Mary Had a Little Lamb." It's not as easy as it sounds! Let's try it together. (PR)

19. When your children are playing, think about what words you might write or what signs you can make to help them learn new words and ideas. For example, if children are playing going to the doctor, you might ask what the name of the doctor is and then make a sign for it, saying the letters as you spell the words. They can write their names (even if it is scribbly) on a sign-in sheet. This is another fun way to help your children get ready to read. (T, PR)

20. When you and your children go shopping, there are lots of opportunities to point out letters. For example, you can choose a letter from your children's names and have your children find it wherever they can. The more they understand about letters and their sounds, the easier it will be for them learn how to read. (T, PR)

21. Show your child how everyone in your family writes their names. Talk about who has the most letters in their names and what letters the names have in common. Let your child help to write lists or draw pictures of things they want to do or make a card for a relative or friend. Writing can be very motivating for children. It also helps them get ready to read. (T, PR)

Asides That Support Vocabulary

1. Vocabulary is knowing the meanings of words. Researchers have found that children with large vocabularies who know lots of different words find it easier to read. As you sing, talk, read, write, and play with your children throughout the day, you can build your children's vocabulary. (ET, T, PR)

2. Today I'll point out some activities we are doing that help children learn new words. *Vocabulary* is the term that researchers give to knowing the meanings of words. It is an important part of understanding what is being read. You can see what we do here in storytime, and you may get some ideas of what you can do with your children throughout the day when you play and talk together. (T, PR)

3. One early literacy component is vocabulary, or knowing the meanings of words. Young children, especially those younger than age two, need direct, personal interaction to learn language and to understand words. Babies also read gestures and facial expressions to understand what is

ET = early talker (newborn to two years old), **T** = talker (two to three years old),
PR = prereader (four to five years old); **[ ]** = directions to presenter, **( )** = optional

going on. These are clues to what words mean. **Talking** directly with your children throughout the day helps them build their vocabulary and language skills. Vocabulary helps children understand what they will read. (ET)

4. Having a large vocabulary helps with reading in two ways. When children are learning to read, they sound out words. It is easier for them to know they sounded out the word correctly if they have heard the word before. The second is that they need to understand what they read. If there are too many words in a text that a child doesn't know, then understanding the whole paragraph or story will be difficult. I will point out some ways to help the children's vocabularies grow when we talk, read, write, sing, and play [choose whichever practices you will be pointing out] with them. (T, PR)

5. Our youngest children learn words that name things they can see, like *milk*, *bottle*, and *juice*. As children get older, they understand words for feelings and concepts, and as they get older still, they understand words for ideas. By **talking** with our children and adding some new words in conversation, we help them understand their world, and later to make sense of what they read. (ET, T, PR)

6. It is important to use all kinds of words, words for things, feelings, and ideas, with children of all ages, even our youngest children. They will not understand all the words you say, but being exposed to the words is the first step in greater understanding later on. (ET, T)

7. Go ahead and use words that are unfamiliar to your children. Don't replace words in books that they may not understand—explain them. When you **talk** with your children, try to use the word for a specific thing. For example, if you see a dog on the street, call it a dog, but also the breed if you know it, like a cocker spaniel. The more words your children know, the easier it will be for them to understand what they are reading. (ET, T, PR)

8. **Talking** with your children, especially as you share books, is one of the best ways to develop your children's vocabulary. In books there may be new words you can explain or pictures of things your children might not otherwise see. Talking with your children about the pictures in a book is a great way to help their vocabularies grow. Good readers know lots of words! (ET, T)

9. What happens when *you* don't know the meaning of a word? What a great opportunity to show your children what we do when we don't know

ET = early talker (newborn to two years old), **T** = talker (two to three years old), **PR** = prereader (four to five years old); **[ ]** = directions to presenter, **( )** = optional something! There's the dictionary, of course, but also you might be able to figure out what the word means from what else is going on or from a picture. **Talk** through your thought process so your children will understand how we find out the answers to questions. These are strategies they can use when they are readers, too. (T, PR)

10. [When handing out board books] When you read with your children, don't just read the words. Talk about the pictures. Use these books as conversation starters. Describe what is going on. Perhaps a picture makes you remember something. Hearing you talk is one of the best ways for your young children to develop a strong vocabulary, one of the hallmarks of a good reader. (ET)

11. The way you **talk** with your children and the words you use, called rich talk, makes a difference in your children's vocabulary. Business talk, or talk to get something done, is not rich talk. Rich talk comes from the extra talk, such as telling your children stories or talking about something that happened, something you remember, something you're going to do. Each bit of extra talking may not seem like a lot, but it all adds up to make a big difference in how much your children will understand when they learn to read. (ET, T, PR)

12. [When using a rhyme or song that names body parts] This is a good rhyme to do as you are bathing or diapering your children. Try to use different parts of the body, such as wrist, elbow, eyebrow, and words for different actions while you talk and sing together. This will help increase your children's vocabulary. Even though your babies don't understand everything you say, it is important for them to hear you talk. The more different words they hear, the larger their vocabulary will be, and the more easily they will later be able to later understand what they read. (ET, T)

13. We just went through the book from start to finish, feeling the rhythm of the text and noticing the sequence between each action. Now let's go through it again. This time we'll read it but also talk about what is happening in the pictures, adding a word or two your child may not know, the way you would with your baby or toddler. This way of sharing books helps your children develop vocabulary, which helps them understand what they are reading once they are in school. (ET, T)

14. One way you can help increase your children's vocabulary is by narrating your day. That simply means talking about what you are doing while you are doing it. Or you can say what your children are doing as they are doing it. You might even add little stories about when you were a child. By

ET = early talker (newborn to two years old), **T** = talker (two to three years old), **PR** = prereader (four to five years old); **[ ]** = directions to presenter, **( )** = optional

doing this, you are exposing your children to lots of language! Leave your children time to reply or react, even if you cannot understand what they are saying. Conversation can help children learn new words. The more words your children know, the more likely they are to understand what they read. (ET, T)

15. Try talking like a sports announcer, giving a play-by-play description of what you and/or your child are doing or thinking as it happens. For example, you might say, "Hmmm, I have to go to the grocery store, the cleaner's, and drop something off at Grandma's. I think we'll go to the grocery store last because I have to pick up some frozen food and I don't want it to melt." Children learn words by hearing many words often.

16. [When using a nursery rhyme or song that has some unfamiliar words, such as "Jack and Jill"] As you can see, singing or saying nursery rhymes exposes children to words that are not used much anymore. Researchers have found that children who know nursery rhymes find it easier to learn to read. (ET, T, PR)

17. By using specific names for things when we talk with our children, like *cat* and *kitten*, you help your children learn new words and understand differences between similar things. This is one way to increase their vocabulary, which is an important part of understanding the written word. (ET, T)

18. [When introducing a book] You can help children understand words they may not know by offering a little explanation as you read the book. If you prefer, you can talk about or explain some words before you start reading the book. Research notes that the more words your children know and understand, or the more vocabulary they have, the easier it will be for them when they begin to read. (T, PR)

19. Children like to hear books over and over again. Every time we read the same book to them we can talk about different words or pictures. This makes repeating the book more interesting to them and to us, and will also help your children build their vocabulary. Children who know a lot of words have higher achievement in reading. (T, PR)

20. Children not only like to hear the same book over and over again; they also need to hear the same book repeated to understand words as we explain some of them and to better understand the story. (T, PR)

21. [With any book in which a character shows feelings] This book allows you to **talk** about feelings. You can turn to a page and talk about what is happening in the picture. How does the child feel? You help your child

ET = early talker (newborn to two years old), T = talker (two to three years old), PR = prereader (four to five years old); [ ] = directions to presenter, ( ) = optional

talk about how he or she feels if you use the words for both what your child is feeling and what you yourself are feeling. Using words for feelings not only develops your child's vocabulary but also is the first step in helping young children identify and then manage their feelings. All of these words will help your children understand themselves, as well as what they are reading. (T, PR)

22. Ask us to help you find some true books on things your children are interested in. We can all learn new words and new things together when we read these books! Factual books often have words that are not found in storybooks, so your children learn more words with them. They need to know lots of words about all kinds of things to be able to understand what they read. (T, PR)

23. [When using a book such as *Dinosaur Roar*, by Paul and Henrietta Stickland (Puffin, 2002)] Even when reading a fairly simple story, there are many words that we don't use in everyday conversation. Even if you don't talk about the meaning of all the unfamiliar words, your children hear the words in the story and get an idea of what they mean from hearing the story and from looking at the pictures. Guessing what words mean from the pictures and the words around them is a strategy they can use when they are reading. (T, PR)

24. Children's books have about thirty-one "rare" words per thousand words. That's three times more than in conversation and 25 percent more rare words than we see on TV shows. The more of these rare words children know, the easier it will be when it comes time for school. This is just one more great reason to **read** books with our children! (ET, T, PR)

25. The more words your children know, the better off they will be when they learn to read. Research tells us that it is easier to read a word that you know. You can use books to help expand your children's vocabulary. As you **read** together, look for words in the book that have the same meaning, or synonyms. If there aren't any used in the book, choose a word from the story and think of a word with a similar meaning. When you start with words your children know, it is easier for them to learn new words, and that makes it easier for them to understand what they read. (T, PR)

26. When you and your children are playing together, add more words to your conversation. Children learn words best in context, or in the moment. Pretending while you **play** gives you lots of opportunities to use new words. The more words your children know, the better, because it is easier to read a word you know than one you don't. (ET, T, PR)

ET = early talker (newborn to two years old), **T** = talker (two to three years old),
PR = prereader (four to five years old); **[ ]** = directions to presenter, **( )** = optional

27. When we **talk** with children about a story after reading it, we are helping them remember what they heard. This helps reinforce new vocabulary words because they have the opportunity to use the words again. The more words they know, the easier it will be for them to understand what they read. (T, PR)

28. When you go to the store, look at the names of different brands. Lots of them, like Hefty trash bags, have meanings aside from the product itself. **Talk** about the meanings of these words—what does *hefty* mean? Take advantage of every opportunity to help your children learn more words, which will help them be good readers. (T, PR)

29. **Play** gives you and your children lots of opportunities to pretend. As you are playing with your children, make a point of adding in a word or two they may not know. You are adding to their vocabulary in a fun way, teaching new words without making them sit down to memorize what words mean. Children will remember these words because they hear them and use them while being involved with them. They will use these words to help them understand what they read. (T, PR)

30. There are many ways at home that you can help your children understand the words for spatial relationships, or positions. You can tell your children where to put something: "Please put this pot on top of the counter (or in the cabinet or underneath the sink)." You can make a game as you play with blocks. You can talk about what you are doing as you do it: "I am putting your clean pants next to your red shirt," or "Your sock is under the bed." All these little activities put together over time help your children understand what these words mean, which will help them understand what they are reading. (T)

31. Talk with your children in the language that you are the most comfortable using. It is best for children to hear language spoken fluently, with lots of words and expression. If children know one language well, they can learn another more easily. The more words they know in both languages, the easier it will be for them to understand what they read. (ET, T, PR)

32. Talk with your children in the language that you feel most comfortable using. Tell them stories, talk about what they are doing, and give them information in your language—the language of the heart. When children go to school, they will very quickly learn English. It is much harder to learn both new ideas and new words at the same time. It is easier to just translate into English the words they already know in your language. Having a strong foundation in your home language will help them be better readers in English. (ET, T, PR)

ET = early talker (newborn to two years old), **T** = talker (two to three years old), **PR** = prereader (four to five years old); **[ ]** = directions to presenter, **( )** = optional

33. Children enter school knowing anywhere from five thousand to twenty thousand words, depending on how much they have been spoken and read to. They can't know too many words! The more words they know, the easier it will be for them to understand what they are reading. (ET, T, PR)

34. When we **read** to children they are being exposed to the language of books. This helps children learn to read more easily once they go to school because the language of books is different from the way we talk. It uses more different words in more complicated sentences than we use in conversation. (T, PR)

35. When we adults **talk** with young children, we most often use nouns, or the names of things. To learn new words children need to be exposed to verbs, adverbs, adjectives, and spatial prepositions, like *on*, *under*, and *beneath*. So, when a child asks, "What's that?" We might say "microwave" and then define it as a kind of machine or appliance that cooks and warms up our food. Children who know a lot of words have an easier time understanding what they are reading than children who don't. (ET, T, PR)

36. Children learn words for things and events that interest them. **Reading** informational books is one way to build on a child's interest while building vocabulary, an important part of being a good reader. (ET, T, PR)

37. Children first learn the meanings of words of those things they can see—like *cup* or *mommy*. As preschoolers, they begin to understand the meanings of words that are abstract or not physically visible, like *courage* or *responsibility*. However, we can still use these abstract words with little kids. They will not understand all the words we use, but exposure to the words is a first step as children learn language and the meanings of words. Knowing the meaning of these words will help them understand what they are reading once they are in school. (ET, T, PR)

38. Children need language, or vocabulary, to think about mathematics. Children need to know the words for numbers and the language of geometry (*shapes*) and words for quantity (e.g., *more*, *less*). The more mathematical language children hear as young children, the more their mathematical knowledge increases over the school year. They can learn a lot of these kinds of words from the way we **read** picture books and informational books with them. There is a lot of reading in math (lots of word problems!), so having a good mathematical vocabulary will help them once they are in school. (T, PR)

39. Children learn words best in a meaningful context. Children need clear information about words—hearing an unfamiliar word is not enough to gain a true understanding of the word. It is important to help make

ET = early talker (newborn to two years old), **T** = talker (two to three years old), **PR** = prereader (four to five years old); **[ ]** = directions to presenter, **( )** = optional

the word meaningful for the child by relating it to something he or she already knows. When we talk with children we can help fill in the blanks in their understanding. The more words they know, the easier it is for them to learn still more! (PR)

40. After reading together, you can ask your child to draw a picture of what you read. Ask your child what the story means and write his or her words down. When you read what you have written back to your child, you can read his or her words and then add new words to help your child's vocabulary grow. The more words children know, the easier it will be for them to understand what they are reading. (T, PR)

41. When children write or draw a picture, we can talk with them about the picture. By rephrasing what they say, we can introduce them to new words. There is no such thing as knowing too many words! Children with larger vocabularies have higher achievement in school. (T, PR)

42. Sometimes we are learning along with our children when we **read** informational books! Reading this kind of book is an easy way to talk about interesting and unfamiliar words, to ask what your child knows about a topic, and to learn together. Sharing informational books offers us many opportunities to add to children's vocabularies, which helps them become better readers. (T, PR)

43. When babies observe things, they use all of their senses. They learn a lot of new words when we talk and play with them. To learn words, they need to hear them over and over again over time. All of these words add up, so when your child learns to read, he or she will be able to understand all of those words. (ET)

44. We should not be afraid to use difficult ideas and words with our children. Informational books have a lot to offer! Research shows that when children are exposed to complex language, it has a positive effect both on children's ability to use language themselves at higher levels and on their later literacy abilities. This exposure will help them to understand what they are reading. (T, PR)

45. When children have hands-on experiences that use both real items and science experiments, they learn new words. When we **talk** with children about the informational books we read and combine them with hands-on activities, young children are getting the necessary context and language to help them more completely understand scientific processes. Understanding what is going on will help them read the words they need when they are learning science. (PR)

ET = early talker (newborn to two years old), **T** = talker (two to three years old), **PR** = prereader (four to five years old); **[ ]** = directions to presenter, **( )** = optional

46. When we read with our children, we shouldn't dumb down new words. Research indicates that young children can learn scientific names for complex ideas. These new words will help them understand what they are reading once they are in school. (T, PR)

Asides That Support Background Knowledge

1. Background knowledge is information that children are taught and gain through experience. It includes different kinds of knowledge. Today I'll point out ways that children can learn [choose one of the following: about information on a particular topic, about how stories work, about the enjoyment of reading, about concepts such as opposites or spatial relationships]. Researchers have found that it is easier for children with strong background knowledge to understand what they read when they are older. It starts now! There are many ways you can develop your children's background knowledge as you sing, talk, read, write, and play with your children every day.

2. Children need background knowledge, or general knowledge about the world, to later understand what they read. Background knowledge includes knowing information about things, understanding ideas and concepts like opposites, having thinking skills like problem solving and predicting, and knowing how stories work. Today I'll point out some ways that we can share information with our children when we talk, read, write, sing, and play with them. (T, PR)

3. Children must have a lot of background knowledge, or knowledge about the world around them, to later understand what they read. Gaining background knowledge begins from birth. Children with strong background knowledge are more likely to understand what they read in the fourth grade and up. They are more likely to become successful readers. When you **talk** with your children about everything you see and do together, explaining what you know, you are helping to develop their knowledge. (ET, T, PR)

4. Even very young children are learning background knowledge. They learn how different items feel; for example, the carpet feels different from the floor. They learn that when they let go of an object, it falls. And by **talking** about their world, you are giving them the background knowledge they need to understand it. If they understand it in life, they will also understand it when they come upon it in a book. (ET)

ET = early talker (newborn to two years old), T = talker (two to three years old), PR = prereader (four to five years old); [ ] = directions to presenter, ( ) = optional

5. Helping your children associate books and **reading** with something enjoyable and positive is supporting print motivation, or a child's interest in and enjoyment of books and reading. Researchers have noted that children who have enjoyable experiences around books are more likely to stick with learning to read even if it difficult. (ET, T, PR)

6. When children say a phrase that is repeated throughout the book with you, they are involved with the story. They also learn the structure of stories—that they have a beginning, a middle, and an end. By making books and reading fun for your children, you are helping them to connect reading with enjoyment. Researchers have noted that this helps children stick longer with learning to read when they get to school. (T, PR)

7. Children are curious about their world. There is so much to know! You help them learn when you share with them what you know and when you help them find new information, by **reading** books, for example. All their knowledge will help them understand what they read when they learn to read in school. (ET, T, PR)

8. Choose books that you enjoy. Your children pick up on your feelings. Talk with your children about why you enjoy what you are reading. This connection between books, reading, and pleasure will help them want to learn how to read. (ET, T, PR)

9. Did you know that talking with your children and giving them time to talk back with you is one way to develop your children's speaking skills? Even though your children may only be babbling or we may not understand all of what they say to us, we still want to encourage their talking. Children who can express themselves with words are better able to later understand what they read. (ET, T)

10. To learn, children need a lot of repetition. They need to hear words over and over again as you do things together. They also like you to read favorite books over and over again. It may get boring for you, but their brains need repetition to learn language. The more words they know, the easier it will be to understand what they read. (ET, T)

11. Often when we **talk** with children, we simply are telling them what to do—"Please pick up your toys," or "It's time to take a nap." This is called business talk. Researchers have found that it is the extra talk that makes a difference in the amount of language and knowledge that children have. Adding information or talking about experiences helps children learn more about their world, which in turn helps them get ready to read. (ET, T)

ET = early talker (newborn to two years old), **T** = talker (two to three years old), **PR** = prereader (four to five years old); **[ ]** = directions to presenter, **{ }** = optional

12. When you're looking at and reading books with your toddlers and even your babies, ask questions like, "What's that?" or "What's happening?" Give them time to respond even if you don't understand what they have said. Then give them the answer by saying, "That's right, it's a frog. Frogs live in ponds," or whatever the picture is. These little tidbits of conversation are helping children learn how language works—that we take turns when we have a conversation. All of these activities build on one another to help children get ready to read. (ET)

13. The ability to retell stories is one of the early literacy skills that researchers say children need to understand what they read. Using things you have around the house to play with as props can help children remember a story and retell it. (T, PR)

14. You may often hear the phrase "read with your child fifteen minutes a day," or "read with your child twenty minutes a day." No one expects young children to sit and be read to for that long at one sitting. It is more important for the interaction between you and your children to be a good one than for it to be long. Keeping the interaction around books enjoyable helps children understand that reading is fun and will keep them motivated to learn to read. (ET, T, PR)

15. The language used in storybooks is different from the language we use when we are talking. Stories also have a certain structure, with a beginning, a middle, and an end. By **reading** storybooks with your children, you help them become familiar with written language and story structure. This will make it easier for them to understand the stories they learn to read in school. (ET, T, PR)

16. Encouraging your children to **talk** will help them later understand what they read. Leaving time for your babies to babble back to you when you talk with them encourages them to talk. For children who are just learning to talk, being patient while they say words is important. When your children are talking fluently, the next step is to help them recount stories or things that have happened in order, or in sequence. (ET, T, PR)

17. When you ask your children questions, give them extra time to think and to answer you. **Talking** back and forth uses four different parts of the brain, so it takes them some time to get their words out. Talking about what you see going on around you can help your children develop background knowledge, which will help them understand what they are reading. (ET, T)

ET = early talker (newborn to two years old), **T** = talker (two to three years old),
PR = prereader (four to five years old); **[ ]** = directions to presenter, **( )** = optional

18. One kind of **play** is dramatic play, or acting out stories. Having young children use their whole bodies when they move and play along with what is happening in a story helps them remember and understand what is happening in the story. They'll be able to tell some stories back to you, especially their favorites, which they like to hear over and over again. This process helps them understand the story, and it will later help them understand what they read. (T, PR)

19. Sharing informational books with your children is one way to build background knowledge. Often, we adults also learn new things as we **read** this kind of book with our children. The more they know, the easier it will be for them to understand what they read when they get to school. Children are naturally curious about all kinds of things. Take advantage of it! (T, PR)

20. Some children who won't listen to stories will love listening to informational books. Ask us (library staff) librarians to show you books on things your children are interested in. You don't need to **read** all the words in these books and you don't have to read them from cover to cover. Using informational books helps children see that books can be used for different purposes, which is an important aspect of background knowledge. The information that children learn from books when they are little will help them understand what they are reading when they are bigger! (T, PR)

21. Informational books are not shelved with the picture books. I would be happy to help you find books on topics that you and your child are interested in. Sharing factual information with children is one of the best ways to develop their background knowledge, which will later help children understand what they read. (T, PR)

22. If you let your children watch television, talk about the shows that you watch together. Listen as your children talk about what is happening. Add your own information and ideas. When you clarify and add information, you are supporting your children's background knowledge, which will help then comprehend what they are reading when they are older. (PR)

23. It is important to talk with children to help them understand concepts like positions—over, under, top, bottom, between, left, and right. This is part of giving them the background knowledge they will draw from as they learn to read and write. (T, PR)

24. When your children **play**, they often use one object for another, such as a block to represent a telephone. This kind of symbolic play is the same type of thinking that allows them to understand that a picture or the

ET = early talker (newborn to two years old), **T** = talker (two to three years old), **PR** = prereader (four to five years old); **[ ]** = directions to presenter, **( )** = optional

written word represents a real thing. This is conceptual thinking, which is part of building your children's background knowledge and contributes to their ability to understand what they are reading once they are in school. (T, PR)

25. When you ask children open-ended questions, ones that cannot be answered with yes or no, you can learn what they are thinking and what they already know. By listening to what they say, you can build their background knowledge by adding more information or ideas as you **talk** together. The more they know about the world around them, the easier it will be for them to understand what they are reading. (T, PR)

26. It is helpful for children to see that we **read** informational books differently from the way we read storybooks. We read them in a nonlinear way, not necessarily in order, dipping in and out of them, using an index. We can **talk** about this when we use this kind of book with them. All of these experiences help them develop their background knowledge, which in turn helps children understand what they are reading. (T, PR)

27. Researchers have learned that children who have had informational texts read to them at a young age are better able to read and write these kinds of texts later on in school. The background knowledge they gain as young children can have a big impact on how they learn when they are older. (PR)

28. We want to encourage children's curiosity about the world and to both respond to and encourage their questions. Share things that you know with your children. The more children know, the easier it is for them to learn new things, because new knowledge is most easily learned when it builds on something they know. **Reading** books together is certainly one way to build knowledge. Your enthusiasm about topics of interest to you often spills over to your children as they learn about the world.

Science and Math Asides

These asides can be used to support background knowledge in science and math. We believe that it is motivating for adults to see that they can help their children develop their higher-level cognitive skills along with their early literacy skills.

1. The motto "wait, watch, and wonder" as you talk with your child is a reminder not to give your child answers but to learn what your child

---

ET = early talker (newborn to two years old), **T** = talker (two to three years old), **PR** = prereader (four to five years old); **[ ]** = directions to presenter, **( )** = optional

knows and to have your child put thoughts and ideas into words. These are activities that strengthen your children's understanding of the world and later of what they read. (PR)

2. Background knowledge is information children are taught and gain through experience. It includes different kinds of knowledge. Today I'll point out ways that children can learn about [information on a science topic]. Researchers have found that it is easier for children with strong background knowledge to understand what they read when they are older. It starts now! There are many ways you can develop your child's background knowledge as you sing, talk, read, write, and play with your children every day. (T, PR)

3. Children need background knowledge, or general knowledge about the world, to later understand what they read. Background knowledge includes knowing information about things, understanding ideas and concepts like opposites, having thinking skills like problem solving and predicting, and knowing how stories work. Today I'll point out some ways we can share information with our children when we talk, read, write, sing, and play with them. (T, PR)

4. Children must have a lot of background knowledge, or knowledge about the world around them, to later understand what they read. Background knowledge begins from birth. Children with strong background knowledge are more likely to understand what they read in the fourth grade and up and are more likely to become successful readers. Today I'll point out some interesting science ideas you might enjoy exploring with your children. (T, PR)

5. Even very young children learn background knowledge. They learn how different things feel—for example, the carpet feels different from the floor. They learn basic scientific principles when they do things like letting go of an object and seeing it fall. By talking about their world, you are giving them the background knowledge they need to understand it. (ET)

6. Children are curious about their world. There is so much to know! You help them learn when you share with them what you know and when you help them find new information by reading books that include information about a scientific concept, like how plants grow or how a car works. All their knowledge will help them understand what they read when they later learn to read in school. (ET, T, PR)

7. Often when we talk with children, we simply tell them what to do, such as "Please pick up your toys," or "It's time to take a nap." This is called

ET = early talker (newborn to two years old), T = talker (two to three years old), PR = prereader (four to five years old); [ ] = directions to presenter, ( ) = optional

business talk. Researchers have found that it is the extra talk that makes a difference in the amount of language and knowledge that children have. Adding information or talking about experiences teaches children about their world. This can include information about science (or counting things and playing with numbers). (ET, T)

8. Sharing informational books with your children is one way to build their background knowledge. Often, we adults also learn things as we read these books with our children. The more children know about topics, including math and science, the easier it will be for them to understand those concepts when they get to school. Children are naturally curious about all kinds of things. Take advantage of it! (T, PR)

9. Some children who don't like to listen to stories will be happy to listen to informational books. Ask us to show you books on topics of interest to your children. You don't need to read all the words in these books, and you don't have to read them from cover to cover. Children see that books can be used for different purposes, which is an important aspect of background knowledge. (T, PR)

10. If you let your children watch television, talk about the shows that you watch together. You can borrow DVDs from the library that will help your children understand the scientific ideas we have explored in storytime. Listen as your children talks about what is happening. Add your own information and ideas. When you clarify and add information, you are supporting your children's acquisition of scientific knowledge. (PR)

11. It is important to **talk** with children to help them understand concepts like more than, less than, bigger, and smaller. This is part of giving them the background knowledge that they will draw from as they learn to read and write as well as express math ideas. (T, PR)

12. When you ask children questions like, "What do you think will happen?" you help them learn how to make predictions, which is an important part of scientific investigation. By listening to what they say, you can build their background knowledge by adding more information or ideas as you talk together. All of this information will help them understand what they read. (T, PR)

13. Young children can learn how to think mathematically. It occurs to many of us to say counting words—such as *one*, *two*, *three*—when we are walking up the stairs or handing something out. This is a start, but children are also able to understand more complex concepts like *more* and *less*. **Talking** about the ideas related to numbers will help them think

abstractly, a skill they need for reading as well as for science and math. Children need to know about all kinds of things to understand what they read. (T, PR)

14. Young children like to look at and explore objects. When we talk with them about shapes and measure how tall they are, we are supporting mathematical thinking, which contributes to their background knowledge. Talking about shape and size takes advantage of both their interest in and ability to learn mathematics. All of this helps build a foundation in math that will help them understand math when they are in school. (T, PR)

15. When you play with your children and sort things into piles, you can talk about not only which pile has more but also which characteristics you are sorting by. For example, if your child has a lot of vehicles, he or she might decide how these items could be grouped, such as number of wheels, color, purpose, length, or weight. This supports both mathematical and conceptual thinking, which children will need once they are in school and have to solve problems. (PR)

16. Naming shapes is a first step for children to understand what makes a shape that particular shape. Talking about what makes a triangle a triangle—the fact that it has three sides—helps children understand the idea behind the shape, not just the word. A strong foundation built when children are young will help them later when they are in school. (T, PR)

17. Cause and effect is a scientific concept. Even babies learn the idea of cause and effect. They learn that the rattle in their hand makes a noise if they move their hand. Tell them what is happening even if they don't understand everything you say. All of the **talking** and interacting you do with your children will help them develop language and math skills, which will help them understand what they are reading. (ET)

18. Young children like to examine objects. Talking about how the object feels, its colors, how heavy it is, and what it does all help children later when they try to match or sort items. Observation is the beginning of scientific thinking. Everything you teach your children now will help them understand what they learn later in school. (ET)

19. Cooking offers lots of opportunities to talk about math and science. Talking about how you are using measuring cups is an introduction to using tools in a scientific way. A handful is also a measurement! When you divide food into portions, you can talk about fractions—half, a quarter, and so on. Understanding how things work helps children understand what they read. (T, PR)

ET = early talker (newborn to two years old), **T** = talker (two to three years old), **PR** = prereader (four to five years old); **[ ]** = directions to presenter, **( )** = optional

20. [When using a counting song like "Five Green and Speckled Frogs"] Singing counting songs give us the opportunity to show children the concept of subtraction, or having one less, as we count backward. Children can also learn one-to-one correspondence as we offer one bug per frog. All of this early math helps lay a foundation for later learning. (T, PR)

21. As you read books with children, you may sometimes pause and count the number of things in a picture. The names of numbers, especially after the number ten, are hard for children to keep track of. With our older preschoolers we can go up to higher numbers. When we count pictures of things in books we read, we can count aloud with our children. We want our children to enter school knowing some basic math concepts. (PR)

22. Young children can make a mental match of objects to things that they can't see. For example, a young child will get two cookies for two children who are in another room. This shows that the child understands the relationship among objects. We can help reinforce this concept by asking children to help do things like setting the table when playing or at home. We can help our children get ready for school when we encourage them to help us out around the house! (T, PR)

23. Exposing young children to mathematical concepts can have a positive impact on their achievement later. When children participate in activities that help them to do things like compare and put objects in order, learn whether objects are of the same size, and use words to describe attributes like size, we increase the likelihood that they will be able to do math in the elementary grades. When we talk, read, and play with them we should try to remember to include activities about math. Don't forget to explain what is going on to your child, too. (ET, PR)

24. Research indicates that young children who have the opportunity to experience different kinds of activities (with enough exposure to activities) can move into more advanced levels of reasoning than previously thought. In other words, young children's minds are more ready to learn new things than we realized! We need to point out math concepts when we talk and read together. I'll point out some in our storytime today. (ET, T, PR)

25. You can think of ways to sort items at home: sorting laundry; unpacking groceries; sorting by what foods go in the freezer, the refrigerator, or the cupboard; at the checkout counter, what is heaviest might be put on the conveyer belt first so that it will go in a bag at the bottom of the cart. As you talk about the way you and your children are sorting, this helps them

---

ET = early talker (newborn to two years old), **T** = talker (two to three years old), **PR** = prereader (four to five years old); **[ ]** = directions to presenter, **( )** = optional

understand categories, which supports both conceptual and scientific thinking and helps them later understand what they read.

26. There are many times throughout the day when we can take advantage of talking about science. For example, in the bath we can talk about what floats and what sinks. When you talk with your young children about scientific things, even if you don't know the answers, you can get them thinking and talking in a scientific way, and trying to figure things out. When you do this, you help them make predictions and then test them or try them out. (If this floats, then this object, which is the same shape, will float.) Children need to be encouraged to ask questions and to try different ways of solving problems, to think like a scientist.

27. Using graphs and charts and pictures to sort and group things is one way to help children put what they are noticing on paper. We can encourage them to share their ideas through their own drawings and writing. We can talk with them about how they are organizing the objects and encourage experimenting with sorting things by other characteristics. This helps them see that print has meaning and develops their science and math skills. (PR)

28. Sometimes we are too quick to solve problems for our young children. We can support their development of scientific thinking by giving them extra time to figure things out for themselves, using their problem-solving skills, before jumping in. If they begin to get frustrated or discouraged, we can encourage them or give a little hint. Remember, if we do this, they may come up with a solution different than ours.

ET = early talker (newborn to two years old), **T** = talker (two to three years old), **PR** = prereader (four to five years old); **[ ]** = directions to presenter, **( )** = optional

chapter 13

Evaluation and Assessment

ASSESSING AND EVALUATING OUR WORK IS KEY TO IMPROVING IT. THOUGHTFUL EVALU-ations can help us improve and expand our early literacy programming. Assessment and evaluation might include some or all of the following elements:

Self-assessment: Are we including the elements that make for a strong, early literacy enhanced storytime? Are adults and children enjoying the storytime?

Library system: Are our storytimes in alignment with the goals of our system and/or department? Have we communicated the importance of these programs so that they are included in the strategic plan?

Patron satisfaction: Are our early literacy enhanced storytime programs well received by patrons? What improvements could we make? What suggestions do our patrons have? Do they understand the early literacy information we are conveying? Do they have suggestions for ways they can "hear" it better? What would they like to learn more about?

Intended purpose: Are parents and caregivers learning more about ways to support early literacy development and why it is important? Does the information they get in storytime help them to support their children's early literacy development? Are we building a community of lifelong learners?

Web extra 13.1 is a checklist that can be used with self-assessments and adapted to performance evaluations for early literacy enhanced storytimes. These elements can be added to whatever checklists or assessments you have in place for the traditional storytime. Other helpful assessment documents, developed by the Arapahoe (CO) Public Library, are included as web extras 10.2–10.4 at www .alaeditions.org/webextras.

Assessments of Impact of Early Literacy Storytimes

The rest of this chapter looks at three library entities and their projects for evaluating the effects of early literacy enhanced storytimes. The Idaho Commission for Libraries, the state library entity, compared parent and caregiver early literacy behaviors between those who had heard early literacy asides and those who had not. It also looked at staff implementation of conveying early literacy information. The Brooklyn (NY) Public Library developed an outcome-based evaluation that surveyed parents who attended early literacy storytime sessions to assess changes in both parent and child behaviors in early literacy development as a result of storytimes. The Douglas County (CO) Libraries conducted evaluation surveys in 2005 and 2006 to assess the effect of early literacy enhanced storytimes.

IDAHO COMMISSION FOR LIBRARIES

Stephanie Bailey-White, projects coordinator

Eighteen public libraries from all regions of Idaho participated in a study exploring the effects of enhanced storytimes on parent and caregiver behaviors, knowledge, and motivation. The Idaho Commission for Libraries designed and supported the study. An enhanced storytime is a regular storytime with the addition of adult asides focused on the six early literacy skills. An adult aside was operationally defined for this study in the following way: A thirty- to ninety-second tidbit of information or a "tip" on early literacy directed at parents that explains some aspect of early literacy skills and may include how an activity supports an early literacy skill.

It was hypothesized that, as a consequence of systematically incorporating adult asides into storytimes over a six-week period, participating parents and caregivers would report having increased knowledge of the six early literacy skills, being more motivated to apply and reinforce the six skills, and making changes in their early literacy behaviors with their children.

A presurvey and postsurvey design was employed (see the surveys at the end of this section) to explore the effects of enhanced storytimes. Librarians and parent or caregiver attendees were surveyed before implementation of enhanced story-times. Library staff then participated in one and a half days of training focused on how to implement adult asides. For an individual storytime there were three adult asides: introductory, example, and closing. (Note: these correspond to the explain, example, and empower asides.) Librarians introduced the literacy skill with the introductory aside. Then at an appropriate point in the storytime, they did the example aside, which illustrated and modeled the literacy skill. The closing aside served to restate the literacy skill and its importance, to provide some helpful tips on how to model and reinforce the skill at home, and to showcase the handout that provided by the Idaho Commission for Libraries for each of the six early lit-eracy skills. Scripts were provided to presenters to guide them in implementation of asides. After training, storytime presenters returned to their libraries, where each week for six weeks they incorporated adult asides into their storytimes. At the conclusion of the six-week treatment period, storytime presenters and parents and caregivers completed follow-up surveys.

The eighteen participating libraries submitted 374 completed parent and care-giver presurveys and 251 completed postsurveys. Counter to the original hypothe-ses, enhanced storytimes did not cause appreciable changes in parent or caregiver behaviors. Most people who attended storytimes in the pre- and poststorytime groups reported that they did the activities before or did not change the amount of time spent on those activities as a result of attending storytimes. It should also be noted that most of the people included in this research study were regular storytime participants. The following are some questions asked in the surveys:

As a result of attending library storytimes, I . . .

   a. Occasionally point out words while reading to my child/children.
   b. Spend more time singing with my child/children.
   c. Spend more time rhyming with my child/children (e.g., rhyming games, fingerplays that rhyme, nursery rhymes).
   d. Build my child's/children's vocabulary by using rare words from books or other sources.
   e. Stop and give my child/children time to talk about what is in the book.
   f. Read more shape and alphabet books with my child/children.
   g. Find my child/children more interested in books.
   h. Am more knowledgeable about the six early literacy skills.
   i. Am more motivated to do things at home that reinforce the six early literacy skills.

Librarians provided extensive comments and opinions about their experi-ences implementing enhanced storytimes. A few had positive experiences, some were neutral on their experiences, and some struggled with implementation and expressed concern that adult asides disrupted their normal storytime routines.

When asked what caused parents to change behaviors, reading the handouts and the storytime presenter's presentations were all identified as causing change. In all instances, higher scores occurred on the postsurvey than on the presurvey, which means that more people recognized the items as change agents after the treatment period. Similar to the entire group, for the matched survey group, the handouts were effective. Storytime presenters appear to be the most effective change agent, but adults' learning about prereading skills is also important. The "storytime presenter made early literacy activities look fun" was ranked the highest factor in this category.

In summary, the Idaho Commission for Libraries' read-to-me coordinators found that the study backed up the training and work done to promote enhanced storytimes. The study also confirmed the importance of reaching non–library users and taking the early literacy message out to underserved families in our communities. For a relatively low investment in time to plan and incorporate three adult asides in storytimes, the payoff in increased knowledge and motivation seems well worth this initial investment. Making handouts available is another relatively quick and cost-effective way to reinforce early literacy skills.

A subgroup of parent and caregiver respondents who did not have prior training in the six early literacy skills and who attended four or more of the six enhanced storytimes did not report appreciable changes in their early literacy behaviors. This ran counter to the original hypothesis, which stated that behaviors would change. The lack of change in behaviors was probably due to the finding that these parents were already doing many of the suggested early literacy behaviors, so changes would be unlikely as a consequence of enhanced storytimes. Results, however, did support the other two hypotheses. Parents and caregivers reported that enhanced storytimes increased their knowledge of the six early literacy skills and their motivation to apply and reinforce the six skills when away from the library. What enhanced storytimes most likely did for these respondents is provide them a foundation and underlying rationale for behaviors that they were already, for the most part, doing. This may be the root cause of their increased motivation. As they learned about the six early literacy skills, parents and caregivers achieved a deeper understanding of the skills' importance, which in turn caused adults to be more motivated to apply and reinforce the skills when away from the library. Importantly, these results were supported by analyses of a subgroup of respondents with whom it was possible to directly match their pre- and postsurveys.

The study concluded that the enhanced storytime model should be further developed because of the strong, positive results supporting two of the three study hypotheses. The results showed that the model in its current form increased parent/caregiver knowledge and motivation.

Presurvey for Parents and Caregivers for Storytime Participants

Instructions: Storytime is an important activity for your children. In addition to participating in a positive and entertaining social activity, children learn important early literacy skills. The purpose of this survey is to learn what you and your child have gained from attending storytime. Please complete the following questions by coloring in the appropriate box. Please use a dark blue or black ink pen to complete the survey. Thank you for providing this important feedback.

1. Name of Library

_____

2. Are you here with your day-care or preschool group?   ☐ Yes   ☐ No

3. Have you previously attended parent workshops provided by your local public library about the six early literacy skills? Oftentimes the workshops are called Every Child Ready to Read Family Workshops.

☐ Yes   ☐ No

4. *Including this week*, how many times have you attended storytime during the past *six weeks*?

☐ 1   ☐ 2   ☐ 3   ☐ 4   ☐ 5   ☐ 6   ☐ **

** Attended more than six times in past six weeks.

5. Please answer all of the following:

AS A RESULT OF ATTENDING LIBRARY STORYTIMES, I . . .	YES	NO	NOT SURE	DID THIS BEFORE*
a. Occasionally point out words while reading to my child/children.				
b. Spend more time singing with my child/children.				
c. Spend more time rhyming with my child/children (e.g., rhyming games, fingerplays that rhyme, nursery rhymes).				
d. Build my child's/children's vocabulary by using rare words from books or other sources.				

AS A RESULT OF ATTENDING LIBRARY STORYTIMES, I . . .	YES	NO	NOT SURE	DID THIS BEFORE*
e. Stop and give my child/children time to talk about what is in the book.				
f. Read more shape and alphabet books with my child/children.				
	YES	NO	NOT SURE	NO CHANGE**
g. Find my child/children more interested in books.				
h. Am more knowledgeable about the six early literacy skills.				
i. Am more motivated to do things at home that reinforce the six early literacy skills.				

* Mark this column if you did this before with your child/children and you have *not increased* the amount of time spent on the behavior since attending storytimes.

** Mark this column if interest, knowledge, or motivation were *strong to begin with* and there has been *no change* since attending storytimes.

6. Please answer the following *only* if you have children *thirty-six months or older.*

AS A RESULT OF ATTENDING LIBRARY STORYTIMES, I . . .	YES	NO	NOT SURE	DID THIS BEFORE*
a. Am more likely to ask my child/children questions that will prompt a retelling of a story.				
b. Spend more time "playing" with letters with my child/children.				
c. Show my child/children the print in signs.				
d. Am more likely to read informational/ nonfiction books with my child/children.				

* Mark this column if you did this before with your child/children and you have *not increased* the amount of time spent on the behavior since attending storytimes.

If you marked *yes* to any items in questions 5 and 6, please answer the following. If not, please skip to question 8.

7. What caused you to change? (Please check all that apply):

☐ Learning about prereading skills
☐ Reading the handouts
☐ The storytime presenter made early literacy activities look fun.
☐ Other (Please list):

8. Did you receive handouts at storytime?

☐ Yes   ☐ No   ☐ Not sure

If you answered *yes* to question 8, please answer *all* of the remaining questions. If you answered *no* or *not sure* to question 8, please skip to question 10.

9. Using the following types, please rate the handouts *you received*:

	VERY USEFUL	USEFUL	NEUTRAL	NOT USEFUL	DON'T KNOW
a. Recommended reading lists					
b. Early literacy information					
c. Library program information					
d. Take home activities (e.g., crafts, rhymes, songs, fingerplays)					
e. Other (please list):					

10. Your comments are important to us. The Idaho Commission for Libraries would like to contact you for follow-up comments. All comments will remain confidential. If you agree to be contacted, please list your name and contact information:

Name:_____

Phone: _____ E-mail: _____

Thank you for completing our survey!

Postsurvey for Parents and Caregivers for Storytime Participants

Instructions: Storytime is an important activity for your children. In addition to participating in a positive and entertaining social activity, children learn important early literacy skills. The purpose of this survey is to learn what you and your child have gained from attending storytime. Please complete the following questions by coloring in the appropriate box. Please use a dark blue or black ink pen to complete the survey. Thank you for providing this important feedback.

1. Name of Library

_____

2. Are you here with your day-care or preschool group?   ☐ Yes   ☐ No

3. Have you previously attended parent workshops provided by your local public library about the six early literacy skills? Oftentimes the workshops are called Every Child Ready to Read Family Workshops.

☐ Yes   ☐ No

4. *Including this week*, how many times have you attended storytime during the past *six weeks*?

☐ 1   ☐ 2   ☐ 3   ☐ 4   ☐ 5   ☐ 6   ☐**

** Attended more than six times in past six weeks.

5. Please answer all of the following:

AS A RESULT OF ATTENDING LIBRARY STORYTIMES, I . . .	YES	NO	NOT SURE	DID THIS BEFORE*
a. Occasionally point out words while reading to my child/children.				
b. Spend more time singing with my child/children.				
c. Spend more time rhyming with my child/children (e.g., rhyming games, finger-plays that rhyme, nursery rhymes).				
d. Build my child's/children's vocabulary by using rare words from books or other sources.				

AS A RESULT OF ATTENDING LIBRARY STORYTIMES, I . . .	YES	NO	NOT SURE	DID THIS BEFORE*
e. Stop and give my child/children time to talk about what is in the book.				
f. Read more shape and alphabet books with my child/children.				

	YES	NO	NOT SURE	NO CHANGE**
g. Find my child/children more interested in books.				
h. Am more knowledgeable about the six early literacy skills.				
i. Am more motivated to do things at home that reinforce the six early literacy skills.				

* Mark this column if you did this before with your child/children and you have *not increased* the amount of time spent on the behavior since attending storytimes.

** Mark this column if interest, knowledge, or motivation were *strong to begin with* and there has been *no change* since attending storytimes.

6. Please answer the following *only* if you have children *thirty-six months or older*:

AS A RESULT OF ATTENDING LIBRARY STORYTIMES, I . . .	YES	NO	NOT SURE	DID THIS BEFORE*
a. Am more likely to ask my child/children questions that will prompt a retelling of a story.				
b. Spend more time "playing" with letters with my child/children.				
c. Show my child/children the print in signs.				
d. Am more likely to read informational/ nonfiction books with my child/children.				

* Mark this column if you did this before with your child/children and you have *not increased* the amount of time spent on the behavior since attending storytimes.

If you marked *yes to any items* in questions 5 and 6 above, please answer the following. If not, skip to question 8.

7. What caused you to change? (Please check all that apply):

☐ Learning about prereading skills
☐ Reading the handouts
☐ The storytime presenter made early literacy activities look fun
☐ Other (Please list):

8. Please rate the handouts you received at storytime:

	VERY USEFUL	USEFUL	NEUTRAL	NOT USEFUL	DON'T KNOW	DIDN'T RECEIVE
a. Print motivation (fun with puppets)						
b. Print awareness (sign bingo and "Wheels on the Bus" chant)						
c. Vocabulary (pointing to animal pictures and "Six Little Ducks" rhyme)						
d. Letter knowledge (name the shapes and playdough recipe)						
e. Narrative skills (draw family picture and "Grandma's Glasses" rhyme)						
f. Phonological awareness (match pictures that rhyme and "Row, Row, Row Your Boat" rhyme)						
g. Other (please list):						

9. Do you recall completing this survey before? If you did complete it, you would have done so about two to three months ago when you attended storytime at your library.

☐ Yes   ☐ No   ☐ Not sure

Your comments are important to us. The Idaho Commission for Libraries would like to contact you for follow-up comments. All comments will remain confidential. If you agree to be contacted, please list your name and contact information:

Name:_____

Phone: _____   E-mail: _____

Thank you for completing our survey!

BROOKLYN (NY) PUBLIC LIBRARY: OUTCOMES-BASED EVALUATION OF BPL'S WEEKEND STORIES FOR PRESCHOOLERS PROGRAM

Funded by the Altman Foundation

Rachel Payne, coordinator, early childhood services

http://ittakesavillagetoraiseareaderpla2012.pbworks.com

Background

For the past four years, Brooklyn Public Library has supported our Weekend Stories for Preschoolers Program using grant funds. This program is an early literacy storytime program that models early literacy practices to parents, presents early literacy activities that children and parents can do at home together, and gives parents tips for developing their children's early literacy skills—all within a storytime program. Our funders often require a rigorous outcomes-based evaluation process to verify that their funds are being effectively spent. The library has developed evaluation tools and strategies that are effective and easy to use.

Outcomes and Outputs

Over the years, we have been able to develop outcomes that we can verify and that show change and growth in our participants. When we first launched the program, we hoped we could show an increase in shared reading between parents and children. Our target audience was busy working parents who could not bring their children to a preschool program during the week. While we were noticing parents were anecdotally reporting that the program was causing growth in the quality of a parent and child's shared reading experience (parents were reporting reading to their children with more expression), we weren't seeing a dramatic increase in the amount of time parents were reading with their children. Busy parents simply could not find more time to read with their children, and many of the families were reading with their children at optimal levels (five to seven times per week).

This being the case, we decided to create outcome goals that showed growth in a child's early literacy development since attending the program. Our current outcomes and outputs are as follows:

- In the fall and spring, Weekend Stories will serve 1,800 discrete individuals (1,000 children and 800 parents) through 168 sessions at 13 libraries and one offsite location, with average attendance of 20 and aggregate attendance of 3,400 (1,900 children and 1,500 parents). In addition, 250 parents will attend three or more sessions with their children.
- Of parents attending three or more sessions, 75 percent will report that their child has either begun demonstrating indicators of early literacy or has shown improvement in at least four of the eight indicators identified on the survey.
- Of parents attending three or more sessions, 30 percent will increase their shared reading at home to five times per week or from five times per week to every day.

Evaluation Tools

The Brooklyn Public Library has strengthened its evaluation methodology since launching Weekend Stories. We use evaluation instruments implemented during and after these programs:

- a baseline survey given to families when they attend their first session
- a weekly self-reporting multiple-choice survey given to all repeat attendees
- a take-home reading calendar
- a final program evaluation given to all repeat attendees who attend the final session
- a telephone survey offered to those who volunteer to be interviewed on the final program evaluation

The surveys are offered in English, Spanish, Chinese, Polish, and Russian.

Baseline Survey

The baseline survey asks eight directed questions to measure growth in common early literacy indicators. We ask parents to self-report whether their children currently demonstrate these indicators. This is helpful to establish a baseline of where the child is before starting the program. Here is the language used on the survey:

Does your child currently show any of these signs of early literacy development?

My child asks to be read to:
☐ Yes   ☐ My child doesn't do this yet.

My child is comfortable handling books:
☐ Yes   ☐ My child doesn't do this yet.

My child pretends to read books aloud or "reads" books from memory:
☐ Yes   ☐ My child doesn't do this yet.

My child understands that words on a page mean something and
recognizes some letters:
☐ Yes   ☐ My child doesn't do this yet.

My child recognizes his or her first name or first initial in print:
☐ Yes   ☐ My child doesn't do this yet.

My child is able to answer questions about things in a book:
☐ Yes   ☐ My child doesn't do this yet.

My child uses words or phrases learned from books:
☐ Yes   ☐ My child doesn't do this yet.

My child is able to label objects or feelings and tell stories:
☐ Yes   ☐ My child doesn't do this yet.

Weekly Survey

The weekly survey asks participants to respond to questions about the quality of their early literacy interactions at home and about the change in their shared activities. Parents fill out this survey each time that they attend the program between the first and last sessions. To track whether children have shown growth in early literacy, we use the same questions on the introductory survey, but we add a check box for parents to indicate growth. This tool also measures parents' understanding of the program concepts and comfort level with the activities.

> Have you noticed growth in your child in any of these areas since you came to Weekend Stories?
>
> > My child asks to be read to:
> > ☐ About the same   ☐ More frequently   ☐ My child doesn't do this yet.

Reading Calendar

The Brooklyn Public Library created the reading calendar as way for parents to document what activities they were doing at home with their children. We gave each family a file folder with a calendar for the time frame of the program (for Weekend Stories it was six sessions). We put the program dates on the calendar as well as simple instructions. Families were also given color coded labels (often used for filing) for "Read," "Songs and Rhymes," "Play," and "Weekend Stories" printed on each of the stickers. When parents and children engaged in one of these activities, they would get to place the sticker on that date of the calendar. Children would get their calendar at the first session, and the very first activity was to decorate it and make it their own.

Since families often forget to bring their reading calendar to each session, it has been difficult to use as a method for tracking outcomes. However, it has been a great way for parents to reflect on the quality of their early literacy interactions. Also, the calendar is a fun way to get children involved in the process! We also share the reading calendars with our funders as a clear example of how engaged families become in the program.

Final Program Evaluation Survey

The final program evaluation survey is quite similar to the weekly survey. We ask parents to share their overall evaluation of the program and leave space for them to share anecdotes about the program's impact. We also ask parents to let us know if they would volunteer their phone number and give us good a time to call them for a telephone interview.

Telephone Interview

As stated already, we recruit parents from the program to participate in a telephone survey. Often, we are able to speak to only about ten parents after each program series, but this is sufficient to gain some good anecdotes about what families have gotten out of the program. Here are the questions we ask:

1. What do you think your child gained from going to the program?

2. When you think back to the time before you attended the program, what are you doing differently now regarding your child's reading and language?

3. Are you still reading to your child as frequently as you were then?
    a. I am reading more.
    b. I am reading somewhat less.
    c. I am reading less.
    Please explain.

4. Do you do fingerplays and sing songs together?
    a. More
    b. Somewhat less
    c. Less
    Please explain.

5. About how often do you go to the library? What do you do there?

6. What would you have changed about the program?

7. Is there anything else you would like to tell us about your experience?

Reporting the Results

No numbers without stories, not stories without numbers.
—The Rensselaerville Institute

The epigraph from the Rensselaerville Institute has always been really helpful to us as we think about how to convey our results to our funders. It is important to include the numerical results, the outputs and outcomes, as well as anecdotes and stories from the participants. The stories humanize the numbers, and the numbers show the breadth of what we have accomplished. Here is an excerpt of how we reported the results of our work to our funders in the spring of 2012 (our project was half completed):

Of the 376 discrete parents and caregivers that attended Weekend Stories programs, 96 returned for three or more programs. 71% of the returning parents reported that their children showed early literacy growth in at least four areas and 23% reported that they had increased the amount of time spend reading to their children at home. [Brooklyn Public Library] revised its evaluation tools this year for a more straightforward, specific and qualitative evaluation of these behaviors. The new evaluation forms include check boxes that relate to early literacy indicators and parents' understanding of early literacy practices. They are easy to fill out and the questions have more clarity. As a result, the reported early literacy growth was 20% higher than evidence of positive behavioral shifts in the previous year. While the rate of return was lower than expected, there was significant variance among the branches and one severely inclement weekend affected the total average.

The fall programs proved to offer profound insights into both constructive parenting practices and challenges related to early childhood learning and family bonding. This is demonstrated by the substantial anecdotal evidence gathered during the project that refers to the program's impact on parent-child literacy and social interaction. After each session, parents and caregivers were given surveys and asked to provide feedback on their impressions of the program and discuss how it has helped them over time. Program staff also made phone calls to parents who shared their contact information with [the library] to collect more detailed accounts. Below are examples of anecdotes from the past six months that demonstrate improved parent-child literacy engagement.

"We love the program—my daughter is recognizing a lot more letters and thinking about sounding out words now."

"As a single parent, singing and rhymes were something that often fell outside my timetable, not a lot of time, but the program made me decide I could manage, and I have learned the words to some of the songs. One favorite is one that involves pointing to body parts."

"I play with things more, make noises from the book, try to keep it interesting, instead of just reading it straight like I did before. We used to read once in a while, now every day, especially on weekends. We go to the library more, too."

"The instructor taught me to be more patient when working with my child. I also learned ways to engage my child in many activities."

"We read, sing, and play more. My son has improved a great deal. We have more fun with everything."

"The program helped me to make reading fun for the kids instead of feeling like a chore."

Tips

- Color code your surveys if you can! Print the baseline, weekly, and final surveys on different color papers. When parents come to the program, you can say, "If it is your first time here, please complete the pink survey. If you have been to this program before, please complete the blue survey."

- Tell parents and caregivers why you are asking them to fill out surveys. Let them know that your programs are grant funded and that filling out the survey could mean more programs!
- If you have a grant to do a program series, take a break midway in your project and look at your outcome data. Are you on track? Are you getting the data you need? If not, this gives you time to regroup and rethink some things.
- Outcomes evaluation is always a process. You may need to change and adapt your evaluation tools from year to year.
- If you can, include photos in your report.

DOUGLAS COUNTY (CO) LIBRARIES

Priscilla Queen, Literacy Department

In 2005 and 2006, Douglas County Libraries embarked on a goal to train all storytime presenters in the Every Child Ready to Read approach to early literacy. When we learned about ECRR (the first edition), we were very excited to find the research and the rationale to optimize our storytime offerings and to train all our storytime librarians in specific ways that kept all the fun but became much more purposeful. The survey was repeated in 2009 with similar results.

By 2007, the libraries were interested in seeing what effects our new focus on early literacy were having and how parents and child-care providers were responding to our efforts. We created and conducted the first early literacy storytime survey; 252 surveys were completed over four weeks' time, with input from our three largest branch libraries.

Our findings included the following:

56 percent of children represented on surveys were from one to four years old

70 percent reported attending storytimes twice per month or once per week

Question: What storytime elements do you use at home with your child? (Percentage who answered yes)

Books	96%
Fingerplays and rhymes	48%
Songs	86%
Storytime take-home sheets	32%
Nothing	0%

Question: Have you read any of the library's information on early
literacy?

       Yes   49%
       No   51%

Question: Do you use the storyteller's suggestions for early literacy
skills?

       Yes   66%
       No   32%

Question: Please circle early literacy behaviors you feel your child has
gained as a result of storytime attendance.

Ages of children for which the following responses were given:

zero to one year old = 30	*three to four years old = 58*
one to two years old = 44	*four to five years old = 48,*
two to three years old = 65	*older than five = 7*

Enjoys library visits	94%
Plays with books	73%
Asks to have books read aloud	66%
Can point to words and pictures	62%
Knows how to hold a book	62%
Increased vocabulary	57%
Tells and retells stories	49%
Describes events and things	43%
Can identify letters by name	32%
Recognizes rhyming words	32%
Knows sounds letters make	30%
Notices signs in environment	23%

Question: How have the storytime experience and early literacy
approach changed how you read at home? While many people
indicated that they already do activities that support early literacy
at home, the responses included these changes:

    "I read slower and don't mind if we don't get to every page or
        finish the book."
    "I learned to read to her even when she's not focused."
    "Repetition is good."

"Books give lots of good new vocabulary."

"Don't have to read every word of the book, especially if hard to
      pay attention."

"Helps interest in reading more books."

"More animated."

"So fun here, helps us love reading even more at home."

"Makes it easier to make the stories lively."

"Use sign language."

"Asking questions of the child as we read the book."

"Reinforces and supports me to read, read, read!"

"Point more to the pictures and follow the child."

"Clap out syllables."

"Read more often at home."

"Use finger to follow the words."

"More questions and more interactive."

"Love getting ideas for more books to read."

"Make sure to use vocabulary."

DOUGLAS COUNTY EARLY LITERACY AND STORYTIME SURVEY 2007

Please fill out this brief survey and return it to the children's desk in your library.
We are interested in learning how our storytimes and early literacy approach
affect your parenting and child-care activities. Thank you!

1. What are the ages of the children you bring to storytimes? _____

2. How often do you attend storytime at Douglas County Libraries?

☐ This is our first time.
☐ Two or more a month
☐ Two or more times a week
☐ Once a month
☐ Once a week

3. How long have you been attending storytime? _____

4. What storytime elements do you use at home with your child?

☐ Books
☐ Fingerplays, action rhymes, bounces
☐ Songs
☐ Storytime take-home sheets
☐ Coloring sheets

5. Have you read any of the library's information on early literacy?

☐ Yes   ☐ No

6. Do you use the storyteller's suggestions for early literacy skills and getting ready to read?

☐ Yes   ☐ No

If yes, what suggestions have been particularly helpful? _____

7. Has the storytime experience and early literacy approach changed how you read books at home?

☐ Yes   ☐ No

If yes, how? _____

8. Douglas County Libraries' storytimes are designed to improve the prereading skills of children. Please check the early literacy behaviors below you feel your child(ren) gained as a result of storytime attendance.

☐ Plays with books
☐ Knows how to hold a book
☐ Enjoys library visits
☐ Increased vocabulary
☐ Can recognize rhyming words
☐ Asks to have books read aloud
☐ Can point to words and pictures
☐ Describes events and things
☐ Notices signs in environment
☐ Tells and retells stories
☐ Can identify letters by name
☐ Knows sounds letters make

Please share your comments and suggestions to improve storytimes. Feel free to use the back of the sheet.

Bibliography

This bibliography includes all resource books mentioned in text as well as others the authors used or recommend.

American Academy of Pediatrics. "Media Use by Children Younger Than 2 Years." *Pediatrics*, October 17, 2011. doi: 10.1542/peds.2011-1753.

Anderson, Richard, et al. *Becoming a Nation of Readers: The Report of the Commission on Reading*. Champaign: University of Illinois, 1985.

Aram, Dorit, and Iris Levin. "Home Support of Children in the Writing Process: Contributions to Early Literacy." In *Handbook of Early Literacy Research*, vol. 3, ed. Susan B. Neuman and David Dickinson, 189–99. New York: Guilford Press, 2011.

Bankstreet College of Education. *Bankstreet College's Guide to Literacy for Volunteers and Tutors*. http://bankstreet.edu/literacy-guide/glossary-reading -terms/.

Barton, Lauren, and Holly Brophy-Herb. "Developmental Foundations for Language and Literacy from Birth to Three Years." In *Learning to Read the World: Language and Literacy in the First Three Years*, ed. Sharon Rosenkoetter and Joanne Knapp-Philo, 15–58. Washington, DC: Zero to Three, 2006.

Bortfeld, Heather, J. L. Morgan, R. M. Golinkoff, and K. Rathbun. "Mommy and Me: Familiar Names Help Launch Babies into Speech-Stream Segmentation." *Psychological Science* (April 2005): 298–304.

Brenneman, Kimberly, Judi Stevenson-Boud, and Ellen C. Frede. "Math and Science in Preschool: Polices and Practice." NIERR Preschool Policy Brief, March 2009, issue 19, National Institute for Early Education Research, New Brunswick, NJ.

Brooks, Jacqueline. *Big Science for Growing Minds: Constructivist Classrooms for Young Thinkers*. New York: Teachers College Press, 2011.

California Department of Education. *Preschool English Learners: Principles and Practices to Promote Language, Literacy, and Learning; A Resource Guide.* 2nd ed. Sacramento: California Department of Education, 2009. www.cde .ca.gov/sp/cd/re/documents/psenglearnersed2.pdf.

Chiong, Cynthia, Jinny Ree, and Lori Takeuchi. "Print Books vs. e-Books: Comparing Parent-Child Co-Reading on Print, Basic, and Enhanced e-Book Platforms." May 15, 2012. www.joanganzcooneycenter.org/publication/ quickreport-print-books-vs-e-books/.

Chiong, Cynthia, and Carly Shuler. "Learning: Is There an App for That? Investigations of Young Children's Usage and Learning with Mobil Devices and Apps." Joan Ganz Cooney Center, Sesame Street Workshop, New York, 2010. www.joanganzcooneycenter.org/publication/learning-is-there-an -app-for-that/.

Christ, Tanya, and X. Christine Wang. "Bridging the Vocabulary Gap: What the Research Tells Us about Vocabulary Instruction in Early Childhood." *Young Children* (July 2010): 84–91.

Clark, Beverly A. "First- and Second-Language Acquisition in Early Childhood." Early Childhood and Parent Collaborative. http://ecap.crc.illinois.edu/pubs/ katzsym/clark-b.pdf.

Collier, Virginia. *Acquiring a Second Language for School in Directions in Language and Education*. Washington, DC: National Clearinghouse for Bilingual Education, 1995.

Conezion, Karen, and Lucia French. "Science in the Preschool Classroom: Capitalizing on Children's Fascination with the Everyday World to Foster Language and Literacy Development." *Young Children* (September 2002): 16.

Copple, Carol. *Growing Minds: Building Strong Cognitive Foundations in Early Childhood*. Washington, DC: National Association for the Education of Young Children, 2012.

Council on Communications and Media, American Academy of Pediatrics. "Media Use by Children Younger Than Two Years." *Pediatrics: Official Journal of the American Academy of Pediatrics* (October 17, 2011). doi: 10.1542/peds.2011-1753.

Cunningham, Anne E., and Jamie Zibulsky. "Tell Me a Story: Examining the Benefits of Shared Reading." In *Handbook of Early Literacy Research*, vol. 3, ed. Susan B. Neuman and David Dickinson, 396–411. New York: Guilford Press, 2011.

Diamant-Cohen, Betsy, and Saroj Ghoting. *Early Literacy Kit: A Handbook and Tip Cards*. Chicago: American Library Association, 2010.

Dickinson, David, Julie Griffith, Roberta Golinkoff, and Kathy Hirsh-Pasek. "How Reading Books Fosters Language Development around the World." *Child Development Research* (2012). www.hindawi.com/journals/cdr/2012/602807/.

Dickinson, David, and Susan B. Neuman. *Handbook of Early Literacy Research*. Vol. 2. New York: Guilford Press, 2006.

Dombro, Amy Laura, Judy Jablon, and Charlotte Statson. *Powerful Interactions: How to Connect with Children to Extend Their Learning*. Washington, DC: National Association for the Education of Young Children, 2011.

Duke, Nell K. "Reading to Learn from the Very Beginning: Information Books in Early Childhood," *Young Children* (March 2003). http://journal.naeyc.org/btj/200303/InformationBooks.pdf.

Evans, Mary Ann, and Jean Saint-Aubin. "An Eye for Print: Child and Adult Attention to Print during Shared Book Reading." In *Literacy Development and Enhancement across Orthographies and Cultures*, ed. D. Aram and O. Korat, 43–53. New York: Springer Science and Business Media, 2010.

Ezell, Helen, and Laura Justice. *Shared Storybook Reading: Building Young Children's Language and Emergent Literacy Skills*. Baltimore: Paul H. Brookes, 2005.

Ghoting, Saroj, and Pamela Martin-Diaz. *Early Literacy Storytimes @ your library: Partnering with Caregivers for Success*. Chicago: American Library Association, 2006.

Ginsburg, Herbert P., Joon Sun Lee, and Judi Stevenson Boyd. "Mathematics Education for Young Children: What It Is and How to Promote It." *Social Policy Report: Giving Child and Youth Development Knowledge Away* 22, no. 1 (2008). National Institute for Early Education Research, New Brunswick, NJ.

Goodson, Barbara, and Carolyn Layzer. "Learning to Talk and Listen." Washington, DC: National Institute for Literacy, 2009. http://lincs.ed.gov/publications/pdf/LearningtoTalkandListen.pdf.

Gronlund, Gaye. *Developmentally Appropriate Play: Guiding Young Children to a Higher Level*. St. Paul, MN: Redleaf Press, 2010.

Hallissy, Jennifer. *The Write Start: A Guide to Nurturing Writing at Every Stage, from Scribbling to Forming Letters and Writing Stories*. Boston: Shambhala Publications, 2010.

Harper, L. J. "Nursery Rhyme Knowledge and Phonological Awareness in Preschool Children." *Journal of Language and Literacy Education* 7, no. 1 (2011): 65–78. http://jolle.coe.uga.edu/archive/2011_1/harper.pdf.

Harris, Justin, Robert Michnick, and Kathy Hirsh-Pasek. "Lessons from the Crib for the Classroom: How Children Really Learn Vocabulary." In *Handbook of Early Literacy Research*, vol. 3, ed. Susan B. Neuman and David Dickinson, 49–65. New York: Guilford Press, 2011.

Hart, Betty, and Todd R. Risley. *Meaningful Differences in the Everyday Experiences of American Children*. Baltimore: Paul H. Brookes, 1995.

Irujo, Suzanne. "What Does Research Tell Us about Teaching Reading to English Language Learners?" *Reading Rockets*. 2007. www.readingrockets.org/article/19757/.

Jones, Elizabeth, and Gretchen Reynolds. *The Play's the Thing: Teachers' Roles in Children's Play*. 2nd ed. New York: Teachers College Press, 2011.

Jones, Ithel, Vickie E. Lake, and Miranda Lin. "Early Childhood Science Process Skills: Social and Developmental Considerations." In *Contemporary Perspectives on Science and Technology in Early Childhood Education*, ed. Olivia N. Saracho and Bernard Spodek, 17–35. Charlotte, NC: Information Age Publishing, 2008.

Juel, Connie. "The Impact of Early School Experiences on Initial Reading." In *Handbook of Early Literacy Research*, vol. 2, ed. David Dickinson and Susan B. Neuman, 410–26. New York: Guilford Press, 2006.

Justice, Laura M., and Khara L. Pence, with Angela R. Beckman, Lori E. Skibbe, and Alice K. Wiggins. *Scaffolding with Storybooks: A Guide for Enhancing Young Children's Language and Literacy Achievement*. Newark, DE: International Reading Association, 2005.

King, Kendall, and Lyn Fogle. "Raising Bilingual Children: Common Parental Concerns and Current Research." *Center for Applied Linguistics Digest* (April 2006). www.cal.org/resources/digest/raising-bilingual-children.html.

Klass, Perri. "Hearing Bilingual: How Babies Sort Out Language." *New York Times*, October 10, 2011. www.nytimes.com/2011/10/11/health/views/11klass.html?_r=0.

Kupcha-Szrom, Jaclyn. "A Window to the World: Early Language and Literacy Development." *Zero to Three*. February 2011. www.zerotothree.org/public-policy/policy-toolkit/early-literacywebmarch1-6.pdf.

Leung, Cynthia B. "Preschoolers' Acquisition of Scientific Vocabulary through Repeated Read-Aloud Events, Retellings, and Hands-On Science Activities." *Reading Psychology* 29 (2008): 165–93.

Lillard, Angeline S., and Jennifer Peterson. "The Immediate Impact of Different Types of Television on Young Children's Executive Function." *Pediatrics: Official Journal of the American Academy of Pediatrics* (September 12, 2011). doi: 10.1542/peds.2010-1919.

Milteer, Regina, and Kenneth Ginsburg. "The Importance of Play in Promoting Healthy Child Development and Maintaining Strong Parent-Child Bond: Focus on Children in Poverty." *Pediatrics* (December 26, 2011). doi: 10.1542/peds.2011-2953.

National Institute for Literacy. *Learning to Talk and Listen: An Oral Language Resource for Early Childhood Caregivers*. Washington, DC: National Institute for Literacy, 2009. http://lincs.ed.gov/publications/pdf/LearningtoTalkandListen.pdf.

National Reading Panel. *Teaching Children to Read: An Evidence-Based Assessment of the Scientific Research Literature on Reading and Its Implications for Reading Instruction*. Washington, DC: National Institute of Child Health and Human Development, 2000.

Neuman, Susan B. "Literacy Development for Infants and Toddlers." In *Learning to Read the World: Language and Literacy in the First Three Years*, ed. Sharon Rosenkoetter and Joanne Knapp-Philo, 275–90. Washington, DC: Zero to Three, 2006.

Neuman, Susan B., and David Dickinson. *Handbook of Early Literacy Research*. Vol. 3. New York: Guilford Press, 2011.

Neuman, Susan B., and Kathleen Roskos. *Nurturing Knowledge: Building a Foundation for School Success by Linking Early Literacy to Math, Science, Art, and Social Studies*. New York: Scholastic, 2007.

Novick, Rebecca. *Developmentally Appropriate and Culturally Responsive Education: Theory in Practice*. Portland, OR: Northwest Regional Educational Laboratory Program, 1996.

Owocki, Gretchen. *Literacy through Play*. Portsmouth, NH: Heinemann, 1999.

Paciga, Kathleen, Jessica Hoffman, and William Teale. "The National Early Literacy Panel and Preschool Literacy Instruction: Green Lights, Caution Lights, and Red Lights." *Young Children* (November 2011): 50–57.

Paris, Scott G. "Developmental Differences in Early Reading Skills." In *Handbook of Early Literacy Research*, vol. 3, ed. Susan B. Neuman and David Dickinson, 228–41. New York: Guilford Press, 2011.

Patton, Susannah, and Madelyn Holmes, eds. *Keys to Literacy*. Washington, DC: Council for Basic Education, 1998.

Payne, Rachel. "It Takes a Village to Raise a Reader: Creating Grant-Worthy, Outcomes-Based Early Literacy Programs." Paper presented at the Public Library Association Conference, 2012. http://ittakesavillagetoraiseareaderpla2012.pbworks.com.

Pianta, Robert, Karen La Paro, and Bridget Hamre. *Classroom Assessment Scoring System Manual Pre-K*. Baltimore: Paul H. Brookes, 2008.

Piasta, Shayne, Laura Justice, Anita McGinty, and Joan Kaderavek. "Increasing Young Children's Contact with Print during Shared Reading: Longitudinal Effects on Literacy Achievement." *Child Development* (May–June 2012): 810–20.

Price, Lisa, Anne van Kleeck, and Carl Huberty. "Talk during Book Sharing between Parents and Preschool Children: A Comparison between Storybook and Expository Book Conditions." *Reading Research Quarterly* 4, no. 2 (2009): 171–94.

Rideout, Victoria. *Zero to Eight: Children's Media Use in America: A Common Sense Media Research Study*. San Francisco: Common Sense Media, 2011.

Rosenkoetter, Sharon, and Joanne Knapp-Philo, eds. *Learning to Read the World: Language and Literacy in the First Three Years*. Washington, DC: Zero to Three, 2006.

Roskos, Kathleen, James Christie, and Donald Richgels. "The Essentials of Early Literacy Instruction." *Young Children* (March 2003): 52–59.

Roskos, Kathleen A., Patton O. Tabors, and Lisa A. Lenhart. *Oral Language and Literacy: Talking, Reading, and Writing*. 2nd ed. Newark, NJ: National Reading Association, 2009.

Rowe, Meredith L., and Susan Goldin-Meadow. "Difference in Early Gesture Explain SES Disparities in Child Vocabulary Size at School Entry." *Science* 323, no. 5916 (2009): 951–53. www.ncbi.nlm.nih.gov/pmc/articles/PMC2692106/pdf/nihms89518.pdf.

Saracho, Olivia N., and Bernard Spodek, eds. *Contemporary Perspectives on Science and Technology in Early Childhood Education*. Charlotte, NC: Information Age Publishing, 2008.

Schickedanz, Judith, and Renee Casbergue. *Writing in Preschool: Learning to Orchestrate Meaning and Marks*. Newark, DE: International Reading Association, 2004.

Schickedanz, Judith, and Molly Collins. "For Young Children, Pictures in Storybooks Are Rarely Worth a Thousand Words." *Reading Teacher* (May 2012): 539–49.

Sénéchal, Monique. "A Model of the Concurrent and Longitudinal Relations between Home Literacy and Child Outcomes." In *Handbook of Early Literacy Research*, vol. 3, ed. Susan B. Neuman and David Dickinson, 175–88. New York: Guilford Press, 2011.

———. "Reading Books to Young Children: What It Does and Does Not Do." In *Literacy Development and Enhancements across Orthographies and Cultures*, ed. D. Aram and O. Korat, 111–21. New York: Springer Science and Business Media, 2010.

Singer, Dorothy, Roberta Golinkoff, and Kathy Hirsh-Pasek, eds. *Play = Learning: How Play Motivates and Enhances Children's Cognitive and Social-Emotional Growth*. New York: Oxford University Press, 2006.

Snow, Catherine E., David K. Dickinson, and Patton O. Tabors. "The Home-School Study of Language and Literacy Development." www.gse.harvard.edu/~pild/homeschoolstudy.htm.

Sousa, David. *How the Brain Learns to Read*. Thousand Oaks, CA: Corwin Press, 2005.

Strangman, Nicole, and Tracey Hall. (2004). *Background Knowledge*. Wakefield, MA: National Center on Accessing the General Curriculum. www.aim.cast.org/learn/historyarchive/backgroundpapers/background_knowledge.

Tabors, Patton O. *One Child, Two Languages*. 2nd ed. Baltimore: Paul H. Brookes, 2008.

Trelease, Jim. *Read Aloud Handbook*. 6th ed. New York: Penguin, 2005–6.

Vermont Center for the Book. *Mother Goose Cares about Social Studies*. Chester: Vermont Center for the Book, 2005.

Wilson, Ruth. "Promoting the Development of Scientific Thinking." *Early Childhood News*. www.earlychildhoodnews.com/earlychildhood/article_view.aspx?ArticleId=409.

Zigler, Edward, Dorothy Singer, and Sandra Bishop-Josef. *Children's Play: The Roots of Reading*. Washington, DC: Zero to Three, 2004.

Recommended Websites

Research

Center for Applied Linguistics (www.cal.org)—bilingual learning

Center on the Developing Child, Harvard University (http://developingchild.harvard.edu)—generates, translates, and applies knowledge in the service of improving life outcomes for children

Children of the Code (www.childrenofthecode.org)—Todd Hart on meaningful differences

¡Colorín colorado! (www.colorincolorado.org)—Reading Rockets, in Spanish and English, with an emphasis on English-language learners

Every Child Ready to Read (www.everychildreadytoread.org)—research and information on how to implement PLA and ALSC's early literacy initiative

Joan Ganz Cooney Center at Sesame Workshop (www.joanganzcooneycenter .org)—investigates and disseminates information about digital media and learning, especially for young children

KIDiddles (www.kididdles.com/lyrics/index.html)—free recorded songs and lyrics

National Early Literacy Panel (http://lincs.ed.gov/earlychildhood/NELP/ NELPreport.html)—reports from the National Early Literacy Panel in their entirety

National Institute for Early Education Research (http://nieer.org)—current research and policy issues about preschoolers

National Institute of Environmental Health Sciences (http://kids.niehs.nih.gov/ games/songs/)—free recorded songs and lyrics

Reading Rockets (www.readingrockets.org)—information on early literacy and how children learn to read; includes resources for parents, teachers, and librarians

Saroj Ghoting (www.earlylit.net)—early childhood literacy consultant

Storytime Share (www.earlylit.net/storytimeshare/)—includes early literacy asides

Storytime Resources

DLTK Growing Together (www.dltk-teach.com)—free reproducibles on all kinds of themes

Everything Preschool (www.everythingpreschool.com)—free reproducibles on all kinds of themes

Sur La Lune Storytime (www.surlalunefairytales.com/storytime/index.html)— books, songs, and fingerplays by a former children's librarian

For a sampling of library storytimes and implementation of early literacy research and practices, visit these websites:

Denver (CO) Public Library Babble, Scribble, Read (http://kids.denverlibrary.org/grownups/early-literacy/index.html)—research and activities to build early literacy in children birth to age five

Hennepin County Public Library (www.hclib.org/BirthTo6/ELSIE.cfm)—features a section on early literacy that includes recommended books with tips on how to share them

Multnomah County Public Library (http://multcolib.org/birthtosix/earlyliteracy .html)—good information about early literacy and some of the practices

Ohio Ready to Read (www.ohreadytoread.org)—includes sample storytimes, some incorporating early literacy information.

Pierce County (WA) Library System (www.piercecountylibrary.org/kids-teens/parents-caregivers/child-care-providers/Default.htm)—offers newsletters with activities and early literacy information.

Saroj Ghoting (www.earlylit.net)—research articles

Storytime Share (www.earlylit.net/storytimeshare/)—asides and storytime ideas

Index

Titles of storytimes are in quotes. Titles of books and CDs are in italic.

You may also be interested in

EARLY LITERACY STORYTIMES @ YOUR LIBRARY
Partnering with Caregivers for Success

Saroj Nadkarni Ghoting and Pamela Martin-Díaz

Storytime is the perfect time to offer guidance to parents so they can better prepare their children to be successful readers—a proven way for adults to enhance children's reading readiness.

ISBN: 978-0-8389-0899-0
272 pages / 7" x 10"

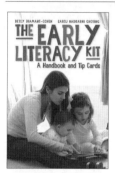

THE EARLY LITERACY KIT
A Handbook and Tip Cards

Betsy Diamant-Cohen
and Saroj Nadkarni Ghoting
ISBN: 978-0-8389-0999-7

TRANSFORMING PRESCHOOL STORYTIME
A Modern Vision and a Year of Programs

Betsy Diamant-Cohen
and Melanie Hetrick
ISBN: 978-1-55570-805-4

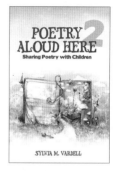

POETRY ALOUD HERE 2: Sharing Poetry with Children

Sylvia M. Vardell
ISBN: 978-0-8389-1177-8

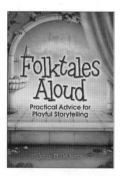

FOLKTALES ALOUD
Practical Advice for Playful Storytelling

Janice M. Del Negro
ISBN: 978-0-8389-1135-8

MULTICULTURAL STORYTIME MAGIC

Kathy MacMillan
and Christine Kirker
ISBN: 978-0-8389-1142-6

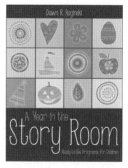

A YEAR IN THE STORY ROOM: Ready-to-Use Programs for Children

Dawn R. Roginski
ISBN: 978-0-8389-1179-2

Order today at alastore.ala.org or 866-746-7252!

ALA Store purchases fund advocacy, awareness, and accreditation programs for library professionals worldwide.